LOST AIKEN COUNTY

LOST AIKEN COUNTY

ALEXIA JONES HELSLEY

THE History PRESS

Published by The History Press
Charleston, SC
www.historypress.com

Cover images: *Front*: Mill employees with Graniteville Manufacturing Company output bundled for shipment, circa 1900. *Courtesy Gregg-Graniteville Photographic Archives, Gregg-Graniteville Library, USC Aiken. Upper back:* Steam locomotive, Graniteville, 1947, near Graniteville Manufacturing Company. *Courtesy Gregg-Graniteville Photographic Archives, Gregg-Graniteville Library, USC Aiken. Lower back*: Main Street (Laurens Street), Aiken, showing Hahn's grocery, an unpaved street with streetcar tracks and electric lines. The PCK series, printed in Germany. *Courtesy Allen Riddick Collection.*

First published 2019

Manufactured in the United States

ISBN 9781467141499

Library of Congress Control Number: 2018960981

To Chaseton Cole Paschal, Keiser Alexia Paschal, Justus Evelyn Paschal,
Evelyn Mae Helsley and Jacob Henry Helsley Jr.

"Behold, children are a gift of the Lord…."
–Psalms 127:3a (NASB)

And to Deborah Tritt Harmon and Allen Riddick,
who made this dream possible.

CONTENTS

PREFACE

Aiken, South Carolina, is more than a place. It is a state of mind—the accumulated wisdom of centuries of living and working in a unique environment. It is also a beautiful place with woodlands and parks, charming vistas and blooming azaleas.

The history of Aiken is long in geologic and human time. The first human beings arrived more than eleven thousand years ago. They created stone tools and shaped utilitarian and decorative pottery from the rich koalin deposits along the rivers. They built communities, hunted and fished for food and left trails for later arrivals to follow.

The Mississippi mound builders also established chiefdoms and built mounds along the Savannah River. Some later settlers admired the strategic value and location of these mounds and the bluffs along the river and, like George Galphin, made them a base for economic development and protection.

The interplay of land, people and economic opportunity is critical for understanding the history of Aiken County, a unique place that lies between the Savannah and North Fork of the Edisto Rivers. As local poet Thomas H. Williams wrote:

> *This land of vineyard, valley and stream*
> *The four square county of Aiken,*
> *Where scenic beauty reigns supreme…*[1]

ACKNOWLEDGEMENTS

One's history is about connections—the associations, serendipitous encounters and unique personalities that are the stuff of life. This project is the result of many connections. In 2002, Dr. Val Lumans employed me to teach history at USC Aiken—the beginning of an exciting and wonderful adventure. Later in 2006, Jane Tuten, a person of great historical vision, employed me to process and arrange the archives of the University of South Carolina Aiken. This book, therefore, is a tribute to the many individuals who have made Aiken a wonderful place to live, work and visit.

The author thanks Professor Deborah Tritt Harmon, instruction/reference librarian and archivist of the Gregg-Graniteville Collection, Gregg-Graniteville Library, University of South Carolina Aiken. Professor Harmon shared her expertise and historical knowledge, as well as the riches of the Gregg-Graniteville Archives. In addition, the author thanks Allen Riddick, Aiken historian, for generously giving her access to his extraordinary collection of Aiken history and sharing his remarkable understanding of that history. Also, special thanks to Bill Benton and Precious Memories for his South Carolina postcard collection and to Curt DuVall, digital assistant, for his work digitizing the collections of the Gregg-Graniteville Library.

Special thanks to the hardworking staff of my former "home"—the South Carolina Department of Archives and History—including Archives and Records Management director Steve Tuttle; Archives Accessions and Records Management supervisor Pat McCawley; Bryan Collars, Electronic

Records and Digital Collections; and archivists Robert Murray, Kim McClure and Elaine Rohr for above-and-beyond research assistance. One can never have too many friends, so thanks, too, to Head of Collections and Curator of Manuscripts Graham Duncan and Visual Materials Archivist Beth Bilderback, South Caroliniana Library, University of South Carolina, as well as to my understanding husband, Terry, for his support and encouragement and, specifically, for proofreading and indexing this book.

PROLOGUE

Aiken is a diverse and beautiful place. Major interstate and state highways crisscross the county. Economically, the county profits from federal investment, a moderate climate, educated labor and good natural resources. It is a forward-looking area blessed with a long and fascinating history. Many are attracted to the award-winning county seat and the verdant hinterland.

But while much is good and much will be better, there are lost chapters in Aiken's history. This book looks at several of these—how they developed, how they contributed to modern Aiken and how we should celebrate, commemorate and remember them.

Modern Aiken stands on the shoulders of lost dreams and dreamers. Like Janus, the Roman god of beginnings and endings, one needs to look deep into the past in order to embrace fully the future.

Chapter 1

LOST FRONTIER

Savanna Town, Fort Moore and Windsor Township

Approximately 11,500 years ago, Native Americans entered the Southeast and began settling along the Savannah River. Initially, small mobile groups, hunter-gatherers, roamed the countryside. In time, with climate change, food supplies increased and populations grew. Some inhabitants became less mobile, enhanced their tool repertoire, developed pottery and expanded their food options. These early Aiken residents enjoyed a varied diet that included hunting, fishing and a variety of plants. For several millennia, they evolved new technologies, adapted to changing conditions, developed new social constructs and faced new challenges.

In 1540, the harbinger of the coming tsunami, Hernan de Soto, and a band of Spaniards crossed the Savannah River near modern Augusta. De Soto brought six hundred soldiers, a priest, a secretary, enslaved African and Native Americans, hogs, dogs and microbes. Seeking new sources of wealth, he landed in Florida and journeyed inland through Georgia, South Carolina and Western North Carolina and reached the Gulf Coast before his death and ignominious burial in the Mississippi River. De Soto's expedition found no gold or silver, but it did gather valuable information about the interior of the southeastern United States.

According to local lore, near Aiken, De Soto spied a vein of mica and assigned his men to explore. The germs the Spaniards inadvertently carried drastically altered the lives of South Carolina's Native American peoples. The malicious microbes spawned several epidemics, decimated populations and depopulated villages. As a result, when the English arrived in 1670, more than a century later, they encountered a greatly altered Native American landscape.

In 1670, when the first English settlers set foot on Carolina soil, the mighty Westos held sway on the Savannah River. Even the coastal tribes, such as the Kiawahs and Cussaboes, feared the Westos and welcomed the English as possible allies. The fearsome Westos were "likely the Erie from western New York" who entered the Savannah River area in 1659.

In 1674, Henry Woodward, one of the first settlers of Carolina, well versed in Native American culture and language, visited the Westos in their village on the Savannah River. By that time, Woodward had already experienced a lifetime of adventures.

A young Henry Woodward was part of the 1666 voyage of Robert Sandford. The eight Lords Proprietors of Carolina sent Sandford to explore the Port Royal area. In 1669, King Charles II granted the eight men, political supporters of the Crown during the dark days of the Cromwellian Protectorate, a vast tract of land, named Carolina in honor of King Charles (*Carolus* in Latin). Sandford sailed along the coastline of South Carolina and interacted with the indigenous people and their rulers. He also wrote a lengthy report of his findings for the Lords Proprietors.

Intrigued with Native American life, Woodward chose to remain in Carolina. He wanted to study the culture and language of the coastal tribes. Spaniards from St. Augustine, however, learned of his presence in the Carolina Lowcountry. They viewed him as an interloper at best or a spy for the British. As a result, the Spanish authorities sent an armed force to capture Woodward and bring him to St. Augustine. Once there, the Spaniards imprisoned Woodward. In 1668, in a bizarre twist of fate, he escaped prison when a privateer attacked St. Augustine. He then joined the crew of the privateer and worked as a surgeon until he was able to return to South Carolina in 1670. His romantic adventures well equipped him for his role as Indian agent and advisor to the fledgling colony.

As a result of Woodward's visit, the early colonists enjoyed a highly profitable trade with the Westos from 1674 to 1680. The Westos supplied the Carolinians with Indian slaves and deerskins. In return, the Carolina traders supplied the Westos with arms, ammunition and European trade goods. The Carolinians viewed the warlike Westos not only as valuable trade allies but also as a bulwark against possible Spanish incursions and Indian threats from the west.

Outfitted with the latest in weaponry, the well-armed Westos terrorized neighboring tribes and enslaved many for the Lowcountry and Caribbean slave market. Unfortunately, this symbiotic relationship was short-lived. A few opportunistic Carolina traders exploited the situation and placed profit above fair trade practices. Their sharp dealings not only antagonized the Westos but also provoked conflict between the erstwhile trading partners. As a result, the Carolinians looked around for other Indian allies. With the support and encouragement of colonial officials, the Creeks and the Savannahs, a group new to the Aiken area, attacked, defeated and killed or captured most of the once-mighty Westos. The Westo remnant first fled northward and joined the Iroquois, but later they returned to the South, where they settled on the Ocmulgee River in Georgia and became part of the Creek Confederacy.[2]

Today, archaeologists and other researchers track these early Americans and the vicissitudes of their existence before and after the arrival of the Europeans, excavating their camp and village sites and studying the stone tools and ceramics they created.

SAVANNA TOWN

Savanna Town on the Savannah River was the home of the Savannahs, a branch of the Shawnees. Lured by the promise of European trade, the Shawnees moved into the Aiken area from Ohio. Savanna (Savana, Savano) Town was one of the earliest identified settlements in what is now Aiken County. Lying on the Savannah River, the strategically placed town occupied the site of the Westos' principal town. Therefore, at least since 1660, Native Americans have inhabited the site of the town.

In 1680, as relations with the Westos deteriorated, the Carolinians recruited the newly arrived Savannahs to help depose the Westos. The Savannahs, interested in the Westo trade connections and territory, readily agreed. But the Savannahs had fewer warriors than the Westos, so in order to succeed, they allied with the Creeks. Together, the Native American allies destroyed the mighty Westos with only limited colonial involvement. Their town subsequently became a major access point on the principal trading route from Charles Town to the Creek, Choctaw, Chickasaw and Lower Cherokee Nations.

The Savannahs gave their name to the river, to this early trading center and, in 1733, to the new capital of the recently organized Colony of Georgia. Unfortunately, their relationship with Carolinians in Charles Town

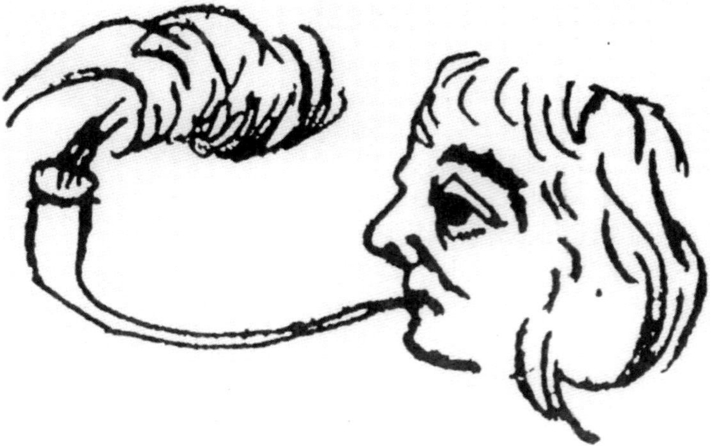

Sketch of pipe-smoking backcountry resident. Joseph Kershaw Papers. *Courtesy South Caroliniana Library, University of South Carolina Libraries, University of South Carolina.*

soured, and within a few years, the Savannahs, like the Westos, had also left the area. Other Native American groups also moved to the Savannah River for trade opportunities. European iron tools and weapons were highly prized by Native American groups. These immigrants included the Yuchis from Tennessee, the Chickasaws from Mississippi, the Apalachicolas from Alabama and Georgia and the Apalachees from Florida.[3]

FORT MOORE

Fort Moore, adjacent to Savanna Town, reflected colonial desperation. Despite years of generally friendly coexistence and trade with various Native American groups within and without the colony, in 1715 the Colony of South Carolina faced the greatest threat to its survival. On Good Friday, April 15, 1715, the Yemassees in Pocotaligo, one of their principal towns, rose in rebellion. The Yemassees were a multiethnic group that at one time lived in Florida. But in 1687, they revolted against Spanish efforts to enslave and convert them.

The disgruntled tribe, with encouragement from Carolina officials and traders in Charles Town, moved into the South Carolina Lowcountry.

There they settled several towns in Old Beaufort District. These Yemassee settlements included Poco Sabo, Pocataligo and Altamaha, and their presence left several Lowcountry place names. By 1715, more than one thousand Yemassee lived in ten settlements in the Carolina Lowcountry and were much-courted trading partners. Traders from the newly formed Stuart Town in the Lowcountry vied to supplant Charles Town's hold on the lucrative Yemassee trade.

Yet once again, greed doomed the relationship. Traders manipulated the exchange, overcharging for trade goods and underpaying for deerskin. These trading practices produced monumental tribal debt. Some estimate that the traders had advanced so much credit that the Yemassees would need years to satisfy the debt. To compound the situation, unscrupulous traders even enslaved Yemassee warriors or their family members to satisfy outstanding debts. Such actions strained relations and set the stage for perhaps the greatest threat faced by any of the thirteen colonies.

In a surprise move, on Good Friday the Yemassee warriors, painted for war, attacked the whites in the village of Pocotaligo. They immediately killed two members of a diplomatic mission whom they had entertained the previous evening. Hearing rumors of Yemassee discontent, colonial leaders had sent a delegation to identify and mediate the Yemassee grievances. The warriors also attacked traders and their families in the town and gruesomely tortured Thomas Nairne, who had served as Indian agent for the colony. Nairne, who had tried to end the exploitation of the Yemassees, died a slow, agonizing death—the equivalent of someone being slowly roasted alive. Some scholars estimate that insurgent Native Americans killed 90 percent of South Carolina's active Indian traders between April and the end of June 1715.

At least one Carolinian, Seymour Burroughs, escaped the initial carnage in Pocotaligo. Although severely wounded, he alerted the inhabitants of Port Royal Island and the new town of Beaufort. Consequently, some three hundred of them escaped by boarding a ship in the harbor and sailing for Charles Town. All were not so lucky, and more than one hundred died in Indian attacks in the area. Raids and deaths continued until the South Carolina militia, including all able-bodied men, black or white, defeated the Yemassee at the Battles of Port Royal and Salkehatchie. With defeat, the Yemassees packed up, abandoned their towns and returned to Florida.

Although the Yemassees abandoned the fray, allied tribes continued their attacks until the Carolinians induced the Lower Cherokee to support their interest. The Cherokee-Creek conflict eased attacks in South Carolina.

Consequently, much of the unrest had calmed by April 1716. In 1718, the Carolinians and Creeks negotiated an end to hostilities. The war left more than four hundred dead in the colony and extensive property damage, lost livestock and interrupted trade. The colony took years to recover.[4]

As a result of this conflict, the South Carolina Commons House of Assembly established a series of three forts to protect the interior of the colony. Fort Moore on the Savannah River was one of those frontier forts. The colony built other forts at the Congarees near modern Columbia and in Beaufort close to the former Yemassee settlements.

Fort Moore, constructed in 1716 near the former site of Savanna Town, was strategically located on the major east–west Indian Trade route. Named in honor of Governor James Moore, the fort had several roles. First, it was an early warning outpost charged with monitoring Indian activities. Second, in the event of Indian attack, it was a refuge for area settlers. Third, the fort was a detriment to French efforts to control the Indian trade west of the Savannah. Finally, the colony saw the fort as a way to regulate the Indian trade and prevent abuses such as those that precipitated the Yemassee War.

Located in the fall zone, the fort stood on a high bluff above the Savannah River across from the site of modern Augusta. The fort featured four bastions, a barracks for housing troops and a storehouse. The fort, as Mark Groover and Jonathan Leader wrote, functioned as "a frontier cultural crossroads."

During its first year of operation, African American militia garrisoned the fort, but this was a short-term solution and white militia garrisoned the fort the remainder of its active life. In its heyday, Native Americans, such as the Yuchis, Creeks and Chickasaws, traded deerskins for textiles, tools, weapons and ammunition. In the 1730s, the colony, in an effort to increase the number of white settlers and provide a buffer between external threats and the capital of Charles Town, established New Windsor Township adjacent to the site of the military fort.[5]

Mark Catesby, an important English naturalist, provided the following contemporary description of one of many challenges that the inhabitants of the fort faced:

> *In Sept. 1722, at Fort Moore, a little fortress on the Savannah River, about midway between the sea and mountains, the waters rose twenty-nine feet in less than forty hours. This proceeded only from what rain fell on the mountains, they at the fort having had none in that space of time. It came rushing down the river so suddenly, and with that impetuosity that it not only destroyed all their grain, but sweeped* [sic] *away* [livestock].

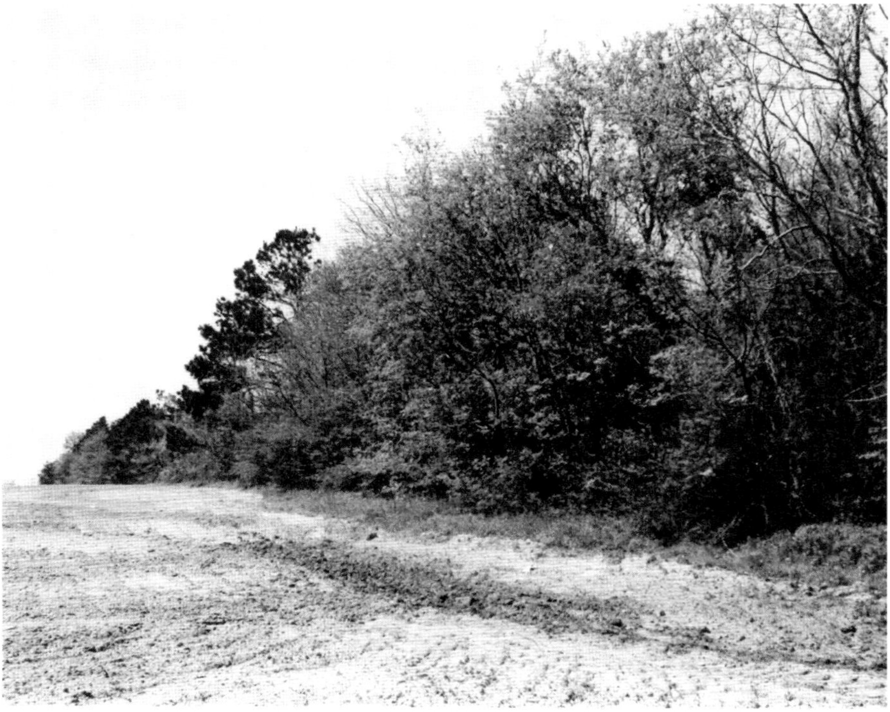

Section of the Cherokee Path. U.S. Department of the Interior, National Register of Historic Places, Calhoun County. *Courtesy South Carolina Department of Archives and History.*

In the 1730s, the development of the new township changed life at the fort. Fort Moore became the centerpiece for the recently laid-out New Windsor Township. Unfortunately, while its commanding location was excellent for defense, its site with the nearby sand hills, bluffs, swamps and slopes offered few agricultural opportunities for would-be farmers. So, settlers in the township faced special challenges.

When European settlement slowed in New Windsor, the colony sought to encourage Native Americans to settle in the area. As a major thoroughfare between the western markets and Charles Town, Indian groups frequently traveled through the area, and some stayed. By 1725, there were groups of Chickasaws living near Fort Moore. The Chickasaw homeland in Mississippi was under attack by Choctaws and pressure from the French, so several bands relocated. A great warrior known as Squirrel King led one group. On September 14, 1713, he and a delegation accompanied the commander of Fort Moore, Captain Gerald Monger, to Charles Town. There, they met with Governor Francis Nicholson. Squirrel King had forty warriors and forty women and children who planned to settle in South Carolina. The Chickasaws and Nicholson exchanged gifts. Nicholson encouraged them to settle along the Savannah River since he, like many South Carolinians at the time, believed that Chickasaw settlements along the Savannah promoted Carolina security.

Edmond Atkin also saw great advantages to Chickasaw settlements on the Savannah River. According to Atkin, "The chief service they are of in that post is the guarding of our traders up and down in time of any danger between their Nation and the Creeks." The Chickasaws were famous warriors, at times at odds with the Choctaws, and did not participate in the great Yemassee uprising.[6]

Around 1738, colonial officials invited the Chickasaw Nation to settle within the bounds of New Windsor. Most declined, but two groups did settle near Fort Moore: a group of twenty within a few miles of the fort and another group of seventy-plus on Horse Creek.

The Horse Creek Chickasaws, under the leadership of the Squirrel King, had a tract of more than twenty-one thousand acres, surveyed in 1739. Relations were not always harmonious between the Chickasaws and the colonists. In 1742, the Squirrel King and his men fought with colonial military units to fend off a Spanish attack on Frederica in Georgia. As a result, Lieutenant Governor William Bull of South Carolina ordered the commander of Fort Moore to treat the Chickasaws with deference and entertain them well when they visited the fort.[7]

In 1746, Governor James Glen and South Carolina leaders tried unsuccessfully to convince representatives of the Creeks and Chickasaws to reduce recent raids and restore peace to the area. Although Glen had requested forts among the Cherokees, Chickasaws, Creeks and Catawbas, the Commons House of Assembly voted instead to establish forts in the most vulnerable townships. Mobile ranger patrols from these forts eventually brought a cessation of hostilities to the frontier settlements.[8]

In 1747, Squirrel King and other Chickasaws traveled to Charles Town to complain that residents of New Windsor and Augusta were destroying their fields and stealing their livestock. Colonial officials paid the Indians for white depredations and gave them gifts.

Although its importance diminished with the founding of the Colony of Georgia in 1733, the fort still protected residents, and in 1747, the officials rebuilt the fort and added platforms for cannons.[9] For example, in 1759 Cherokee raids drove traders to seek refuge at Fort Moore or one of the other backcountry forts and interrupted connections between the frontier troops.[10]

In early 1759, one of the groups seeking sanctuary at Fort Moore was a group of settlers from the Long Cane. These settlers included the Calhoun family and others who had moved from the Shenandoah Valley of Virginia to South Carolina's contested frontier. Although in 1747 South Carolina purchased from the Cherokee land between Long Cane Creek and Little River, some settlers preferred the more fertile land beyond the Cherokee line. For example, in 1756, the Calhoun family and others moved in, but rather than settling in the ceded land, they had land surveyed on the west side of Long Cane Creek. In 1758, the Cherokees, aware of the incursions, unsuccessfully asked the governor of Georgia to intervene.

As the French and Indian War escalated conflicts in the English colonies, several of the colonies worked to recruit Cherokee warriors to aid the English against the French and their Indian allies. Some of these allies in 1758, after fighting at Fort Duquesne, raided and plundered settlements in Virginia on their way home. These raids prompted a domino effect of more raids and reprisals, with Cherokees and colonists both dying.

In 1759, South Carolina's governor, William Henry Lyttleton, demanded satisfaction for the dead colonists. A number of Cherokee headmen traveled to Charles Town to discuss the situation. Lyttleton refused to waver on his demands but promised safe passage for the Cherokee leaders. Instead, the Carolinians took the Cherokees hostage and imprisoned them in Fort Prince George. Lyttleton led an expedition to the fort. It was a blighted expedition. Men deserted and many became ill and carried smallpox back to the colonial capital. But in December, the governor and the Cherokees agreed to peace, and trade between the Cherokees and the colony resumed.

Nevertheless, many of the Cherokees resented the terms of the treaty, and the peace did not hold. Raids commenced in January 1760. With the frontier under threat, the Calhoun family and their neighbors left Long Cane trying to reach safety at Fort Moore. En route, on February 1, 1760, a party of Cherokees ambushed the wagon train. According to a news report in the *South Carolina Gazette* (the earliest account of the massacre), there were 150 Long Cane settlers fleeing their homes. Several hours into their trip, the settlers encountered muddy terrain. While they were trying to free their wagons, about 100 Cherokees surprised them. With their guns in the wagons, few of the men were able to defend the wagons, and overwhelmed, they "were at last obliged to fly." This first report listed seven wagons lost and 40 deaths, mainly women and children. Later, Patrick Calhoun, a member of the ill-fated flight, increased the number of settlers to 250 and revised the number killed to 23, primarily women and children. One of those who died on that fateful day was seventy-six-year-old Catherine Calhoun, the matriarch of the Calhoun family. Patrick Calhoun placed a monument at Long Cane honoring her and the others who died that day.

Frontier uncertainties continued for several years. Eventually, though, the Cherokees and Carolinians signed another peace treaty. The new treaty included another land cession. The new Cherokee boundary was the modern boundary between Abbeville and Anderson Counties.[11]

CAPTAIN DANIEL PEPPER

South Carolina garrisoned the fort, generally with ten to twenty-five men, through 1766.[12] One of the more colorful fort commanders was Daniel Pepper. Governor Thomas Broughton commissioned Daniel Pepper as captain and commander of Fort Moore on October 5, 1737.[13] Pepper oversaw fort operations from 1737 to 1745. He was perhaps overzealous in performing his duties, and he lacked discretion. Commissioned a justice of the peace, Pepper saw his new responsibilities as an opportunity to clean up the fort and the township. For example, he pursued traders, such as Martin Campbell and William Tobler, who had unpaid accounts in Charles Town and outstanding judgments on file. As a result, many of the traders, rather than satisfy their debts to Charles Town merchants, instead moved their operations across the river to the more friendly confines of Augusta. Those who stayed plotted Pepper's downfall, and he was in time replaced. Pepper's tenure, replete with indebtedness, drunkenness, dunking and stocks, offers a rare insight into the vagaries of daily life on the Carolina frontier.[14]

Reverend Thomas Lamar operated a ferry at "Fort Moore Bluff" across the Savannah River from his plantation. With the ferry, goods, livestock and passengers could cross from the fort and New Windsor into Georgia. In 1824, Abner Whatley petitioned the South Carolina legislature to renew the charter for the ferry. The original charter had vested the ferry in Lamar and his heirs and executors. Whatley had married a Lamar heir and, as a result, operated the ferry.[15] Lamar was one of the area settlers who had occupied former Chickasaw Indian lands on the Savannah. Lamar had befriended the Chickasaws and ground their corn at his mill.[16]

Conflicts took their tolls on the fort, as did the uncertain livelihood of the Indian trade. The establishment of Georgia and peace with the Cherokees reduced threats on South Carolina's western frontier. In the late 1760s, the colony ceased garrisoning the fort, and by 1775, Bernard Elliott noted that Fort Moore had no garrison and neither the stockades nor the barracks were usable.[17] Another chapter in the shifting landscape of the frontier had closed.

NEW WINDSOR TOWNSHIP

In 1729, South Carolina officially became a royal colony. The first royal governor, Robert Johnson, was ironically also the last proprietary governor. In 1731, the new governor proposed a township plan to the Board of Trade. He and others before him, such as John Barnwell of Beaufort, saw a township plan as the answer to several persistent problems. The colony could use free land to recruit free white Protestants and thus improve the racial balance in the province, which by 1720 was over 50 percent African American. An increase in the number of white settlers would lessen fears of a slave rebellion. In addition, the townships, if placed along the colony's exposed frontiers, would provide protection for Charles Town from the French to the west, Spaniards in Florida and Native American groups. The men and women of the new townships would be South Carolina's first ring of defense.

While Governor Johnson requested twelve townships, the Board of Trade in London only approved ten townships for South Carolina. The other two proposed townships became the nucleus of the new colony of Georgia, which James Oglethorpe founded in 1733.

The first of Johnson's new townships was Purrysburg on the Savannah River in the Lowcountry. Jean-Pierre Purry was the guiding light for the new settlement. Purry, a native of Switzerland, was a merchant who had traveled extensively. As a result, Purry had interesting ideas about the importance of climate in colonization efforts. He also had theories on how to create and locate settlements in order to optimize the best climate for agriculture. Unsuccessful in enlisting French or Dutch support for his ideas, in the 1720s Purry approached the English—with the result that three hundred or so French- and German-speaking Swiss immigrated to South Carolina to settle a new township.[18]

With settlers working to make the Purrysburg Township successful, the colony turned to laying out others. In 1735, the colony laid out New Windsor Township, another western township. The township, one of the 1730 townships, lay along the Savannah River and included Fort Moore and Savanna Town. Savanna Town was a trading depot on the eastern side of the Savannah across from Augusta, Georgia. That same year, settlers established the town of Augusta, Georgia, across the Savannah River from the fort.

The new township reflected the efforts of Sebastian Zouberbuhler to locate a home in Carolina for Swiss Protestants. In November 1734, Zouberbuhler landed in Charles Town and spent six months surveying possible township sites and conferring with Lieutenant Governor William Bull and the Council. After due deliberation, in July Zouberbuhler and Bull reached an agreement whereby he guaranteed to bring, within eighteen months, one hundred families to settle the new township at Fort Moore. Specifically, on July 17, 1736, Zouberbuhler signed a contract to settle a "Township up the River Savanna on a Place formerly an Indian Village, then called Savanna Town (at present New Windsor) and for bringing over one hundred Protestant Familys [*sic*] in the space of one Year."[19]

The bounds of New Windsor Township, one of the western townships and the second (after Purrysburg) with Swiss roots, extended from the "mouth of Town Creek to a point about seven miles above Fort Moore," and most of it "was laid out with fort in its northwestern corner." Most of the new township lay between the fort and Silver Bluff. Silver Bluff lay ten miles below the fort. Surveyors laid out the town of New Windsor with Fort Moore as its northwestern corner.

To encourage immigration, the colony promised the new immigrants free land, livestock and food supplies until they could plant and harvest their own crops, as well as the equipment needed to build homes and clear land for farming. Zouberbuhler anticipated that several hundred more immigrants would follow the first group. Despite the organizers' expectations, only 50 families (192 persons) actually traveled from Switzerland under Zouberbuhler's contract. In August 1736, the hardy immigrants under Bartholomew Zouberbuhler and Johannes (John) Tobler departed Switzerland. Tobler (1696–1765), a former government leader, left Appenzell-Ausser Rhoden, Switzerland, due to political difficulties (his party fell out of favor) and immigrated with the others to South Carolina. It was a difficult trip for the would-be immigrants, with a number of bureaucratic delays. As a result, Tobler and his party did not arrive in the port city of

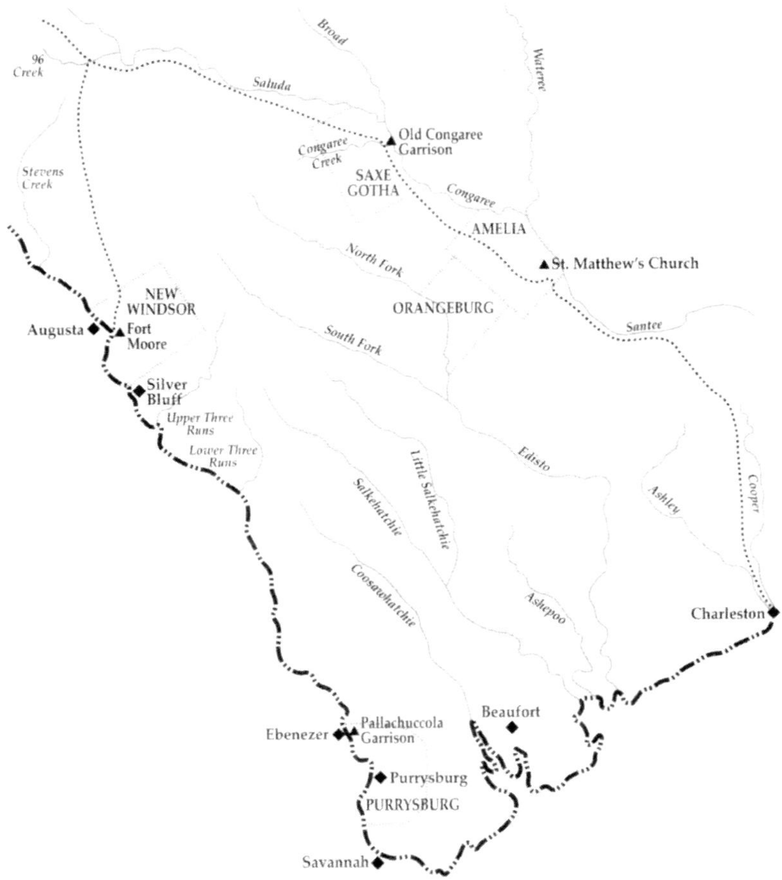

Map, *South Carolina's Eastern Townships, 1730s*. Tim Belshaw, 2003. *Courtesy the author.*

Charles Town until February 1, 1737. Of the 250 individuals who embarked on the trip, 2 died in transit.

Once in South Carolina, Tobler led a party of twenty-five persons directly overland to New Windsor. A trading path connected Charles Town with Fort Moore. He encountered unpredictable hospitality, high prices, ferry delays and bad weather. Setting out on foot, within a few days, he purchased a horse. Fort Moore was 144 miles from Charles Town, and that was a long way to walk. Yet his party reached Fort Moore more expeditiously than the remaining Swiss, who chose to travel by boat. By boat, the trip from Charles

Town to New Windsor took six weeks. In the unaccustomed heat, many became ill and forty died. It was an inauspicious beginning for many seeking to make a new life on the Carolina frontier.

In addition to the German-speaking Swiss, individuals involved in the Indian trade also settled in the township. Good agricultural land was scarce in the township, so location and other forces integrally linked the township's economic viability to the Indian trade. By 1748, two groups of Chickasaws, invited by the Council as a defensive buffer, lived near New Windsor.

In the years between 1732 and 1738, twenty-two German settlers and twenty-six other persons with non-German surnames had land surveyed in the township. At least ten of those who had land surveyed there were involved in the Indian trade. By 1738, about three hundred persons lived in New Windsor. Many of the township's settlers were Indian traders or worked in other occupations connected with the Indian trade. They chose to live in the township because it was convenient to the trade route.

Consequently, the Indian trade was a major factor in the life of the township. When times were good, the township prospered, and when the trade declined, so did the township. But while the traders were intermittent residents—as they spent most of their town in the Indian villages—periodically, they did return to Savanna Town or Augusta for supplies or to visit friends and family. Among the more permanent township residents were the storekeepers who operated year-round businesses that catered both to the traders and to the settlers trying to eke out a living farming.

One of the more important early Indian traders in the area was Patrick Brown, who traded with Archibald McGillivray and Company. Archibald McGillivray left South Carolina in 1744, but his company still traded under the leadership of Brown and his relative Lachlan McGillivray. Patrick Brown, who was licensed to trade with the seven upper Creek towns, had as a result a virtual monopoly on the Indian trade with the western tribes. Brown maintained his trade position but spent most of his time in Augusta, and in 1747, he acquired an indigo plantation south of Augusta as he managed the transition from Indian trader to planter. Brown used the port of Charles Town for his importing and exporting but had stores and warehouses in Augusta.

Among his most valuable business associates were John Rae and George Galphin. Galphin entered the Creek trade and by 1744 had the license for the Lower Creek towns. He became a lifelong friend of Lachlan McGillivray's, and in 1747, he purchased four hundred acres from McGillivray. The four-hundred-acre tract included Silver Bluff, where Galphin built his home and established the seat for his trading empire.

By the early 1740s, New Windsor was almost a wasteland. Most of the traders had moved across the river to Augusta. One of the major reasons for the shift was the controversial leadership of Captain Daniel Pepper, as mentioned earlier. Augusta was a better-managed place. When Governor James Glen arrived in 1743, he immediately heard tales of woe from Fort Moore and New Windsor. Among the complaints levied by leading residents (including a justice of the peace) against Pepper were cattle rustling, changing cattle brands, "criminal conversation" with married women, placing individuals in the stocks for trivial matters and employing members of the fort's garrison to work his farm. Glen, new to the colony, may not have fully understood the significance of the charges and, in a spirit of compromise, removed Pepper as a justice of the peace but left him in command of Fort Moore. He also removed from office the justice of the peace who brought complaints against Pepper!

Augusta was an enticing location in the 1740s for a number of reasons. First, there was no Captain Pepper and no inexperienced Governor Glen. There also was no prosecution in Georgia for South Carolina debt claims, an affliction suffered by many traders. In addition, with the departure of General James Oglethorpe, the strong founder of Georgia, there was a "power vacuum" in the Georgia hinterland. Colonial officials in Savannah suspected (justifiably) that various colonial regulations, such as the bans on rum and slave labor, were being broken in Augusta and its surrounding territory.

At the same time, the major traders in Augusta ceased their competitive aggressiveness and adopted cooperation. As a result, seven Indian trading concerns united under the leadership of Patrick Brown and John Rae. The new company did business as Brown, Rae & Company. Rae maintained his involvement in the company even after Brown retired to his indigo plantation.

An inn, one of several establishments geared to the transient visitor, stood on Town Creek to entertain itinerant travelers and traders. But in time, the Swiss disappeared from New Windsor due to the limited agricultural opportunities. Nevertheless, Galphin and other Indian traders continued to maintain homes in the area. For example, trader Alexander Wood lived at Point Comfort, Upper Three Runs Creek near Silver Bluff. When Wood died in 1757, the inventory of his estate reported six hundred horses, an equal number of cattle, hogs and African American and Native American slaves. The figures suggest a man who had transitioned from trading to planting.

While many of the Indian traders moved their base of operations to Augusta, several continued to live and work in New Windsor. Even Galphin, whose primary business activities were in Georgia, maintained his home at Silver Bluff in South Carolina. During the 1740s, Jeremiah Knott had a store in New Windsor, and part-time Indian trader Isaac Motte lived there at least some of the time. John Fallowfield was another storekeeper in New Windsor. He also served as a justice of the peace. When Fallowfield died, his personal inventory included luxury items such as glassware, plate, decanters, teapots and a chocolate pot, as well as clothing, household furnishings and a looking glass. The value of his personal property and his stock-in-trade exceeded £200.[20]

John Tobler, the former Swiss governor, had a survey for 650 acres at Beech Island. On this land, Tobler built his home near a swamp in the river bend. His son, John Jr., had a grant for an adjoining track. Two of his sons, first William and later Ulric, operated his store. Ulric Tobler was also a justice of the peace and a deputy surveyor. When John Tobler Sr. died, the store had outstanding debts of more than £1,000. Neither his agricultural nor mercantile enterprises was markedly profitable.[21]

Yet Tobler adapted well to his new home in New Windsor and became an active member of his community. He was interested in cultural, agricultural and community activities. He sponsored religious services in his home, ran a store, planted, edited an almanac for forty years, invented "a machine for cleaning rice" and "built a fort." In effect, John Tobler was a Renaissance man of the Carolina frontier.

In 1753, John Tobler, by then a long-term inhabitant of New Windsor Township, wrote "Beschreibung von Carolina" ("A Description of Carolina"), which was published in a Swiss almanac in 1754. Although Tobler had left Switzerland in 1736, he maintained close connections with his homeland. His published description seems far more positive than the realities of life in the challenging environment of New Windsor.

Tobler's goal was to increase immigration into South Carolina. In his description, Tobler commented on various areas in the state, as well as discussing climate, religion, geography and economic activities and opportunities. He wrote, "New Windsor is likewise [referring to Ebenezer] located on the Savannah River and is a town with a good worth and a royal garrison." In addition, Tobler noted that with Charles Town, New Windsor (especially when compared with the town of Augusta) was "one of the best trading towns in the province." The Savannah River, which separated New Windsor and Charles Town, was a great highway for commerce. Packhorses brought deerskins from the interior. Merchants then shipped the skins down the river to the ports of Savannah and Charles Town. According to Tobler, the round-trip from New Windsor to Savannah took "only three weeks," while a round-trip to Charles Town could take five weeks.

Concerning New Windsor, Tobler wrote, "I think there is no better place in Carolina." To support his position, Tobler added, "Everything planted grows quite well and yields much fruit, which, along with the trade makes this place famous." Even so, the writer acknowledged the challenges of flooding and the attendant periodic loss of livestock. The latter he attributed to a lack of sufficient manpower to drive the animals to higher ground and suggested that an influx of settlers would remedy that situation. He was quite the salesman!

In 1753, he reported only five German-speaking families in the area and noted that the community had no church and no pastor. Nevertheless, the residents on Sunday, "according to the Swiss rites," held three church services. Nevertheless, he noted, "The sermons are only read aloud and the service is held in my house." On occasion, Reverend Zublin (John Zubly), Tobler's son-in-law, visited from Wando and held services in German and English.[22] Zubly, the husband of Tobler's daughter, was an ordained minister.

Despite Tobler's rhetoric, the township grew slowly. New Windsor was the least populous of the 1730s townships and by 1756 had an estimated population of three hundred.

During the Cherokee War of 1759, Carolina troops had difficulty obtaining needed supplies and foodstuffs. Consequently, at New Windsor, resident Ulric Tobler used tobacco, knives, salt, rum, pipes and other highly coveted trade goods to entice Chickasaw warriors to fight with him. He then led his fighting men to the Congarees rendezvous with Governor William Henry Lyttleton and the main South Carolina army.[23]

In 1760, according to the *South Carolina Gazette*, news reached Charles Town of an incident near Fort Moore. On February 15, a band of eighteen Cherokees operating in groups of three or four ambushed, killed and scalped Captain Ulric Tobler, John's son. The militia captain was traveling between his father's home and the fort. The Cherokees also wounded William Calhoun, but other members of the party escaped unharmed. The Cherokees who killed Tobler "left a Hatchet sticking in his Neck, on which were 3 old Notches [*sic*], and 3 newly cut."[24] Circumstantial evidence suggested that the Cherokees had killed and scalped six individuals—three in the past and three more recently.

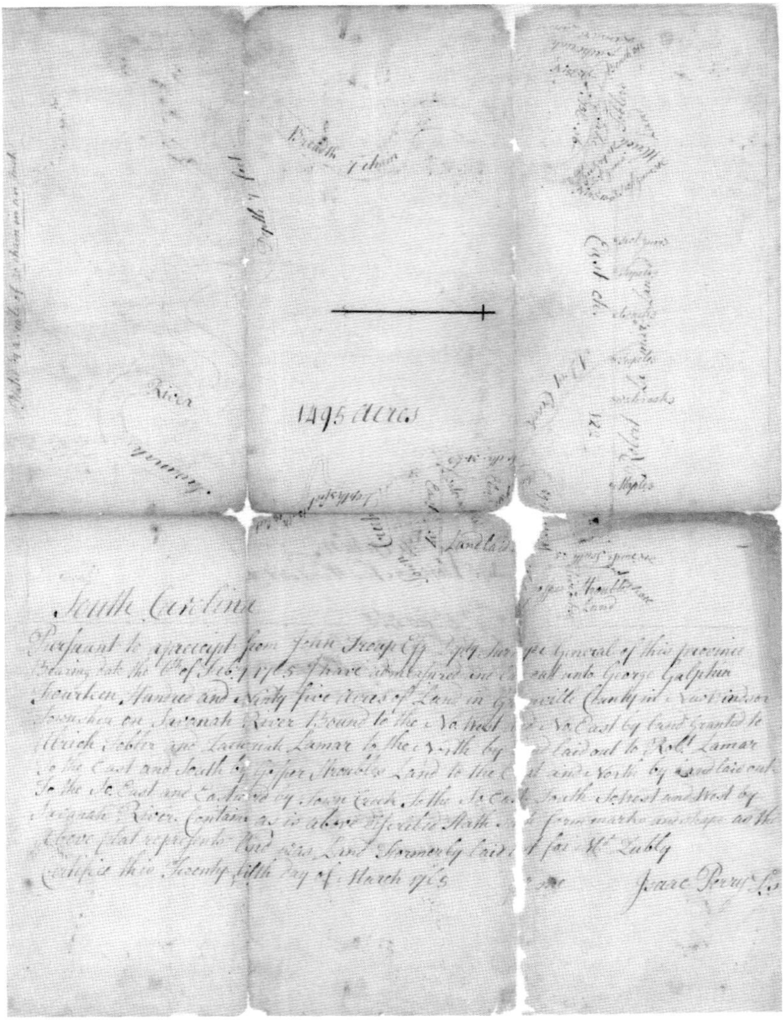

Plat of George Galphin for 1,495 acres on the Savanah River, Granville County, in New Windsor Township, bounding Town Creek and lands granted Ulric Tobler and others. Records of the Secretary of State, Surveyor General, Colonial Plats, Duplicate Series. *Courtesy South Carolina Department of Archives and History.*

The death of John Tobler's son Ulric in 1760 was a major transition point for the area. The dream of opportunity and safety east of the Savannah was shifting. Fort Moore was in decline, its days of usefulness at an end. New Windsor, with its economic challenges and fluctuating populations, sank into stagnation and decline.

Chapter 2

LOST LIVELIHOOD

George Galphin and Silver Bluff

Silver Bluff is a geographic area in Aiken County about thirteen miles south of Augusta. Today, the location is near Jackson, South Carolina. Traditionally, the name reflects a legend of silver ore in the area. When sunlight struck the vein in the river bluff, the minerals sparkled like silver. Research later revealed that the sparkling minerals were mica, not silver, but the name persisted. A plat surveyed for John Fraser on August 17, 1737, may be the earliest reference to the place name recorded in South Carolina land records.[25]

George Galphin, a native of Northern Ireland, immigrated to South Carolina in 1737. Galphin was one of many who crossed the Atlantic or traversed the Great Wagon Road southward seeking economic opportunities on the Carolina frontier.

He arrived during the golden age of the Indian trade. Long a major economic engine for the young colony, trade with the Indians for deerskin and later slaves made a few South Carolinians wealthy and provided a livelihood for many more. The stakes were high and the rewards great. For example, in 1748, the Colony of South Carolina exported 160,000 deerskins worth £300,000. Many sought wealth on the Carolina frontier. Some succeeded; other lost not only their opportunities but also their lives. Galphin, however, was one of the successful incomers.[26]

Born in Tullamore, Ireland, he found fame and fortune as an Indian trader and later Indian agent for the Continental Congress and in the state of South Carolina. In addition, he was a diplomat, land speculator, planter

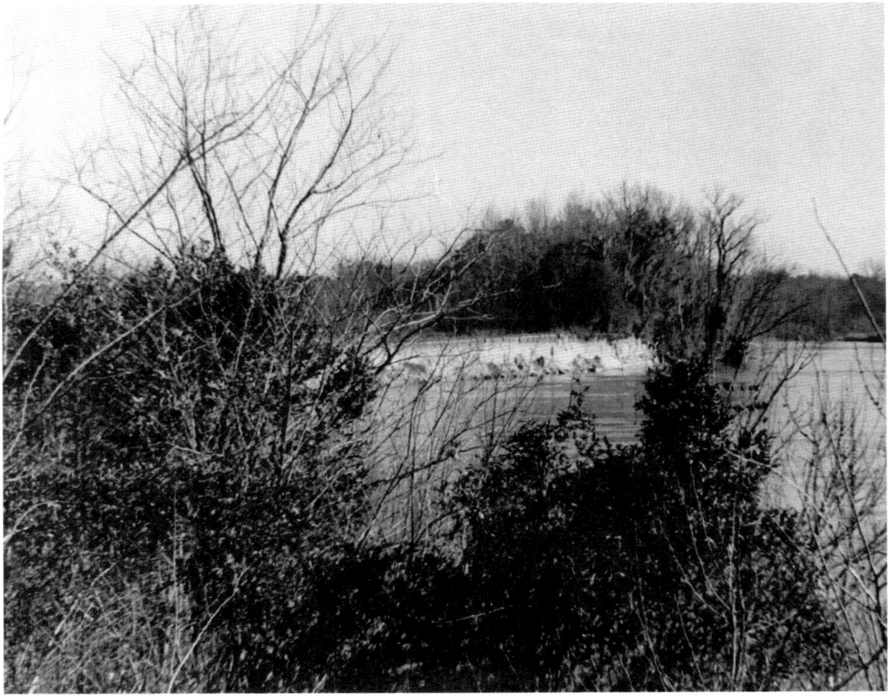

Silver Bluff, home of George Galphin's Trading Post and compound. U.S. Department of the Interior, National Register of Historic Places, Aiken County, South Carolina. *Courtesy South Carolina Department of Archives and History.*

and entrepreneur. In the 1740s, Galphin established a trading post and compound at Silver Bluff, a steep bluff overlooking the Savannah River near New Windsor Township, where he reared a large, multiracial family. He purchased the site on Silver Bluff, about twelve miles downriver from Augusta, from Patrick Brown. In addition, the Colony of South Carolina granted him more than two thousand acres. Later, he also acquired extensive landholdings in Georgia and at one time owned forty-seven slaves. He built an imposing brick house, a rarity in the Carolina backcountry, at Silver Bluff. The house was a landmark for travelers.

Galphin was one of the elite Indian traders who gained not only great wealth but also significant political influence. A large landowner, he also oversaw a far-flung trading empire that extended far into the interior. He cultivated indigo, raised cattle and operated a sawmill, a gristmill and other commercial enterprises. He entertained widely, and before the Revolution, his home on Silver Bluff was a well-known destination for his contemporaries.

For example, Henry Laurens—former slave trader, planter, South Carolina's first vice-president and president of the Continental Congress—was one of Galphin's visitors. In 1770, Laurens wrote Galphin a letter of "hearty" thanks for Galphin's "politeness & civilities" when Laurens was "lately at your Hospitable Castle"—his large brick mansion.

From archaeological excavation, it appears that the Galphin compound, which covered 175 acres, included not only a large trading post but also a "residential area in the north portion of the post," as well as cultivated land. In addition, Galphin was a family man. He had a large family in South Carolina, and he also encouraged several sisters with their families to immigrate to South Carolina. Therefore, the Galphin compound was home to a large interrelated family.

According to the National Register nomination, the Galphin homestead included pens for livestock, the trading post, several houses and cabins, docks and an inn for travelers. Galphin traded extensively with Creeks and Cherokees and oversaw a network of trading connections with tentacles that reached the Gulf Coast and the Mississippi River. Galphin possibly fortified the site in the 1760s, a time of great unrest in the South Carolina backcountry. According to his will, Galphin owned and operated gristmills and lumber mills.

By 1745, Galphin was also an Indian agent for the Colony of South Carolina. He represented the interests of the South Carolina Commons House of Assembly, the lower elected house of the South Carolina legislature, to the Lower Creek Nation. He entertained Creek leaders and shared governmental messages and concerns with the Creeks. Headmen of the Lower Creeks respected and trusted Galphin. For example, in 1750, he witnessed a controversial land cession from Creek leaders to Mary Musgrove Mathews Bosomworth (Oglethorpe's part-Creek interpreter) and Thomas Bosomworth, her third husband. The cession gave the Bosomworths title to several Sea Islands off the coast of Georgia: St. Catherine, Ossabaw and Sapelo. The Colony of Georgia later contested the legality of the cession but eventually compromised with the Bosomworths and allowed them to retain possession of St. Catherine.[27]

Nevertheless, by the 1760s, the heyday of the Indian trade was past. Galphin and other traders, such as John Rae, diversified their efforts and focused on land speculation, agriculture and local markets. For Galphin, New Windsor Township offered great commercial opportunities.[28]

In addition, Galphin was also involved with land speculation in Georgia. In January 1767, he and fellow Indian traders Lachlan

McGillivray and John Rae petitioned the governor of Georgia for a grant of fifty thousand acres. The men, former partners in Brown, Rae & Company of Augusta, Georgia, saw economic opportunity in the growth of Augusta and the colony of Georgia. The men wanted to establish a township (Queensborough) for Irish immigrants. Both Galphin and Rae had emigrated from Ireland and entered the lucrative Indian trade. In addition, both men had invested in Georgia prior to the 1767 petition. Since 1750, Galphin had been acquiring land in Georgia opposite his South Carolina property. By 1764, he owned almost two thousand acres. He had established first a cow pen and later a trading post known as Old Town or Galphin's Old Town.

The settlers of Queensborough had challenges with the neighboring Creeks. On one occasion, in October 1771, tiring of the unresponsive Georgia government, residents pursued horse thieves, killed one and whipped the other. The Council ordered magistrates in Augusta to issue warrants to arrest those responsible. Nevertheless, James Habersham, the president of the Council, also wrote to Galphin and urged him to use his negotiating skills and intervene with the settlers and with the Creeks. Galphin successfully resolved the issue.

In December 1771, Galphin faced a greater diplomatic challenge. A Queensborough settler had entertained a Creek, and after spending the night, the Creek had killed his host. The dead man's son ran to Galphin at his cow pen with the news. Galphin and his slaves pursued the Creek but lost him in the swamps. Nevertheless, apparently the Creeks held Galphin in such high regard that they seized and executed the perpetrator, with other Indian traders as witnesses.[29]

When delegates to the Continental Congress signed the Declaration of Independence, the Congress moved to address defensive needs of the new states. On July 12, 1775, fearing a British effort to exploit the Native Americans' dependence on "the colonists for arms, ammunition, and clothing," the Continental Congress divided the new states into three departments (northern, southern and middle) and designated five commissioners for the southern department. The Continental Congress also appropriated funds to finance "treaties and presents" for the Native Americans. The Congress authorized three commissioners for South Carolina.

The Council of Safety, with approval of the Provincial Congress, appointed three Indian commissioners for South Carolina. The Security Council named Edward Wilkinson as commissioner to the Cherokees. In October 1775, the Council of Safety also named Galphin commissioner of

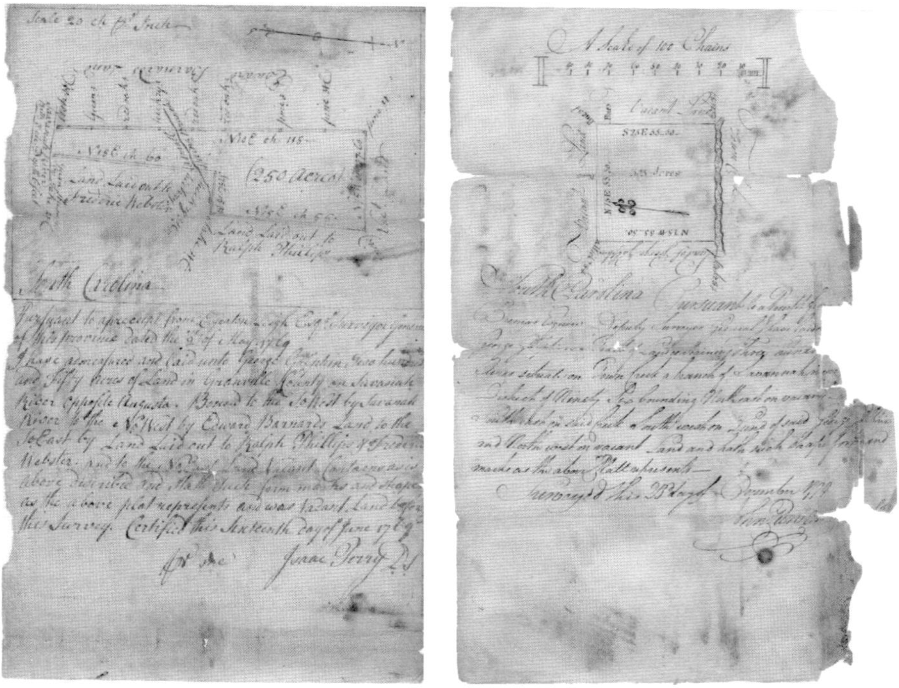

Left: George Galphin survey for 250 acres, "Savannah River Opposite Augusta," 1769. Records of the Secretary of State, Surveyor General, Colonial Plats, Duplicate Series. *Right*: George Galphin survey for 305 acres on Town Creek, a branch of the Savannah River, 1777. Records of the Secretary of State, Surveyor General, Colonial Plats, Duplicate Series. *Courtesy South Carolina Department of Archives and History.*

Indian affairs for the Catawba tribe. The Council of Safety on behalf of the Provincial Congress deputized Galphin to negotiate with Native Americans "in the name & on the behalf of the united Colonies in order to preserve peace and friendship with the said Indians." The third commissioner was Galphin's partner Robert Rae.[30] During the Revolution, Galphin was a Patriot and used his Indian connections to limit Creek support of the British Crown and foster support for the Patriot cause. Given his work experience with the Creeks, Galphin recognized the critical role of "presents" in cementing relationships, so he reminded the Creeks that the colonists had always supplied their needs. He also warned them that the English and their king wanted to interrupt the shipments of ammunition and goods. Nevertheless, he reassured them that the South Carolinians would supply all Creek needs.[31]

With that promise on the table, Galphin stressed the necessity of delivering the needed powder and ammunition. He reminded Charlestown officials that "if thy [they] finde we tell them Lys [lies] thy [they] will not belive a talke that is Sent them." Unfortunately, the Provincial Congress needed arms and ammunition to defend Charlestown and consequently advised Galphin that "rum & good words" must suffice. John Stuart reported Creek displeasure with their meager supplies to British officials. Nevertheless, such was Galphin's influence that he arranged meetings with the Cherokees for April 16 and the Creeks for May 1, 1776.[32] In addition to Galphin's long years of trading with the Creeks, he had also married into a prominent Creek family. He and Metawney, his Creek spouse, were the parents of three children: George, Judith and John.

Despite Galphin's efforts, the Georgians refused to supply the Creeks, and the South Carolinians dragged their feet. Completely exasperated, in April 1776, Galphin in desperation threatened to resign his commission if South Carolina did not address the issue. As a result, the Security Council reallocated resources, but when Galphin met with the Cherokees in April and the Creeks in May, he had little for them except rum and promises. Galphin noted to his superiors that he did not know how long the Creeks would remain neutral without the badly needed ammunition.

Some Cherokees under Dragging Canoe attacked frontier settlements. They saw opportunity, and when British warships appeared off the coast of Charlestown in June, some of the Cherokees attacked backcountry homes.[33] Cherokee dissatisfaction with trade and land issues eventually led to disastrous war. The South Carolina military was successful in destroying the Lower Cherokee towns in South Carolina, and on May 20, 1777, the Cherokees signed a treaty ceding their rights to lands in the state.

In addition to negotiating with the Cherokees and Creeks, Galphin also furnished intelligence about the movements and plans of the British agents to the Security Council.[34] Given the precarious state of the backcountry, at some point Galphin fortified his home. Galphin and his contemporaries knew the fortified home as Fort Galphin. Colonel Barnard Elliott was captain in the Second Regiment, South Carolina Troops. In 1775, Elliott traveled the backcountry enlisting support for the independence. Along the way, Elliott crossed the "Savannah River at Perry Ferry" and proceeded to Galphin's compound at Silver Bluff. During his time there, he enlisted two men and found Galphin's hospitality "so great" that he had difficult extricating himself. Elliott commented on Galphin's fields of indigo, his sawmill and the pleasant experience of dining with Galphin's multiracial daughters.[35]

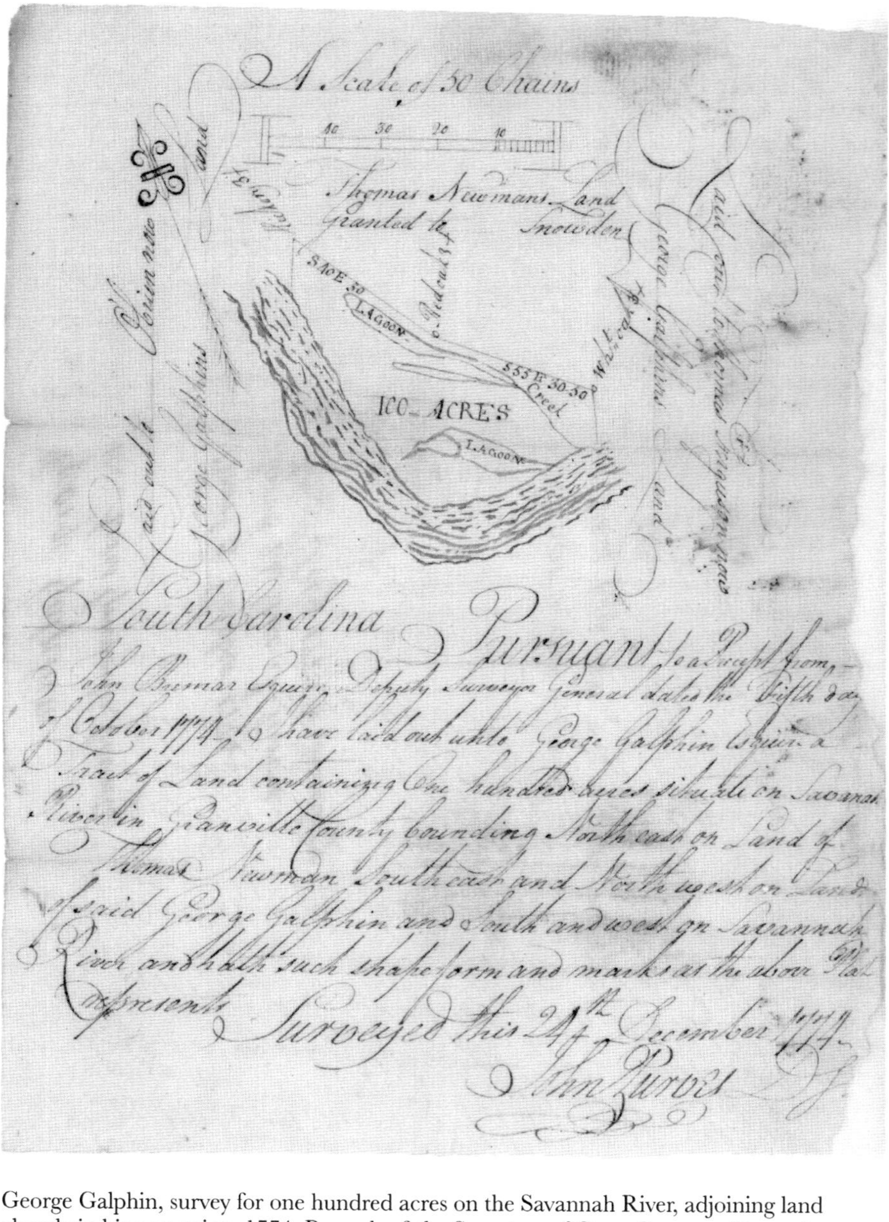

George Galphin, survey for one hundred acres on the Savannah River, adjoining land already in his possession, 1774. Records of the Secretary of State, Surveyor General, Colonial Plats, Duplicate Series. *Courtesy South Carolina Department of Archives and History.*

William Bartram, a naturalist, visited Galphin in 1776. Bartram described Galphin as a "gentleman" and commented on his "liberality" and his extensive trade network. In 1776, with the Cherokees at war, Loyalists, such as Thomas Brown, attempted to establish a Loyalist base in the backcountry of South Carolina and Georgia. Thomas Brown, an immigrant from England, imported seventy indentured servants and established a settlement near Augusta. He sided with the Crown and recruited his own regiment of rangers.

As part of his effort to develop a Loyalist base near Augusta, with little British support, Brown and his followers recruited roughly two hundred Upper Creek warriors to attack Georgia settlements in an attempt to divert colonial attacks on the Cherokees. The Upper Creeks resented settlement on ceded territory, and the settlers sought excuses for war with the Creeks in order to gain access to additional Indian land.

Yet when Brown and his force reached the Lower Creek towns, the Creeks there not only refused to join his campaign but also threatened to attack British forces in Florida unless the Upper Creeks rescinded their support. Galphin's influence saved the day. As he wrote in October 1776, "I have a hard task to keep the Creeks our friends, when both our enemies and the people that should be our friends want us to be at war with them."[36] A subsequent dispute in 1777 did not end as well. According to John Lewis Gervais, although "every thing promised fair for peace with the Creek Nation," men in Georgia had once again brought the new state to the brink of war. Apparently, Galphin had conducted ten Creek emissaries to Charlestown and then returned with them to Silver Bluff. There, while outfitting twenty or so horses with goods for the Creeks, Creeks in Georgia, resentful of settler incursions on their lands, killed Captain Thomas Dooley of Wilkes County, Georgia. Seeking revenge, Dooley's brother, Colonel John Dooley, and others crossed the river and raided the Galphin compound, seized the Creek emissaries and imprisoned them in Augusta. To Galphin and the South Carolina leaders, this action was a challenge to the authority of the state as well as an affront to the Creek Nation.[37]

Given the extent of Galphin's influence, the British Superintendent of Indian Affairs, John Stuart, worked diligently to undermine Galphin's influence and reputedly even encouraged several efforts to assassinate Galphin. For example, Stuart warned Creek leaders that Galphin could not deliver on needed supplies. According to Stuart, the Creeks' only hope for "plenty" was the subjugation of the Patriots.

Galphin suffered a personal setback in the fall of 1776. The family man had encouraged several of his sisters to bring their families and join him at

Silver Bluff. His sister Margaret Holmes and her son immigrated to Silver Bluff. Galphin employed his nephew David in the Indian trade and in time gave him major responsibilities for the trade with the Lower Muskogee Creeks. Then in the fall of 1776, David Holmes switched sides and joined the Loyalist faction in Georgia.[38]

When the Creeks disregarded Stuart's threats, Stuart allied with Patrick Tonyn, the governor of East Florida, to neutralize Galphin's influence. In 1777, Governor Tonyn dispatched Samuel Moore and a group of Florida Loyalists to Georgia to address Stuart's concerns. General Lachlan McIntosh learned that the Florida Loyalists were "after Mr. Galphin" and rallied Continental troops to intercept the Loyalists. That effort failed, and Moore and his men reached Galphin's Silver Bluff compound, where they planned to ambush Galphin when he left for the Creek Nation. Instead, Galphin learned of the threat, and a group of Georgia militia commanded by Captain John Gerard took Galphin's place to escort several Creeks from his Silver Bluff home. The Florida Loyalists, unaware of Galphin's absence, attacked the group and killed Gerard. The remaining militia and the Creeks chased Moore and his men into the swamps. In August 1777, Stuart wrote the Board of Trade that there was a rumor that Galphin was dead.[39]

Nevertheless, by August 29, 1777, Stuart knew that Galphin was alive. In an intercepted letter to David Taitt, he urged Taitt to work to "frustrate the machinations of Mr. Galphin and his associates in the new Superintendancy." Writing from St. Augustine, Stuart also admonished his colleague to "be particular in your informations [*sic*] and attentive to the proceedings of Mr. Galphin & his Associates of which furnish me with the most authentic accounts."[40] By late 1778, Galphin, fearful for his life, did not travel away from home without guards.[41]

After the British captured Savannah and Augusta, Georgia, Galphin's situation was perilous. He was not only cut off from Patriot military assistance but also had few supplies on hand for his Creek allies. He evacuated his family to safety and then returned to Silver Bluff to face the British.

After the fall of Savannah to the British in 1778, Loyalists entered the backcountry planning to attack Indian agents who had raided with and aided the Patriots. To add insult to injury, when Sir Henry Clinton landed his army in Georgia, he planned to feed his army from the cattle of Patriot sympathizers. Thomas Brown, Galphin's nemesis and a prominent Loyalist from Augusta, suggested that Clinton begin by appropriating Galphin's cattle from his Ogeechee herd. In addition, he mentioned Robert Rae, a trading associate of Galphin's, as another Patriot with cattle to feed British troops.[42]

Subsequently, in May 1780, after the fall of Charlestown, Sir Henry Clinton sent Galphin's longtime nemesis, Thomas Brown, back to the Augusta area to capture Galphin. Brown proceeded to Silver Bluff, found Galphin at home, occupied Silver Bluff and worked to destroy Galphin and end his influence with the Creek. Alexander Campbell refortified the compound and renamed the Galphin brick home Fort Dreadnought ("Fearless"). In addition, he placed Galphin under house arrest until Crown authorities could try him for treason.[43] From the British perspective, Galphin, since his appointment as an American Indian commissioner, had virtually single-handedly kept the Lower Creeks from supporting the British.[44]

After the fall of Charlestown, on April 2, 1780, the British governor of Georgia confiscated Galphin's property. In addition to his nephew, two of his sons, seeking personal advantage, also defected to the British. So, at the end of his life, the man who had built an empire from meager beginnings faced betrayal and financial ruin. Yet Galphin continued his work with the Native Americans. Creek friends visited him at Silver Bluff. Therefore, the Patriot spent his last days threatened with execution. Awaiting trial for treason, the great agent Galphin died of unknown causes on December 1, 1780, at his home, leaving the British in control of Silver Bluff.

In 1776, Galphin wrote his last will and testament. Times were uncertain, and Galphin feared for his life. With the push for independence, loyalties were fragile and Galphin understood the uncertainties of life in this western Carolina crucible of revolution. However, at the time he wrote his will, Galphin was an extremely wealthy man. His will included bequests to his children and his extended family, many of whom had joined the Galphin enterprise at Silver Bluff. There were more than two thousand acres of land in South Carolina and Georgia, a cow pen in Ogeechee, a sawmill, a gristmill, horses and cattle, slaves and monetary gifts to his family and friends in South Carolina and in Ireland.[45]

Before he wrote the will, Galphin had executed a deed of trust dated February 2, 1775. By this deed, Galphin conveyed to Lachlan McGillivray, James Parkinson, John Graham, Alexander Wylly, George Galphin (the younger) and John Galphin a gristmill and sawmill, a "new brick house," slaves, livestock and considerable acreage in South Carolina and Georgia, in trust "for love and affection" to Thomas, son of Rachel Dupree. After Galphin's death, his heirs and executors proved the deed and then had it recorded in Charlestown on July 7, 1787.[46]

Nevertheless, by the time he died in 1780, much of Galphin's life work was gone. In the desperate months after the fall of Charlestown, he had exhausted his storehouse making gifts to maintain Creek neutrality. The governor of Georgia had confiscated his lands there. The fate of Galphin's empire was uncertain. Consequently, at the time he died, Galphin did not know whether his family would ever enjoy the fruits of his years of work.

After Galphin's death, Patriot forces partially redeemed their pledge to Galphin. On May 21, 1781, Major Michael Rudolph, under the command of Lieutenant Colonel Henry "Light-Horse Harry" Lee, besieged Fort Galphin. In addition to Rudolph's command, the Patriot attackers included other detachments from Lee's Legion, as well as two companies of the Lower Ninety Six Regiment and one from Roebuck's Battalion.

Fort Galphin, also known as Fort Dreadnaught, was the site of George Galphin's trading post. Fortified by the British, the site occupied a strategic location on the Savannah River. Captain Samuel Roworth of the King's Rangers commanded the fort's defenders, forty-two rangers plus Loyalists from New Jersey and local Loyalist militia. The siege was successful. Roworth surrendered the fort, and reportedly, the only Patriot casualty was a man who died from heat stroke. The victorious Patriots captured 180 Loyalists.[47]

Galphin's family worked to salvage his dream for their future security. They recovered some of his land, and in 1794, his son Thomas Galphin and William Dunbar, executors of Galphin's estate, petitioned the South Carolina legislature for assistance. They cited Galphin's significant influence with the Creeks and Cherokees and his appointment as a commissioner for the management of Indian affairs for the southern department. In addition, they reminded the legislators that Galphin was so "firmly attached to Liberties of America" that he accepted no compensation for his work as commissioner. Nevertheless, in 1780, the British arrested Galphin, occupied his home and "destroyed a very considerable part of his property in South Carolina[48] and Georgia." In addition, the British removed large numbers of Galphin's slaves. Not only was Galphin's estate depleted before and after his death, but also there was a judgment against the estate "for a very large sum of money (for which he was security) to satisfy the demand of a British creditor." Galphin's executors, therefore, asked the General Assembly to grant appropriate compensation for his valuable services.

The death of Galphin ended his dream, but it also signaled the end of an era—the final curtain falling on a major economic engine for the young colony, the Indian trade. What his death did not end was the struggle for independence. When the British finally evacuated Charlestown in December 1782, Galphin's dream of an independent South Carolina was a reality. However, by the time of Galphin's death, his trading empire was gone and so was the heyday of the Indian trade. The new state of South Carolina would not need gifts to ensure harmonious relations with Native American groups. The Cherokees were gone from South Carolina, and the Catawba Nation were Revolutionary War allies. An era had ended.

Chapter 3
LOST STREETSCAPE

Downtown Aiken

Historic Aiken, the county seat of Aiken County, owes its existence to the railroad. Named for William Aiken Sr., president of the South Carolina Railroad, the South Carolina General Assembly incorporated the town in 1835. Aiken, a native of Ireland, dreamed of a rail route that would connect Charleston with Hamburg on the Savannah River.

A native of Northern Ireland, William Aiken Sr. immigrated to South Carolina. Aiken became a cotton merchant, diversified into banking and purchased land for rice cultivation. He also served in the South Carolina legislature and in 1828 served on a committee exploring the possibility of a rail connection between Charleston and the Savannah River. He and others wanted to revive Charleston commerce by tapping into the lucrative Augusta, Georgia market. In 1828, Aiken and others petitioned the South Carolina General Assembly for a charter for the South Carolina Canal and Railroad Company. Petitioners chose Aiken as the first president of the railroad. As the major investor in the plan, Aiken oversaw the selection of a route linking Charleston and Hamburg, across the Savannah River from Augusta. Unfortunately, he died in 1831 and did not see his dream realized.[49]

The route of the railroad crossed the Edisto River, six creeks and swamps, traversed nine miles north of Barnwell and reached Wise Creek, twenty-one miles south of Edgefield, and from there to Hamburg. The major bridge over the Edisto River was four hundred feet long. In Hamburg, Henry Schultz donated six acres for the construction of two "depositories" of brick roofed with zinc.[50]

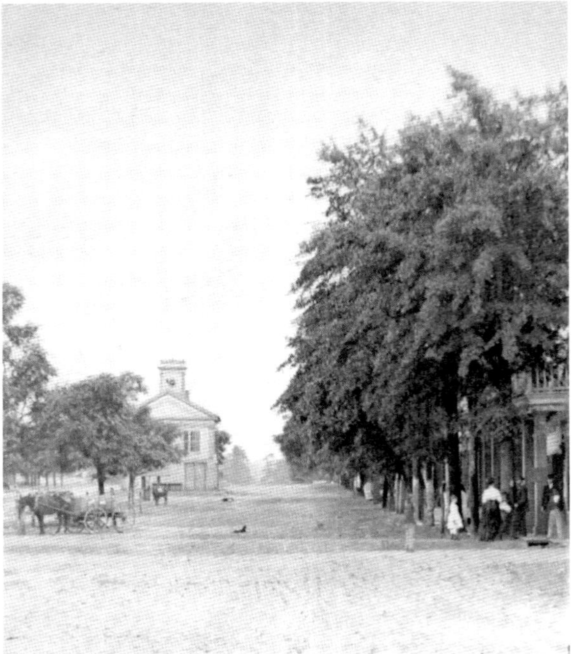

Main Street (Laurens Street), with City Hall/ Fire Department. *Stereoscopic Views of Aiken and Vicinity*. Photographed by J.A. Palmer, City Hall, Aiken. *Courtesy Allen Riddick Collection.*

The South Carolina Canal and Railroad Company planned to build a 136-mile railroad track from Charleston to Hamburg. In 1833, the company hired civil engineers Andrew Alfred Dexter (then of Boston) and Cyril Ouviere Pascalis (of New York) to supervise the construction of the railroad through Aiken. James Achille de Caradeuc surveyed the railroad route.

In 1834, at the request of railroad agent Major Alexander Black, civil engineers Andrew A. Dexter and C.O. Pascalis surveyed the route. They also laid out the town of Aiken on a grid—"in a checkerboard pattern" with the east–west avenues named for South Carolina counties The original survey of Aiken had twenty-seven blocks bounded by Edgefield Street on the north, Rail Road Avenue on the south, Williams Street on the east and Newberry Street on the west. Pascalis and Dexter dated their survey September 19, 1834.

ANDREW ALFRED DEXTER

Andrew Alfred Dexter (circa 1809–circa 1853) was the son of Andrew Dexter and Charlotte Martin. Born in Nova Scotia in 1833, Dexter was an engineer for the South Carolina Canal and Railroad Company.

His father, Andrew Dexter, was a banker who owned the Boston Exchange Bank and built the 150-room Exchange Coffee House hotel. The elder Dexter, according to some sources, demonstrated "for the first time in the New World how to wreck a bank." His father owned other banks, including the Farmers Exchange Bank of Gloucester, Rhode Island, that also failed. To escape prosecution after the bank failures in 1809, Dexter moved his family to Windsor, Nova Scotia.

In time, they returned to the United States, and eight years later, Dexter's father purchased the future site of Montgomery, Alabama, at the Milledgeville, Georgia sales of Indian land and moved his family to Alabama. In 1837, bankrupt, he died of yellow fever in Mobile. Dexter's mother died in 1819, and her family buried her at Oakwood Cemetery, Montgomery.

After the railroad opened from Charleston to Hamburg, other areas of the state petitioned for branches. In 1833, interested citizens in Columbia organized the Columbia Rail Road Company. The South Carolina Railroad authorized the Columbia Company to build the line from Charleston to Columbia. According to the agreement, construction must begin by May 1, 1834, and be finished by May 1836. The Columbia Rail Road Company named a committee to develop a route for the railroad branch. That committee employed Dexter and C.E. Detmold to make the survey.

Dexter married and settled in the Aiken area. In October, he and other residents of Barnwell District petitioned the General Assembly to improve transportation between Aiken and Columbia in order to aid "the Traveler, the Planter, and the Merchant." Specifically, the petitioners wanted the General Assembly to make the stretch of the "Two Notch Road" that ran between Merritt's Bridge and Sharp's on the stage road a publicly maintained road. Although enumerated on the Barnwell County census of 1840, by 1850 Dexter had moved his family to Alabama, where he died in 1853.

CYRIL OUVIERE PASCALIS

Cyril Pascalis, a resident engineer for the Charleston-Hamburg railroad, was born in Philadelphia. A graduate of Harvard, he moved to the Aiken area in 1832. His father, Dr. Felix Ouviere Pascalis, a naturalized Frenchman, was an eminent naturalist, scholar and researcher. He researched silk horticulture, corresponded with noted scientists of his generation, joined an abolitionist society in Philadelphia and researched and published on such disparate subjects as yellow fever and peach production. In 1803, he sent an interesting letter to Thomas Jefferson about the Louisiana territory that the United States had recently acquired from France. Pascalis wrote the president that the United States needed to encourage settlement in the territory and further commented that in order

> *to procure a perfect description of Louisiana, it would require the enterprizing* [sic] *perseverance of men of prudence and of general information. They should be acquainted with all the branches of public Economy, and especially with the comparative results of Commerce and Agriculture. Natural philosophers and tried friends to the Federal governement* [sic] *they might be like political missionaries, capable of influencing a people perhaps corrupt by Loyalty and priesthood. They should be versed in the French and Spanish Languages.*[51]

It is interesting to note that Pascalis's letter of August 18 mirrored President Jefferson's thoughts, as he had just dispatched Meriwether Lewis and William Clark on their famed "Voyage of Discovery" in June 1803. Dr. Pascalis had been involved with the Haitian Revolution and abolitionism in Pennsylvania and never owned a slave. In 1801, while living in Philadelphia, he married Elizabeth Harris McKlintock.[52] Therefore, it is ironic that his widow and son would invest his bequest in a slave plantation in South Carolina.[53]

The Renaissance man Dr. Felix Pascalis, in a handwritten will dated May 21, 1833, named his son, Cyril, as the heir to his estate. Dr. Pascalis died on July 22, 1833, in New York City. His daughter and son-in-law also died in 1833. Consequently, in 1835, Pascalis's widowed mother Elizabeth acquired 790 acres and built a home, known as Pascalina, for herself, her son and her two orphaned grandchildren in the Aiken area. In 1850, she is listed as a seventy-year-old farmer in Barnwell District. By 1860, the Nova Scotia native lived alone and owned real property valued at $5,600 and personal property (including slaves) worth $1,260.

Cyril O. Pascalis continued his work for the railroad. In 1836, while traveling by riverboat on the Mississippi River, Pascalis mysteriously disappeared. Although presumed dead, no one ever found his body. Nevertheless, based on the efforts of Dexter and Pascalis, the planned town of Aiken had wide streets with grassy medians for cattle to graze. Later, residents transformed the medians with trees and shrubs, so that modern Aiken has a unique garden atmosphere.

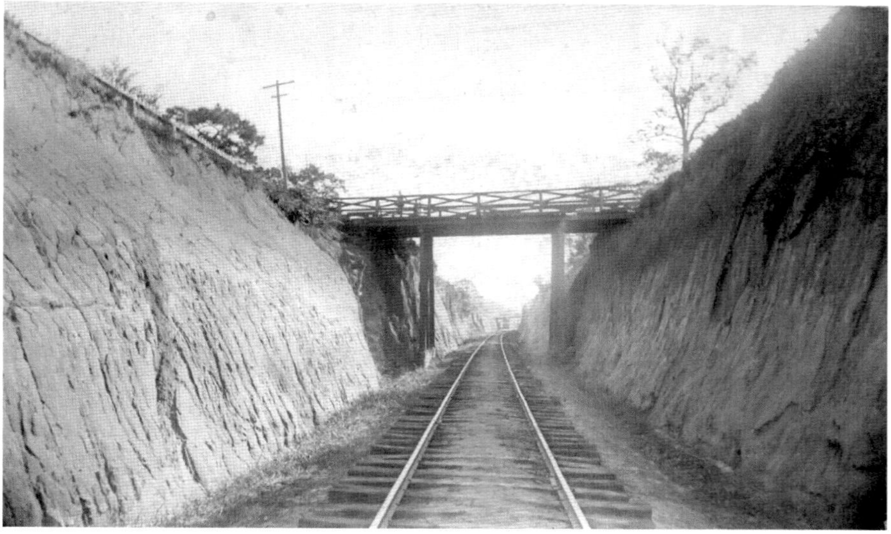

Railroad cut, dug in 1852. Photographed by J.A. Palmer, Aiken. *Evening News* steam print, Augusta, Georgia. *Courtesy Allen Riddick Collection.*

As traditionally reported, romance played a role in the site selection for the new town. Allegedly, local landowner William Williams advised Andrew Alfred Dexter that if Dexter wanted to marry Williams's daughter Sara, the route of the train needed to pass through his property. True or not, the train track traversed the Williams land—and the young couple did marry. But the route had its challenges. For example, until 1852, engines needed a second steam engine to pull the train up the steep grade from Horse Creek Valley. In 1852, a slave-dug ditch lowered the track and eliminated the need for the backup engine.[54]

A NEW TOWN

Shortly after officials laid out the town, concerned citizens in the new town petitioned the legislature to incorporate Aiken. The petitioners stated that they were "frequently disturbed by disorderly persons" because they lacked the ability to develop and promulgate the municipal ordinances necessary to ensure "peace and good order."[55] Consequently, on December 19, 1835, the South Carolina General Assembly duly incorporated the town of Aiken.

William Finlay was the first mayor. A native of Beaufort, Finlay moved to Aiken for the town's climate. Within a few years, town leaders were asking the legislature to alter the charter to give the new town powers similar to those found in Barnwell's charter, so that Aiken could have both the responsibility and the wherewithal to maintain "public highways, streets & alleys" within the town limits.[56]

In August 1838, an anonymous visitor commented on Aiken and its potential: "Aiken is still going ahead, her cotton trade is rapidly increasing." In the visitor's mind, all Aiken needed to be a success was a bank, and he expected city leaders to supply that deficiency soon. Aiken was in a good place in August 1838.[57]

The visitor was correct that plans were underfoot to secure a branch of the Bank of South Carolina for Aiken. On May 30, 1838, about ninety residents from Barnwell District, including twenty-six from the village of Barnwell and fifty-three subscribers from Aiken, petitioned the legislature for a branch bank. The petitioners stressed the location of Aiken on the Charleston railroad, so that it was "the natural outlet for the Trade" for those living in the northwestern parts of the state. In addition, the petitioners included specifics about the amount of cotton that passed

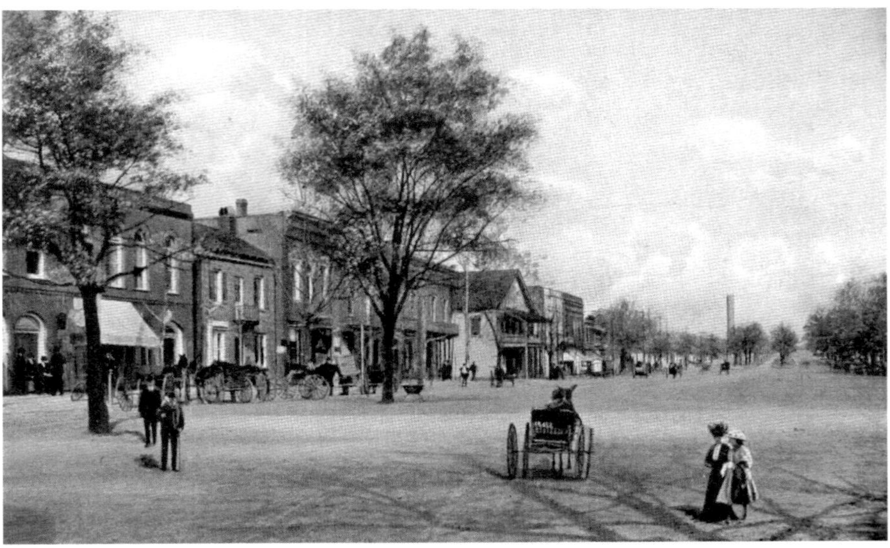

Laurens Street (Main Street) looking north from Park Avenue. Building second from the left, Toole & Toole law office, is one of the oldest remaining structures downtown. "Main Street" was the shopping area between Park Avenue and Richland Street. Hugh C. Leighton Company, manufacturers, Portland, Maine. *Courtesy Allen Riddick Collection.*

through Aiken during the winter of 1837 and spring of 1838—$350,000, and merchants sold an additional $200,000 of goods. These supporters—local businessmen, planters and boosters of the local economy—argued that with access to "Bills of our own Bank," trade and sales would increase. At present, they stated that considerable trade moved through Hamburg to Augusta and down the Savannah to the benefit of Georgia. A branch bank in Aiken would, in their opinion, divert much of that trade to Aiken and keep the profit in South Carolina.

Without a direct connection to Columbia, residents of Aiken, Barnwell or Barnwell District did not have access to banking facilities in the Capital City. In addition, they closed with the assertion that a favorable response to the petition would confer a "great and permanent benefit" on the western and northwestern districts of the state. Several early Aiken civic leaders, such as Francis Schwartz and R.C. Fowke, signed the petition.[58]

The young town continued to thrive until 1839. Just as the new town was gaining momentum, a major disaster struck. A great fire consumed "thirty-six houses, including Stores, Dwellings and Out Houses," as well as a recently constructed "beautiful commodious Market House and Council Chambers." In another petition, Aiken residents more poetically referred to the fire as a "calamitous visitation of Divine Providence," which transformed the "so prosperously flourishing" town of Aiken, the "ornament and chief market" of the area into "a heap of smouldering ruins." In a few short hours, the conflagration destroyed more than $100,000 of property and consumed all but "*a single store* in the business part of the town." Even in legal documents, the pain of loss is evident.

On the heels of the devastating fire, the intendent and city council—James Moseley, A.M. McCane, Lewis Jones and Francis Schwartz—petitioned the South Carolina legislature for increased powers to collect fines and levy taxes in order to, among other matters, organize a fire department. The petitioners cited the "growing Commercial importance" of the town as well as the "salubity [*sic*] of its climate, and convenient location directly upon the Charleston and Hamburg Rail Road" as evidence of the town's importance. They also noted that Aiken was a "desirable resort for invalids" and a summer haven for Charlestonians and other residents of the state. The increased powers were therefore essential to "foster" the economic vitality of the town, promote "health, peace, order and good government" for its citizens and provide "comfort" for its visitors.[59]

Either the legislature did not grant the 1839 petition or the remedy it provided was inadequate, as in 1841, Intendent (mayor) Richard Fowke and the town wardens (council) petitioned again. According to the petition, the "financial resources" of the town were inadequate for "maintenance" and "absolutely incapable of cancelling the heavy liabilities which paralyze the operations" of the Aiken Town Council. Approved by a town meeting, the intendent and wardens asked for several revenue opportunities. First, they wanted a sales tax "not exceeding one eight of one percent on all sales of merchandise" within the town. Second, they wanted to tax all slaves working as laborers or mechanics in Aiken, all free persons of color and all slaves employed by their owners.[60]

In addition to Aiken's leaders seeking legislative relief, in 1840 citizens of Barnwell, Edgefield and Orangeburg again petitioned for the creation of a new judicial district. The petitioners cited the results of the state census of 1839 and specifically of Barnwell District, whose population had grown much faster than any other inland districts and was second only to the population of St. Philip and St. Michael Parishes in Charleston. Barnwell District reported a population of 2,261 versus 2,484 for the two named Lowcountry parishes.

The petitioners also noted that the new judicial district would include areas with the greatest population jump in Barnwell County. That is, the areas enjoying the "stimulating effects of the Rail-Road and the creation of Aiken, and improvement of Hamburg, as commercial points." For example, in 1840, the population of Aiken, including transients, was 973. Of which, 798 were residents. Yet for so many residents to be so far from courts was a major challenge for the citizens of the thriving region.

The proposed new judicial and election district's boundaries were as follows:

> *Commencing at the mouth of Foxes Creek, on the Savannah, thence up said creek to Landrum's Pottery; thence in a direct line to the corner of Edgefield and Orangeburg Districts, on North Edisto River; thence down said river to the old Columbia or Granby Road, below the mouth of Black Creek; thence to Guignard's Bridge on South Edisto River; thence by a direct line to the head waters of Tinkers Creek thence down said Creek to the Upper Three Runs; thence down said Runs to the Savannah River; thence up said river to the place of beginning* [sic].[61]

In 1850, several merchants, such as Salles Randell, operated in Aiken, and the town had at least one hotel. There was also a shoemaker and a doctor, Amory Coffin, who spent his life in Aiken. In 1850, according to

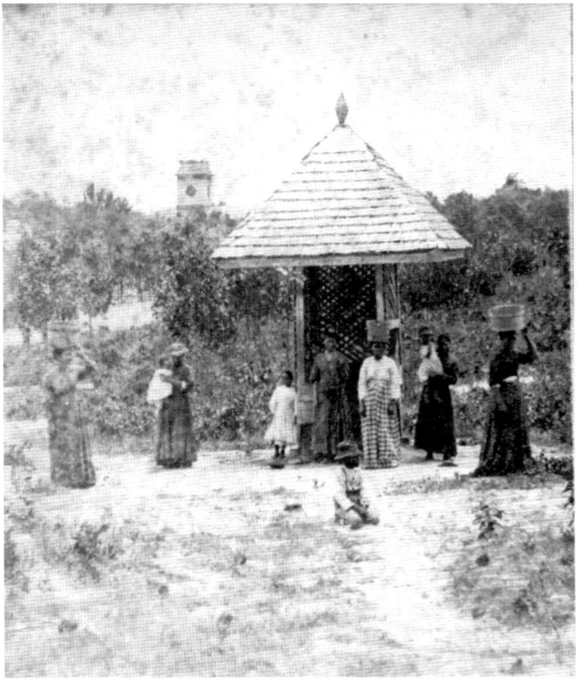

Women at the well. "Gossiping at the Well." Characteristic Southern Scenes. Photographed by J.A. Palmer. St. Thaddeus Church is in the background. The well stood in the middle of the intersection of Laurens Street and Richland Avenue. *Courtesy Allen Riddick Collection.*

the slave schedule, Dr. Coffin owned four slaves. He died on January 12, 1884, and his body lies in the cemetery of St. Thaddeus in Aiken. In 1850, C.H. Lanneau and James Randall operated hotels in Aiken. Lanneau also owned five slaves. Among the forty-year-old Randall's guests in 1850 were two firemen, James Hampton and Sam Edney, and a clerk, Wash Mosley. Randall owned eight slaves in 1850. In addition, in 1850, John A. Harber operated a mercantile establishment. His household included his wife, Hannah, who after her husband's death had a hotel in Aiken, and their son, William, who was a clerk.

In addition, Reverend John Hamilton Cornish appears on the 1850 census. Cornish, a native of Massachusetts, studied at the General Theological Seminary in New York City and then became a tutor on Edisto Island, where he also operated a school. Ordained in 1843, three years later, he became rector of St. Thaddeus Church in Aiken. He remained rector there until his resignation in February 1869. His family buried him at the church cemetery.[62]

In 1854, concerned citizens moved to address their corporate concern about another fire disaster. On December 9, they petitioned the South Carolina legislature to incorporate Aiken Fire Company No. 1. According to the petition, concerned for the "preservation of the property of said town," city council with "voluntary subscriptions" had purchased a fire engine and dug two "fire wells" in the town. The petitioners also stated that they planned to "sink other fire wells in other parts" of Aiken.

The initial members of the company were John N. Mims, George E. Steedman, M.H. Collins, B.T. Rodgers, L.W. Williams and A.T. Wise. The legislature granted the charter, and the following year, the members of the newly incorporated fire company petitioned the legislature for exemption from militia duty. At that time, there were thirty-four members of the fire company, and the members had elected John F. Cutter president, John N. Mims vice-president and Julius Roumillat secretary and treasurer.[63]

The Products of Industry census schedule for 1870 lists three water-powered sawmills and gristmills in Aiken Township. The owners/operators of the mills were T.L. Walker & Son, W.E. Prothro and M. Courtney. The mills produced lumber from the logs and flour and meal from the wheat and

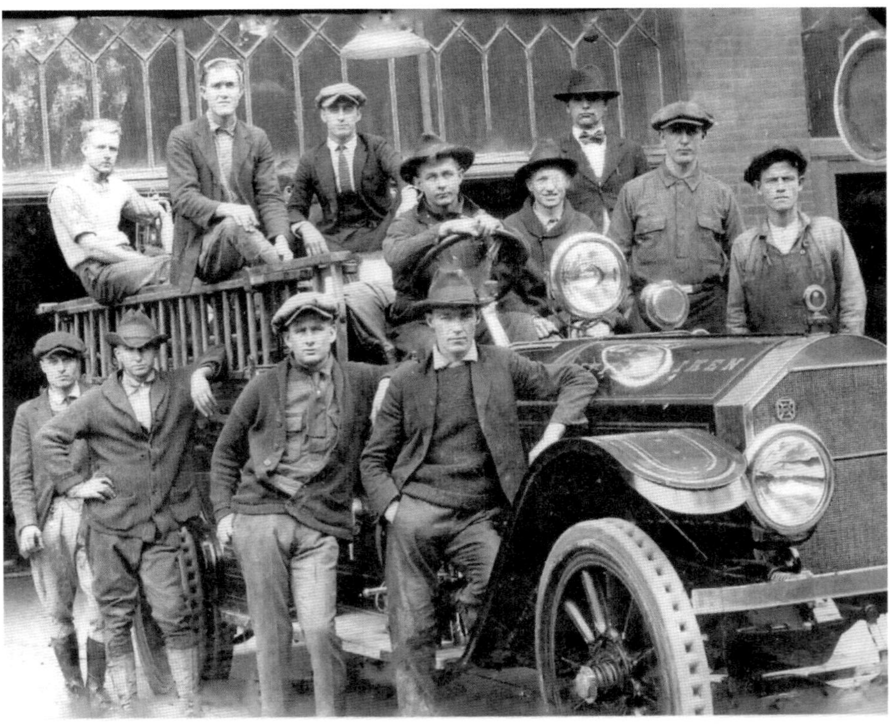

Firefighters with engine, old fire station, circa 1920. The building once housed the opera house, an old movie theater and, until recently, city offices. *Courtesy Allen Riddick Collection.*

corn. By 1880, there were still three milling operations in Aiken Township. The owners/operators were Courtney and Johnson, C.L. Walker and Gunther Lawrence.

Aiken in 1860 was a town with an active business community, several medical doctors and two attorneys-at-law, W.P. Finlay and Edward Smith. Residents included a baker, several schoolteachers, a bootmaker, a blacksmith and butchers. J.M. Gibbs operated a boardinghouse, and the English-born Hannah Harber was the only woman listed as operating a hotel. Willis Burkhalter was the town marshal, John Evans was a barkeeper, C.F. Nurnberger kept a tavern, Thornton Randall was a fireman for the railroad and the town had four ministers in residence. Hasford A. Duncan and M.W. Sams were Baptist ministers, Alexius M. Forster ministered to the Methodist Episcopal congregation and John Hamilton Cornish, discussed earlier, was the Episcopal rector of St. Thaddeus.

Smyrna Baptist Church in Barnwell ordained M.W. Sams, a native of Beaufort, to the ministry. Around 1870, Sams moved to Decatur, Georgia. He died in 1899, and family buried both him and his wife in Decatur. Before

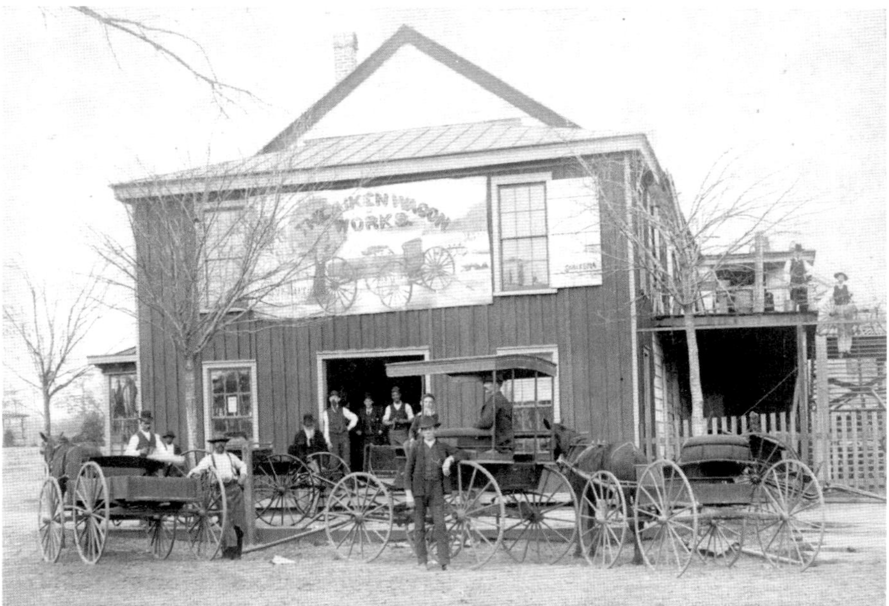

The Aiken Wagon Works, Park Street Extension. Busch House buggy in front, 1880s.
Courtesy Allen Riddick Collection.

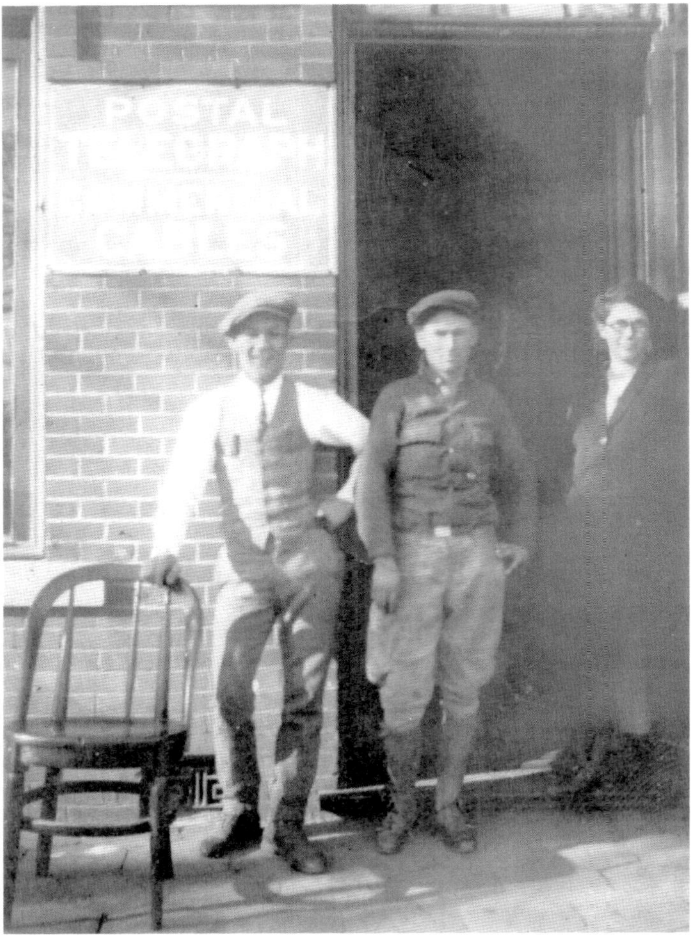

Left: Aiken residents outside post office, advertising "postal telegraph, commercial cables," Park Avenue, Aiken. The date is prior to 1912, when officials built a new post office on the other side of Park Avenue. *Below*: Dr. E.J.C. Wood was the proprietor of the new drug and stationery store. Stereograph, Woods & Company. From *Perkins & Pelot's Photographic Scenery of the South. Courtesy Allen Riddick Collection.*

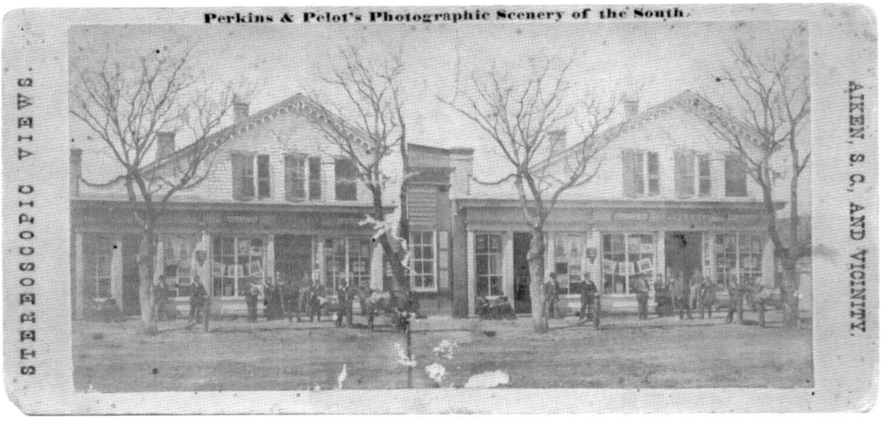

moving to the Aiken area, Alexius M. Forster ministered in York, Winnsboro, Georgetown, Cheraw, Darlington, Marion and Walterboro, South Carolina. His ministry in South Carolina began in 1837.[64]

Many residents pursued the building trades as carpenters and bricklayers. The town boasted several mechanics, a bookkeeper and numerous merchants. Several households of free persons of color also lived in Aiken. For example, William Desorrie was a barber, and Jacob Green operated a livery stable and possessed real estate valued at $1,000. Others were farm laborers. Reflecting the town's railroad origins, J.E. Marley and C.H. Banlett appear as railroad agents; Henry G. Raworth, Nathan Calderbank and Garret Wise are noted as engineers; and T.J. Heyward listed his occupation as "U.S. Officer, Courthouse."

While most town residents were born in South Carolina, there were a sizable number of foreign-born, including merchants and artisans from Germany, Ireland and Bermuda in the Caribbean. Engineer Calderbank was a native of Bolton, England, a mill town in Greater Manchester.

HENRY G. RAWORTH AND ADAM PERRY

Railroad engineer Henry G. Raworth was a native of Charleston. In 1850, the census lists him as a thirty-year-old engineer living in St. Michael and St. Philip Parish, Charleston. By 1860, Raworth had moved to Aiken, where he resided for many years, before moving to Augusta, Georgia, where he died.

In 1834, Raworth began his career with the South Carolina Railroad and worked for the company until failing eyesight necessitated his retirement in August 1888. Born on December 15, 1811, he began his long career apprenticed to Nicholas W. Darrell,[65] another man who served with the railroad from its beginning. In 1831, when a fireman's error caused the boiler of the "Best Friend" to explode, Julius D. Petsch[66] took the wrecked engine parts to Darrell's shop. There, Raworth worked with Petsch to rebuild the destroyed engine. The rebuilt engine bore the appropriate name "Phoenix," as it, too, arose from the ashes.

Raworth was the first engineer to drive the "Phoenix" and served the South Carolina Railroad continuously except for a ten-month stint during the Seminole War. The United States had requested an engineer from the South Carolina Railroad. Railroad officials sent Raworth, who operated a steamboat in the Everglades that transported troops. After that detached duty, Raworth returned to his regular work with the railroad.

In 1871, William H. Brown interviewed Raworth, accompanied him on his familiar route and met Raworth's long-serving black fireman, Adam Perry. According to a letter from Raworth to Brown, prior to emancipation, Major John Schmidt[67] of Barnwell owned Perry and hired him out to the railroad. Initially, Perry worked for George B. Lythgoe, an assistant civil engineer, but he later became a fireman. By October 1872, Perry had worked nineteen years with Raworth. Raworth commended Perry as "faithful, industrious" and "temperate." Over the course of his thirty-seven-year career with the railroad, Perry also worked other positions.

In addition, for seventeen years, Raworth also had a white fireman, Thornton Randall. In 1860, Randall, based on the census, was a twenty-six-year-old fireman living in Aiken with his wife and four young children. According to the Mortality Census Schedule for Barnwell District, Randall, a farmer, died in Aiken in May 1870.

According to Raworth, "when running on Aiken Hill, he had both firemen" working. Traversing the hill was a challenge and required extra power, at least until the 1851 cut. Yet during his long career, Raworth only

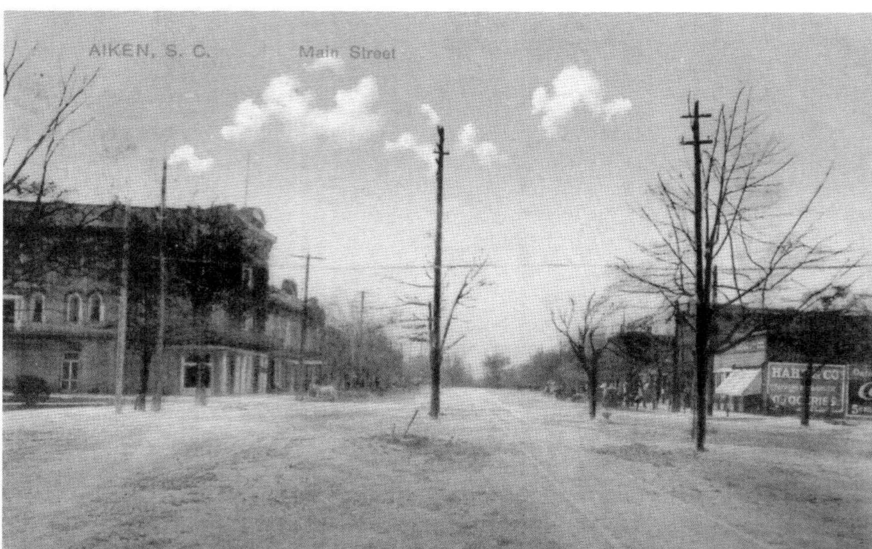

Main Street (Laurens Street), Aiken, showing Hahn's grocery, an unpaved street with streetcar tracks and electric lines. The PCK series, printed in Germany. *Courtesy Allen Riddick Collection.*

had one accident. A washed-out culvert in 1852 caused his only mishap. He also claimed that he hit fewer livestock than other engineers. At his death, many considered Raworth the oldest living engineer in the United States.[68]

During the 1880s, the town of Aiken saw more fires. In 1887, a "whipping fire storm" consumed eight buildings. Apparently, most of the buildings lost were frame. For example, although fire threatened Powell's store, the brick building survived. Some of the affected merchants, such as Courtney & Company, were able to relocate.[69]

Also during the 1880s, the great Charleston earthquake of August 31, 1886, damaged buildings in Aiken and destroyed two milldams.[70]

WORLD WAR II POW CAMP

The World War II years were challenging ones for the United States. Faced with high mobilization, fighting in Europe and Pacific, rationing and shortages at home and ramped-up war industries, the United States also found itself facing the issue of prisoners of war (POWs). Following the Geneva Convention of 1929, the United States assigned the U.S. Army the responsibility for establishing and managing POW camps.

In early 1942, the U.S. Department of War sent all POWs with one exception to the United States for internment. The exception focused on POWs captured by the U.S. Navy. By the end of 1942, the government was housing almost two thousand POWs in the United States. Campaigns in North Africa and the invasion of Normandy greatly increased the number of prisoners needing American "homes." Consequently, the Joint Chiefs of Staff first established internment camps in old Civilian Conservation Camps. Given wartime security, there were restrictions on locations of POW camps. For example, POW camps could not be located near critical industries, in blackout areas along the coast or near U.S. borders with Canada and Mexico. As a result, roughly two-thirds of the initial camps were located in the South and Southwest.

By June 1, 1944, there were fourteen camps in Georgia, including a major facility at Fort Gordon. But within a few months, five small camps opened in South Carolina. Housing roughly 250 POWS, one of those small camps was at Aiken under the administration of Fort Gordon. By mid-1945, Fort Jackson administered the camp. In time, the Aiken camp became one of twenty-one POW camps in South Carolina.

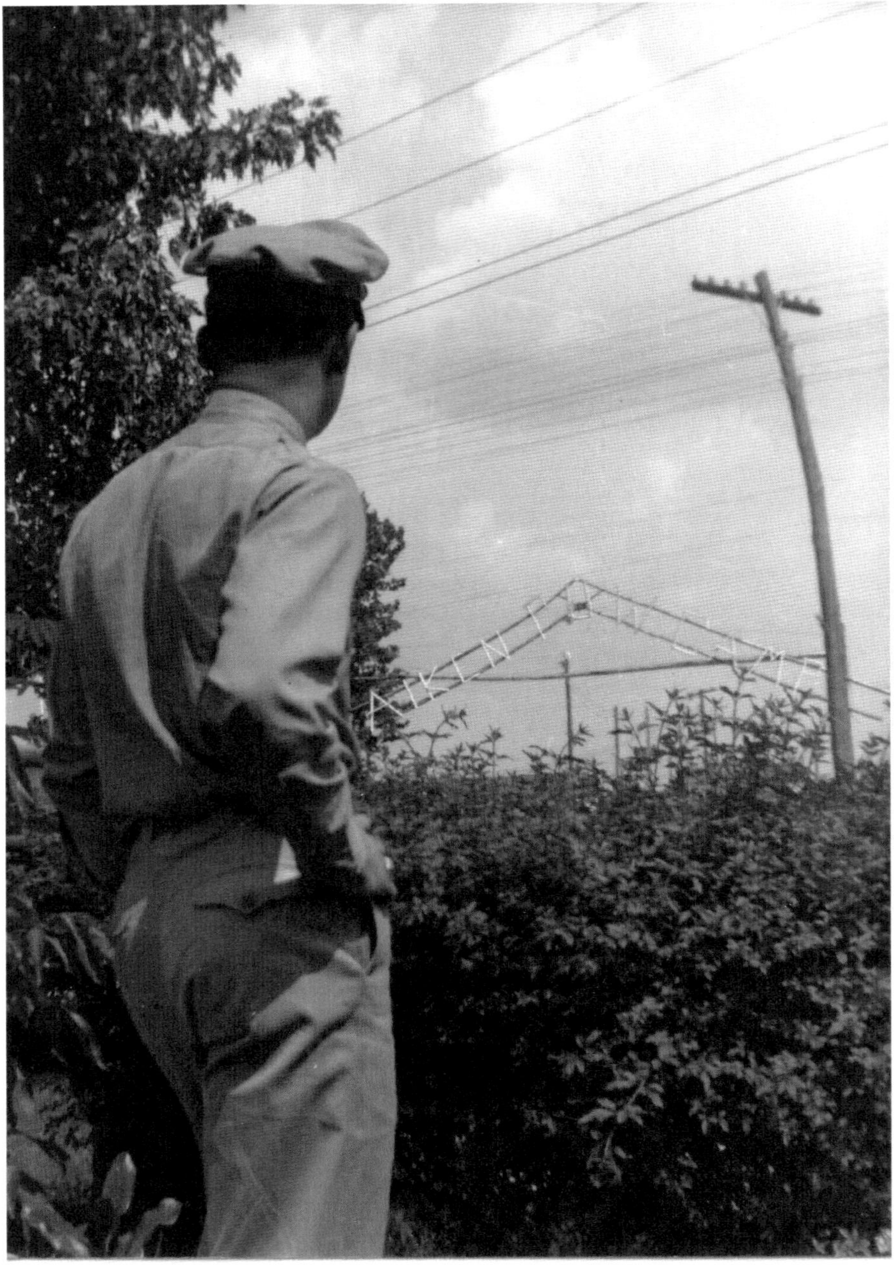

Army officer viewing the Aiken POW camp, Highway 19, 1940s. *Courtesy Allen Riddick Collection.*

Processing POWs involved compiling a personnel record that included a medical examination, a photograph, fingerprints and an interview. One of the big challenges for army personnel was identifying Nazi POWs and separating them from non-Nazi German prisoners. It was not always easy for army staff processing prisoners to identify specific ideological motivations. Not all Germans were Nazis, but not all Nazis wanted their captors to know their political allegiances. Perhaps they feared lack of privileges in the American POW camps, or perhaps they thought there was more room for "fifth column" activities if housed with the general prisoner population. Military officials generally housed known Nazi POWs in Oklahoma. As Command Historian Kathy Roe Coker noted, "This particular concern would later plague Camp Gordon and its Aiken branch camp."

Generally, the prisoners worked within their camps. However, at times, they also worked in off-camp activities such as harvesting and logging. For example, in 1944, Camp (Fort) Gordon sent 246 POWs to the Aiken camp to "work in the pulp-wood industry."

Although originally the Aiken camp housed German soldiers captured in North Africa, as the war dragged on, the camp also held additional German prisoners captured in Italy and France. Most worked in timber-related or agricultural jobs and earned eighty cents per day. For entertainment, the POWs attended classes, engaged in sports or attended concerts. The Aiken camp was a tent city. The prisoners lived in tents with wooden floors. The camp stood on Laurens Street, SC Highway 19, which in 2018 was the site of PruittHealth.

In 1944, someone murdered one of the German POWs at the Aiken Camp. On April 6, 1944, someone hanged Horst Gunter. There was an unexplained eight-hour delay before personnel from Fort Gordon investigated the death. Although at first investigators suspected suicide, the inquest returned murder. Two other German POWs first strangled Gunter and then hanged his body from a telephone pole in a feeble attempt to suggest suicide.

The investigation found several possible causes for the murder. Some alleged inequality in food distribution, while others thought that Gunter had reported a planned "work stoppage to authorities." Perhaps he was too much at home in his new environment, as some mentioned his love of jazz, a distinctly American musical genre, as a factor in his death.

Correspondence with a former Camp Gordon internee suggested another, more chilling scenario. Radbert Kohlass, a long-term detainee at Camp Gordon, described a "dangerous" undercurrent to camp life especially for "active church members." Kohlass cited "Nazi persecution" as a factor in the death of Gunter at Aiken in the spring of 1944. In addition, he alleged that he and other prisoners foiled an attempt to kill a priest in Camp Gordon. After the end of World War II, the Federal Bureau of Investigation investigated Gunter's death, and agents apprehended and punished the killers. Later reports supported the "persecution" possibility, as they found "seven celebrated Nazi-inspired murders" in U.S. POW camps. Even across the broad Atlantic, German POWs could not escape the ideological strife of their homeland.

From news accounts, at least one POW escaped from the Aiken camp. On Monday, January 24, 1944, Gurd Guzstat escaped from a work detail in Hitchcock Woods. Described as blond-haired and blue-eyed, Guzstat had carefully planned his escape and managed to elude capture until Wednesday. Apprehended at the Aiken trash dump, authorities reported that the prisoner planned to steal an airplane and effect his escape.

Gunter Liebelt was an English-speaking German POW who worked part time on the farm of R.H. Holstein Sr. Holstein was the grandfather of Dick

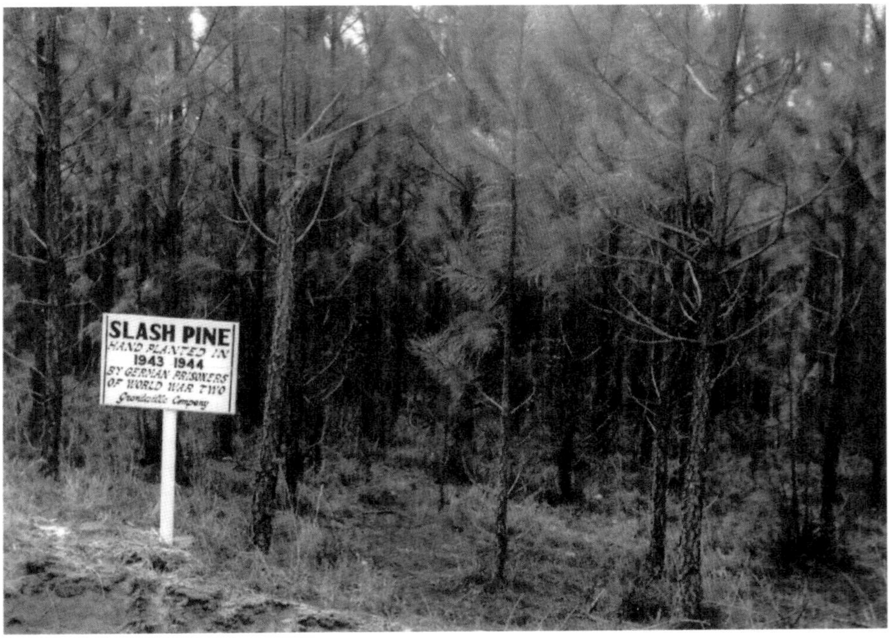

Slash Pine forest, Graniteville Company, planted by German POWs, 1943–44. The army hired out prisoners to assist local companies and farmers. *Courtesy Allen Riddick Collection.*

Holstein, who remembered talking with the prisoner at the camp. Dick Holstein and Liebelt corresponded, and years later, members of Liebelt's family visited the Holsteins in Aiken.

The Aiken POW camp closed in 1946. Today, a historical marker commemorates this little-known chapter in Aiken's long history.[71]

GAS EXPLOSION, 1953

On January 27, 1953, tragedy again struck the city of Aiken. A gas leak on Laurens Street sparked a major explosion. The leak apparently began in the basement of Jones Electric Company on Laurens Street. The explosion triggered a major fire that not only destroyed several other buildings but also killed ten Aiken residents. The next morning, four adjoining buildings—McCreary Dry Goods, Diana Shop, Platt Drugstore and Liles Drugs—were smoking ruins.[72]

An estimated ten thousand vehicles drove through Aiken days after the explosion. Great numbers of sightseers came to view the site of the disaster. Consequently, Frampton Gregory, Aiken police chief, stationed patrolmen at all major intersections. The patrolmen worked to maintain the peace and keep traffic flowing. As one of them pointedly observed, "It looked like every car in Georgia and South Carolina was in Aiken to see the site of the deadly catastrophe."

Local concerns and questions grew as news accounts revealed that the gas company was aware of the leak before the disastrous explosion. Meanwhile, in Columbia, the South Carolina Public Service Commission (PSC), at the request of Aiken mayor Charles Jones, investigated the explosion. Chief Engineer J.C. Lathrop coordinated the commission's investigation. The commission reported that the gas company, Atlanta Gas Light Company, had received two reports of gas leaking in the basement of Jones-Electric Company before the explosion.

According to the PSC investigation, which lasted a week, the company received two reports of gas leaks from the building: the first report at 5:15 p.m. on January 27 the day before the explosion and the second at 8:35 a.m., a scant five minutes before the disaster. The explosion at 8:40 a.m. disrupted downtown Aiken. Despite the reports, the company took "no action." Any gas leak would be noticeable. South Carolina law, for safety reasons, required liquefied gas to be "doubly odorized." While the commission could

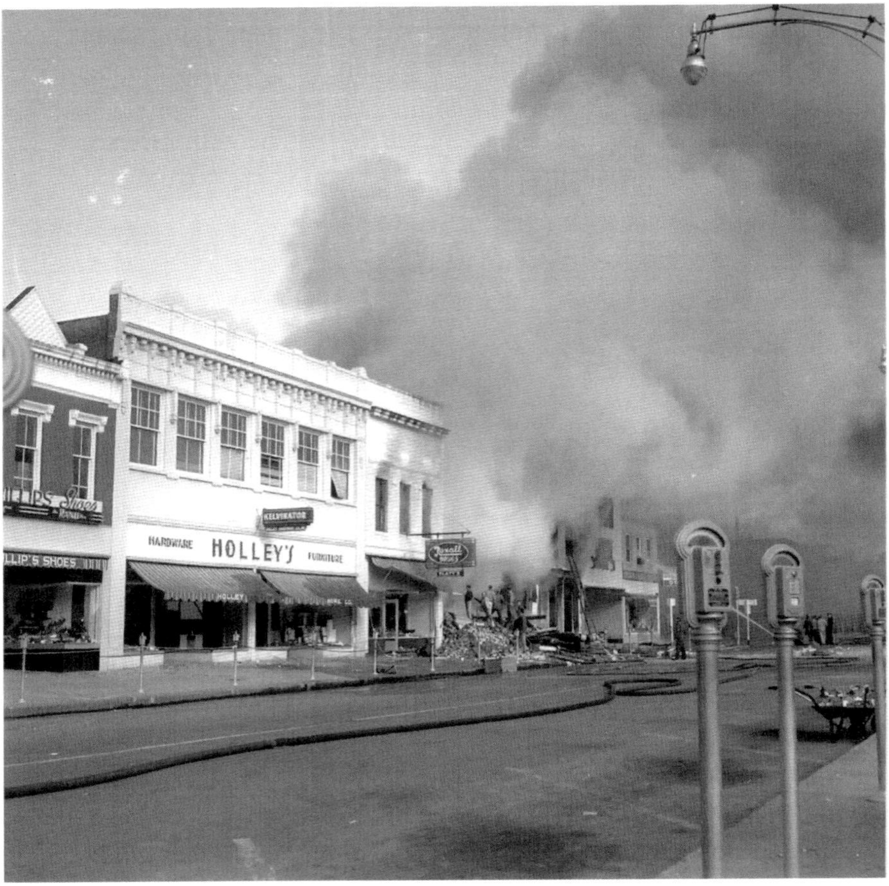

Gas explosion, Phillip's Shoes, Holley's hardware and furniture store and a Rexall drugstore on the left, 1953. All buildings to the right of Holley's were destroyed and replaced. *Courtesy Allen Riddick Collection.*

investigate the facts of the matter, it lacked the authority to establish liability or responsibility.[73]

The PSC may have lacked authority to assign blame, but the Aiken County coroner did not. Coroner J.L. Gregory convened an inquest into the blast. After five hours of testimony, the coroner's jury found that the leak caused the explosion. As part of their deliberations, the members of the jury interviewed eight witnesses. The witnesses included W.O. Jones, owner of Jones Electric Company, and two company employees, Harry G. Tritapoe and Elmer Hittinger. Jones testified that he had smelled gas the afternoon before the explosion, reported the leak to the gas company

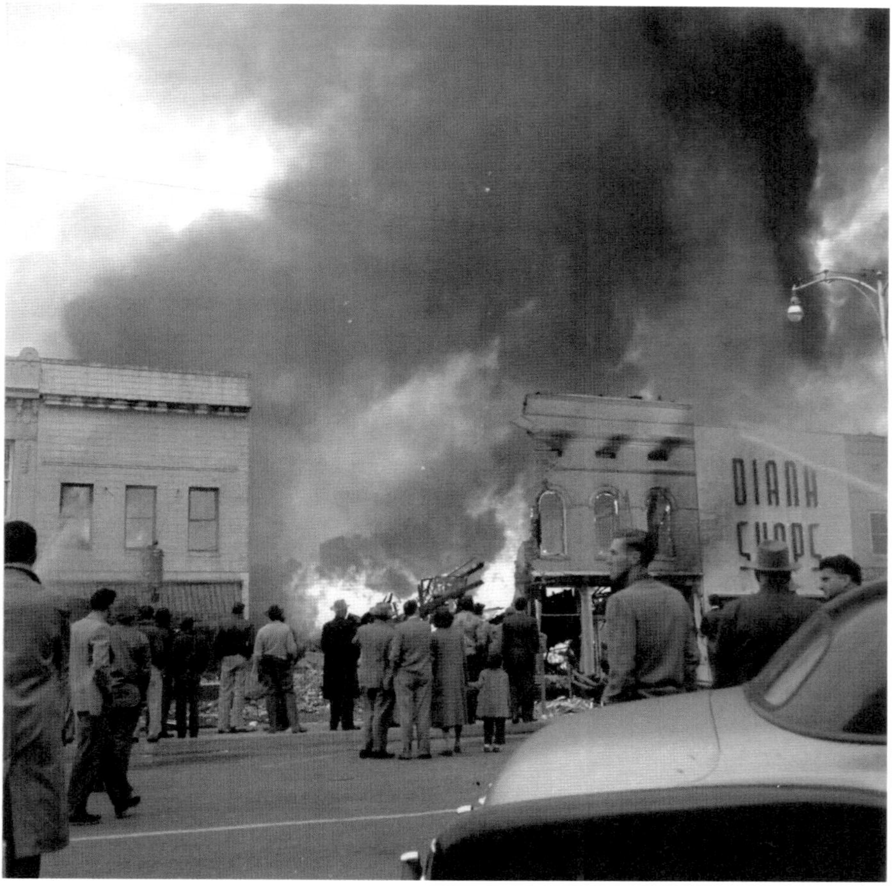

Inferno destroying Jones building, with Diana Shop on the right, 1953. *Courtesy Allen Riddick Collection.*

(three times, he said) and cut off the gas line to his business. His employees supported Jones's account. Hittinger also reported that he heard a hissing noise that sounded like escaping gas. When he investigated the alley outside the building, he found a broken gas pipe that did not connect with the Jones gas meter but instead connected with the meter for Alcoholics Anonymous, which occupied offices upstairs.

George Dunbar Boyd, Aiken manager for the gas company, reported that he personally had received no calls from Jones Electric until within minutes of the explosion. Nevertheless, he did acknowledge that an answering machine had recorded a call on Monday before the disaster. In 1940, the

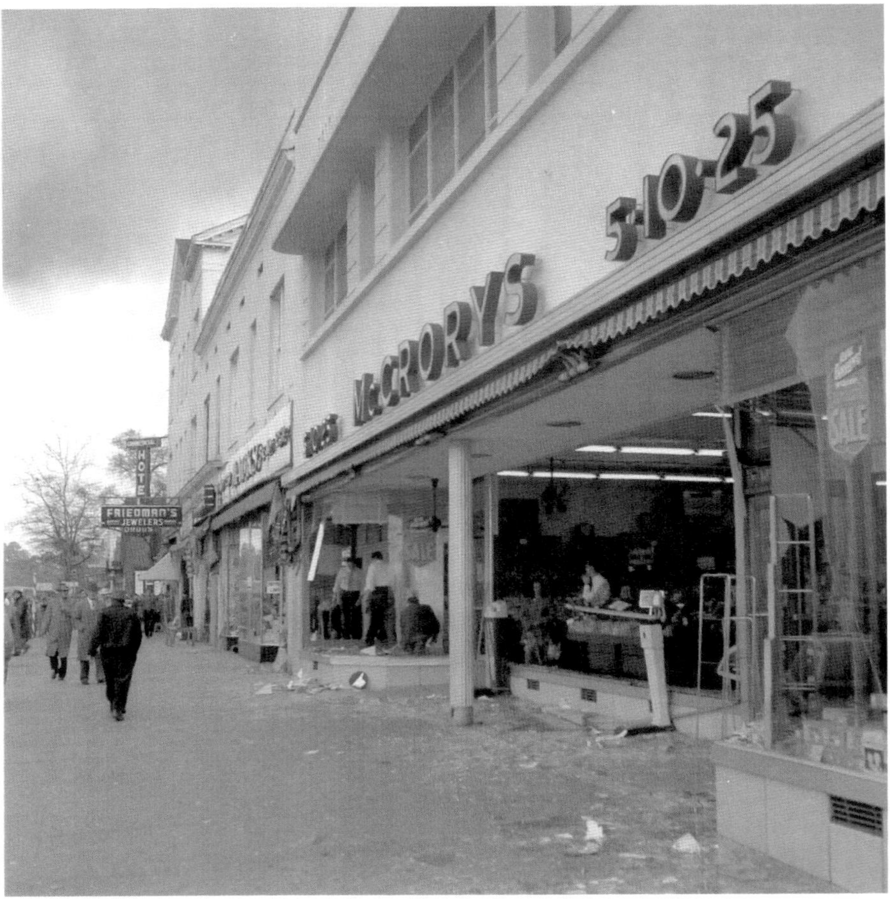

Gas explosion damage, McCrory's, 1953. McCrory's stood almost directly across the street from the site of the explosion. Today, it is an antique mall. *Courtesy Allen Riddick Collection.*

twenty-eight-year-old Boyd, a native of Georgia, lived with his wife and family on Newberry Street in Aiken.[74]

In addition to property damage from the explosion and fire, ten individuals died at their places of work. The victims ranged in age from twenty-one to sixty-seven years. The names of the victims were Lula Mae Weeks (aged sixty-seven), John Henry Neibling (forty), David O. Rutland (forty-three), Emilie McCarter (fifty), James Calhoun Watson (fifty-four), Jack Everette Holley (twenty-five), Ruth Osborne (Mrs. Hugh) Madrey (twenty-one), James "Bubba" Mosley Jr. (twenty-four), Lena Maude (Mrs.

William) Dunkin (forty-nine) and Charles Nelson Long Jr. (twenty-eight). All the casualties, with the exception of Lula Mae Weeks, worked for Jones Electric Company, the primary site of the explosion. Weeks was a clerk in a dry goods store (MCreary's). Long and Neibling worked as electricians for Jones Electric. Madrey, Dunkin, Holley and Rutland worked in sales for Jones Electric. Mosley was the janitor, and McCarter and Watson worked as bookkeepers and clerks. According to their death certificates, all of the casualties died from third-degree burns, except Long and Neibling, who died from compound fractures of the skull.[75]

After the explosion, Jones Electric operated out of a warehouse in downtown Aiken. On October 15, Jones Electric Company began a three-day reopening celebration. The company, owned by W.O. Jones and his son J.O. "Jimmy" Jones, reopened in new facilities on the corner of Greenville Street and Hayne Avenue. The three days of celebration featured prizes and an organ concert by Kay McAbee, a versatile and talented young man.[76]

SAVANNAH RIVER PLANT

When the Atomic Energy Commission announced plans to build a mammoth facility along the Savannah River, residents of Aiken had mixed reactions. Many shared the sentiments of Lester Moody, secretary of the Augusta Chamber of Commerce: "The development will revolutionize the Savannah river basin." He also predicted a major influx of "educated people, technicians, professional men, highly skilled workers, Yankees and Middle Westerners with other viewpoints....We may not enjoy all the changes, but it is impossible to be conservative about our future." Leaders in both Aiken and Augusta saw a future of economic growth, population expansion and change.

Yet Aiken leaders feared the impact of such massive development on its prized Winter Colony. They did not want the city to "lose its character as a pretty, quiet winter resort for wealthy and socially prominent sportsmen from the North." In 1950, many of Aiken's main streets were unpaved, more suitable to horse than automobile traffic.

In December, change was at hand. A Columbia concrete company planned to build a plant in Aiken. On another front, bulldozers were clearing land for forty new homes to house an expected influx of plant-related workers.

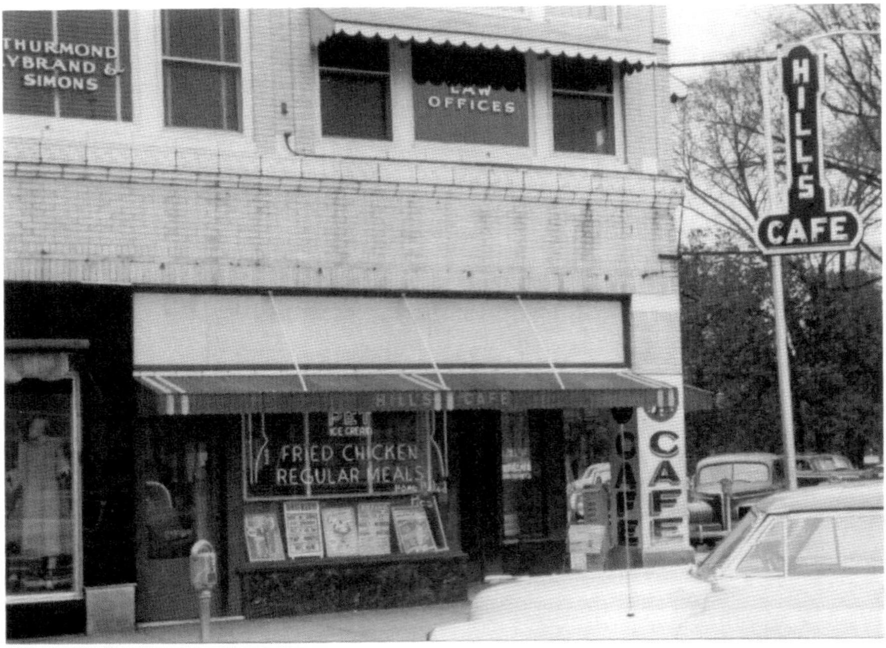

Hill's Café, one of Aiken's few early cafés, with law offices of Thurmond, Lybrand & Simons. Laurens Street at Park Avenue, Aiken, 1940s. *Courtesy Allen Riddick Collection.*

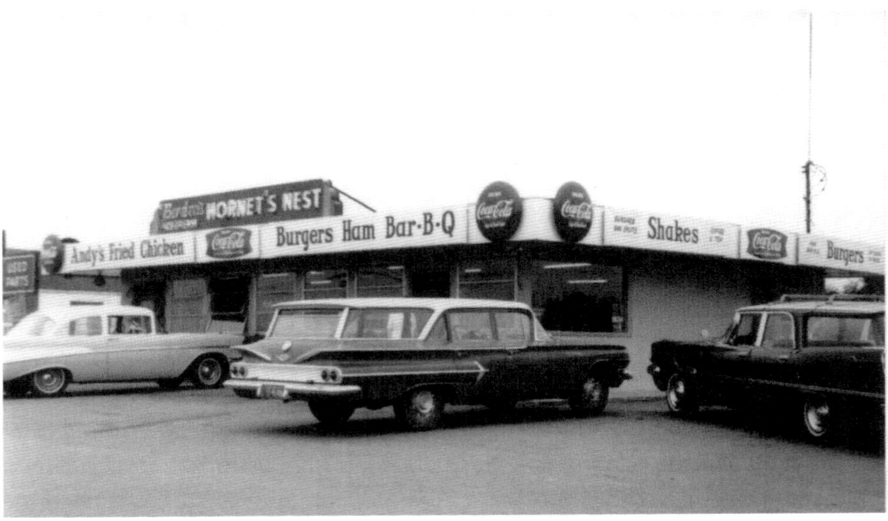

The Hornet's Nest, drive-in restaurant featuring "Drinks 'Good for Atomic Ache.'" Corner of Rutland Drive and Highway 1. Proprietors Andy and Jonesy, 1950s. One of the earliest fast-food restaurants in Aiken. Located near the recently opened high school. *Courtesy Allen Riddick Collection.*

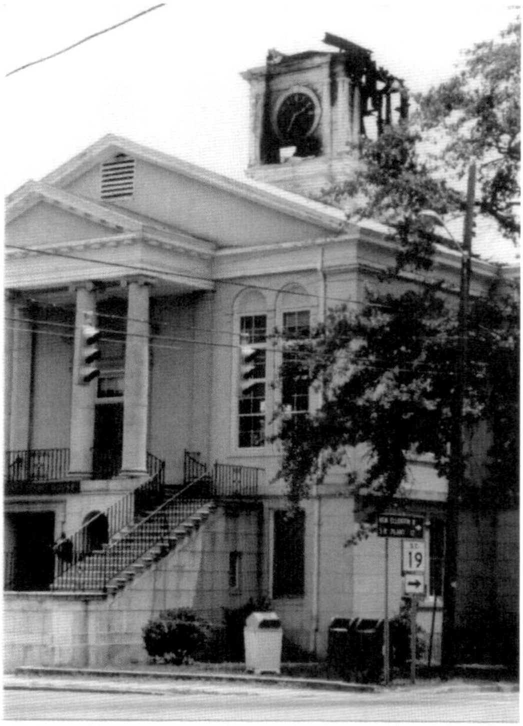

Right: Aiken County Courthouse, built in 1881. In 1981, lightning struck the bell in the cupola and damaged the cupola. *Courtesy Allen Riddick Collection.*

Below: Cars driving on flooded Richland Avenue corner of Blake's Drugs/Hotel Aiken, circa 1964. The car on the left displays an Ohio 1964 license tag. *Courtesy Allen Riddick Collection.*

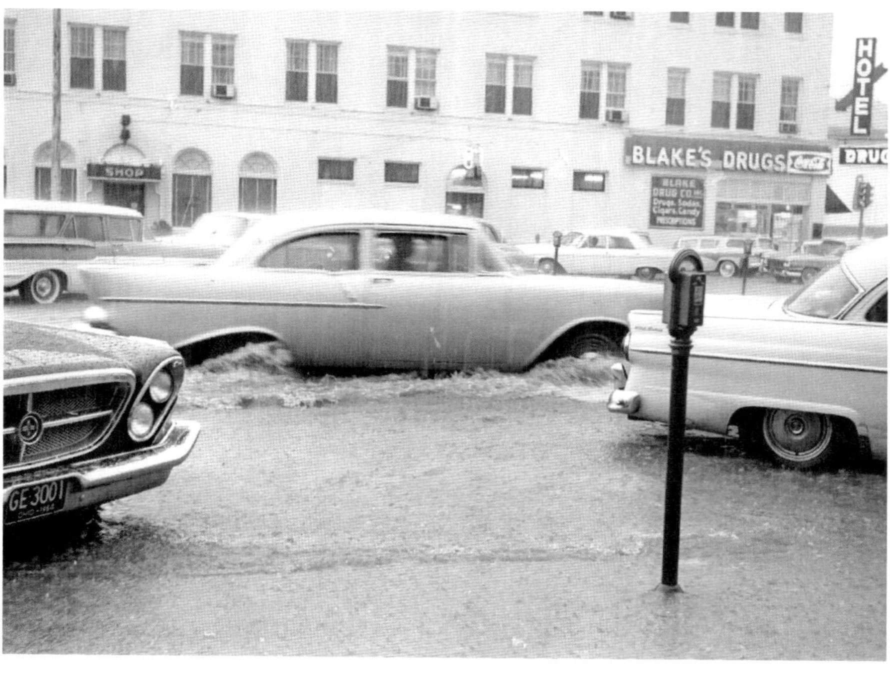

Aiken mayor H. Odell Weeks foresaw a population boost of 4,000 that would give the city a year-round population of 7,000. Nevertheless, Weeks added, "we are hoping to keep our Northern visitors, too." Winter Colony visitors averaged 2,500, but were usually only in Aiken between "New Year's and Easter."

Despite Weeks's assurances, some Winter Colony residents spoke of moving. Mrs. Robert H. Wilds countered, "Nonsense. Some people will believe every cockeyed rumor rather than the truth. I am all for this thing, provided the development is intelligently handled."[77]

The Savannah River Plant was only one of many change agents that have altered the streetscape of downtown Aiken. Yet the layout of the city, the historic business district and the tree-lined medians offer glimpses of the Aiken that was and hints of the Aiken to come.

Chapter 4

LOST GRANDEUR

Highland Park Hotel and Hampton Terrace Hotel

Aiken's salubrious climate attracted visitors from the city's earliest years. Some came for specific health reasons, others to escape the summer miasma of the Carolina Lowcountry. As poet Thomas H. Williamson wrote, Aiken was "secure from tides and ocean mists and free from sleet and snow."[78]

Aiken, located in the fall zone, has sandy soil, a lack of insect-borne diseases and a clean water supply. The South Carolina General Assembly incorporated Aiken in 1835, and by the 1840s, the town boasted a well-deserved reputation as a health and summer retreat. Many considered Aiken a healing place, with an ideal climate for those suffering from tuberculosis and other debilitating illnesses. In 1852, the *Boston Medical and Surgical Journal* praised Aiken not only for its climate but also as a respite for northerners, as the town had "many of the northern comforts of…home."

On August 1, 1838, an anonymous visitor commented on the drought, as the area had not had any rain in weeks. Although some were concerned about the cotton crop, the wheat crop was doing well. He further noted that although the temperature was roughly the same in Charleston as Aiken, to him the air in Aiken "braces rather than debilitates." He also spoke positively of the "celebrated Coker Springs," with its copious and healing "sparkling draught." At that time, Mary Schwartz operated a boardinghouse near the entrance to Coker Springs, while another boardinghouse operated at the "outlet of the village." Both lodging possibilities had all their rooms filled in March but were also expecting more visitors.[79]

A visitor to Aiken in 1849 provided a window on Aiken as a health resort. Charlotte Hixon accompanied her sister-in-law to Aiken and spent two weeks there at a local boardinghouse in May and June 1849. Hixon traveled to Aiken by rail from Charleston. Her description of the terrain may remind a few modern road warriors of I-20: the "country through which we passed was barren and desolate, principally covered with pine forest." The trip from Charleston took almost seven hours. The exhausted travelers stayed in a boardinghouse operated by Mary Schwartz. The 1850 census listed her as a hotelkeeper with real estate valued at $2,500. Among her household members were J.B. Schwartz, a medical doctor, and Francis Schwartz, who served several terms on the Aiken City Council. Schwartz attracted an elite clientele from New England, New York and the Lowcountry.

Life in Aiken was quiet. Hixon and her sister-in-law frequently went horseback riding. Hixon also attended services at the Episcopal, Baptist and Methodist churches and frequently commented on the weather. On May 5, she wrote that the day began at seventy degrees and a cold wind blowing. Surprisingly, by noon, snow had begun to fall and fell for two hours, covering everything. So much snow fell that tree limbs bent under the weight. As Hixon noted, "Ripe strawberries and fresh snow! How incongruous!" In typical South Carolina fashion, by 7:00 p.m., the unseasonal snow had melted, and by the end of May, she was complaining about the heat. On June 7, Hixon and her sister accompanied other lodgers and their landlady on an excursion to Augusta. They traveled by rail to Hamburg and then by omnibus to Augusta for shopping. She also mentioned a trip to Graniteville. Of interest, however, is that she did not mention a trip to Coker Springs, a major health destination, or treating her sister-in-law with the waters there.[80]

In March 1855, Joshua Hathaway visited Aiken. Like many visitors, he commented on the weather. He noted thunderstorms and "very hot, sultry weather." Then he shared his impression of his boarding arrangements. Concerning the food, he wrote, "We are not faring very well—meats seldom cooked properly and served up badly always—tea generally weak as water (then our coffee is strong enough to make it up)." Hathaway also had a jaundiced view of the Aiken residents. He wrote that the residents were "ignorant and common, but respectably connected (every body [*sic*] is, in the south)." Citing a steady diet of pork and cornbread, Hathaway reassured his correspondent, "You would not think we could live here now but taking all things into consideration, we are as well or better off here than at any other Boarding house in Aiken or the Hotel." Hathaway continued that the hotel had declined greatly over the winter and that "[b]oarders complain of very short fare."[81]

In the postbellum years, the town sought to regain its status as a major health resort. The 1870s marked the beginning of a major change for the town. Celestine Eustis brought her ward, Louise Eustis, to winter in Aiken for her health. Louise Eustis loved the Aiken climate and the access to equestrian pursuits. Later, Louise Eustis married Thomas Hitchcock, a well-to-do New York sportsman. She convinced him to winter in Aiken, and the future of this "quiet, pretty, and sleepy country village" changed. As she spread the word about the climate and beauty of Aiken, others traveled from the Northeast, renting, boarding and building the homes that became Aiken's Winter Colony.

Visitors lauded Aiken as an uncrowded winter resort where incomers had breathing space, freedom and access to the town's "unrestricted playground." In 1914, social activities in Aiken included golf, horseback riding, motoring, trapshooting, foxhunting, concerts, dancing and bridge.[82] Most agreed that Aiken's climate was the "mainspring that" kept Aiken in motion.[83]

To meet the demands of visitors, Aiken had a long tradition of boardinghouses and hotels. One of the larger antebellum hotels was the Clarendon. Also known as the Park Avenue Hotel, the hotel stood across Park Avenue from the train depot. Many guests, as a result, arrived courtesy of the South Carolina railroad. Some consider the two-story structure a harbinger of the larger, magnificent hotels of the late nineteenth and early twentieth centuries.[84]

HIGHLAND PARK HOTEL: THE "QUEEN OF WINTER RESORTS"

Aiken's grandest resort was the first Highland Park Hotel, built a few years after the end of the Civil War. Benjamin Pulaski Chatfield (1827–1901), a native of Connecticut, and other investors envisioned a "grand hotel and sanitarium" in Aiken. Workers erected this sprawling resort during 1869–70. The hotel stood "on a plateau" between Highland Park Drive and Hayne Avenue at the end of Park Avenue with a wonderful view.

The planned sanitarium/hotel had one thousand beds. P.A. Jewett, also of Connecticut, had served on the staff of Yale University. Consequently,

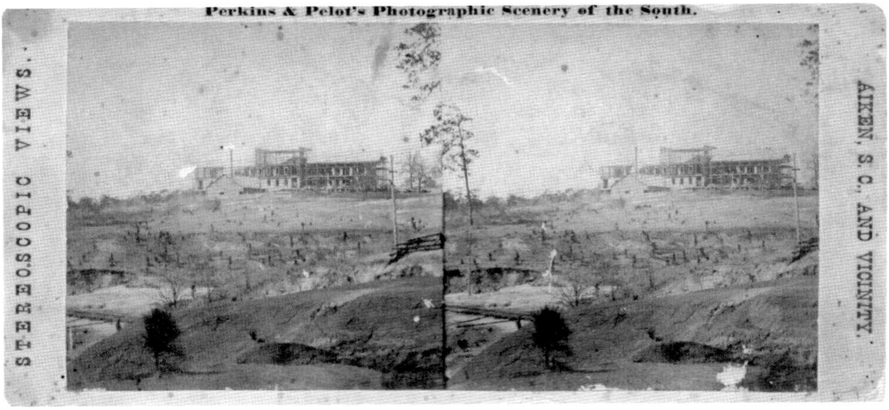

Highland Park Hotel under construction at the head of the old incline, 1869–70. Prior to development of the Winter Colony, Aiken was a well-known health destination. From *Perkins & Pelot's Photographic Scenery of the South. Courtesy Allen Riddick Collection.*

he was an experienced health administrator and a good choice to oversee the health facility. Unfortunately for Jewett, who was a major investor in the sanitarium, while the hotel was successful, the sanitarium closed in two years. Discouraged, Jewett returned to Connecticut.

Family members also enjoyed the amenities of the Highland Park. For example, on March 30, 1892, investor Chatfield's mother-in-law, Mrs. Sarah R. Bristol, also of Connecticut, died at the Highland Park Hotel. Mrs. Bristol was eighty-nine years old.[85]

In 1879, Chatfield, the president and proprietor of the Highland Park Hotel Company, wrote a prospective client about the hotel's accommodations. As Chatfield explained, room rates varied according to location. For example, the rate for rooms "up one flight" ranged from fourteen dollars to twenty-five dollars per night; "up two flights," rates ranged from twelve dollars and fifty cents to twenty dollars per night. The hotel did not have fuel surcharges or charge extra for room service. At the time, E.H. Tomlinson was manager/secretary and treasurer of the hotel company. Highland Park also prided itself on having "a large and well stocked Livery Stable connected with the House."[86]

In succeeding years, the owner added several additional wings to the original building. For example, in 1897 during the off-season, the owners added eighty rooms. As a result, when the hotel opened on December 17, 1897, the hotel could accommodate four hundred guests.[87] The hotel was several floors tall and featured sweeping porches that afforded guests

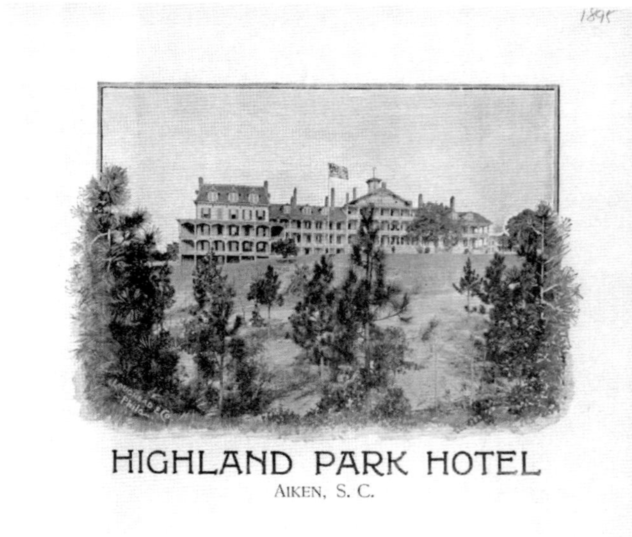

Highland Park Hotel. Published by W. Reid Kirkland, Aiken. *Courtesy Allen Riddick Collection.*

panoramic views. The Highland Park operated between November and June and offered guests a variety of amenities. Entertainment options included billiards, bowling, tennis, croquet, horseback riding and hiking trails. Guests also had easy access to alcoholic beverages. The Highland Park Hotel was one of only seven South Carolina hotels that had dispensaries. Under South Carolina's dispensary law, only approved state outlets could retail liquor and other alcoholic beverages. Also, in 1897, a cyclone struck Aiken and, over the course of thirty-five minutes, damaged the roof of the Highland Park Hotel.[88]

Ads for the hotel, managed by A.C. Judd, claimed "the Driest Climate east of the Rockies" and touted the freshness of the milk, as the hotel had its own dairy. The hotel also featured spring water, bells in every room and bathrooms on each floor. In print, the hotel boasted, "Highland Park Hotel Aiken in the Land of the Pines South Carolina: the Queen of Winter Resorts."

Then, in 1898, disaster struck. The recently renovated frame hotel burned on February 6, 1898. According to news reports, the fire began in the laundry room. At the time, there were 168 guests sleeping quietly in their rooms. Once alerted, all the guests were able to exit safely from the hotel with their baggage. Although the owners had the hotel insured for $98,000, the loss amounted to $165,000. Apparently, "in the excitement of the fire," a hotel employee "shot and badly wounded" Thomas Fallon of Boston. As a tribute to the fame of the hotel, the story of the fire made the front page of a section of the *New York Times*.[89]

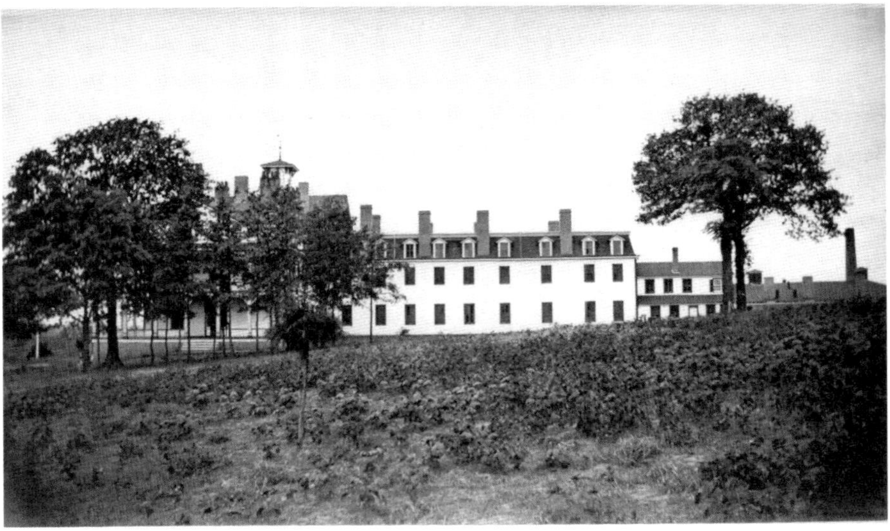

Side view original Highland Park Hotel. Photographed by J.A. Palmer, Aiken. *Courtesy Allen Riddick Collection.*

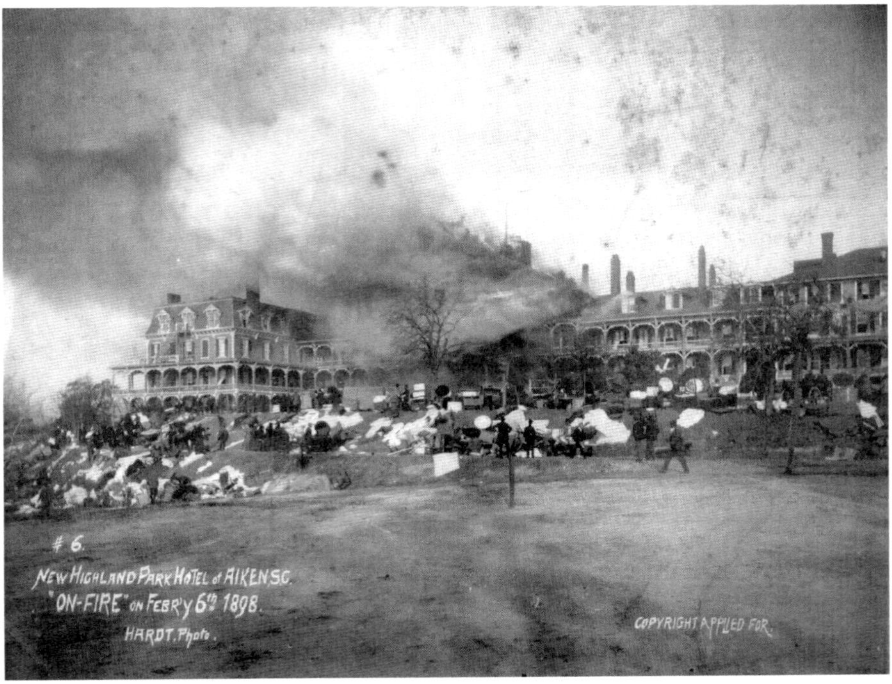

Fire destroys the new Highland Park Hotel, February 6, 1898. *Courtesy Allen Riddick Collection.*

In 1900, Benjamin P. Chatfield, former hotel proprietor, lived on Pendleton Street in Aiken. His household included his wife of fifty years, Sarah, and his widowed son-in-law, Julian Taft. Chatfield was also an inventor, and on September 11, 1878, he filed a patent with the United States Patent Office for a filter. Chatfield died in Aiken, and friends returned his body to Connecticut for burial at Riverside Cemetery in Oxford.[90]

In a way, it is ironic that Chatfield spent much of his life in Aiken and died there. His brother, Colonel John Lyman Chatfield, was a Civil War hero. Colonel Chatfield led the Third and Sixth Connecticut Regiments and fought at Bull Run and with the Federal expeditionary force that seized Port Royal Harbor in South Carolina in 1861. On July 18, 1863, Colonel Chatfield fell mortally wounded in the charge on Fort Wagner during the Second Battle of Morris Island, South Carolina.

PARK-IN-THE-PINES HOTEL

Shortly after the first Highland Park Hotel burned in 1898, developers, undeterred, erected another grand hotel, the Park-in-the-Pines. The new hotel was a worthy successor to the lost Highland Park Hotel. The Park-in-the-Pines stood between Edgefield and Hampton Streets on two hundred wooded acres. The elegant resort boasted three hundred rooms for a discerning clientele.

In 1901, the hotel opened for the "season" on January 10. Leased by the Harry W. Priest Company, John A. Sherrard was the manager for the season. Sherrard was a professional hotel manager and proprietor with extensive experience in Massachusetts. For example, he managed the Colonial Arms Hotel, Eastern Point, Gloucester, Massachusetts, and in 1909 was the proprietor of the Hesperus Magnolia Hotel, North Point, Gloucester. In the 1910 city directory of Swampscott, Massachusetts, Sherrard of Aiken, South Carolina, was listed as the proprietor of the Hotel Preston in Swampscott. According to the 1910 census, thirty-nine-year-old John A. Sherrard, a native of Canada, was a naturalized citizen who lived on Monadnock Street in Boston with his wife and three children.

An advertisement stressed the hotel's accessibility. By rail, Aiken was only twenty-two hours from New York City. Despite its location and great amenities, a nemesis lay in wait. On February 2, 1913, another fire claimed the Park-in-the-Pines Hotel.

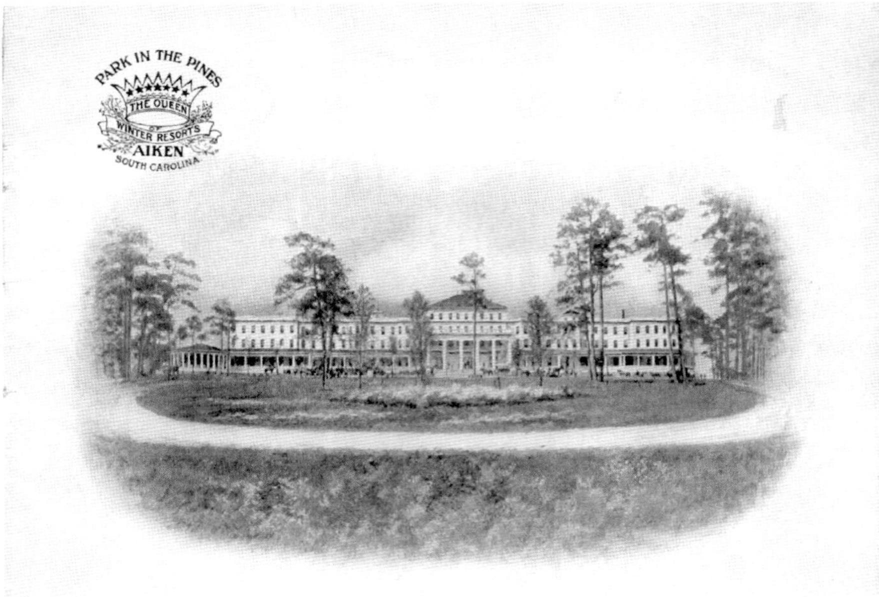

The elegant Park-in-the-Pines Hotel. Promotional brochure. *Courtesy Allen Riddick Collection.*

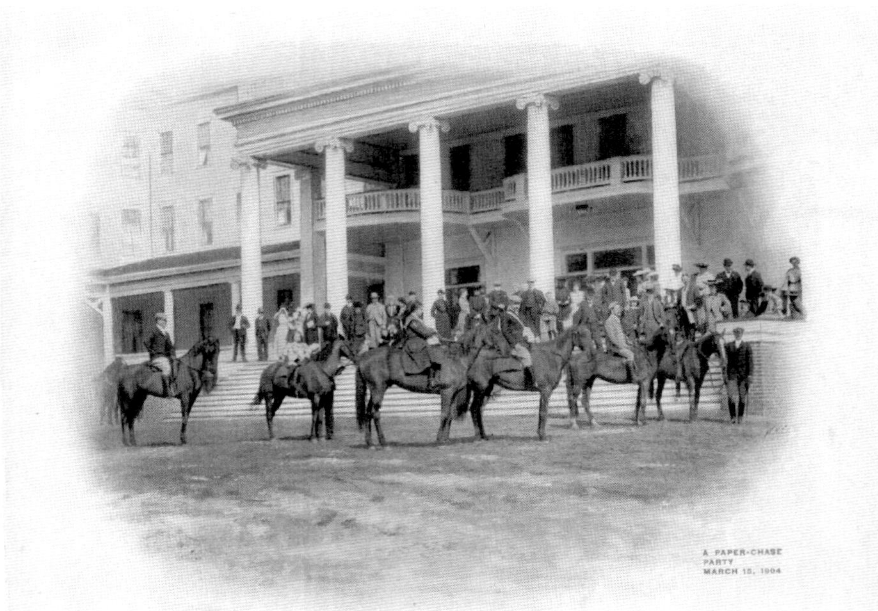

Equestrian entertainment, Park-in-the-Pines Hotel, March 15, 1904. Promotional brochure. *Courtesy Allen Riddick Collection.*

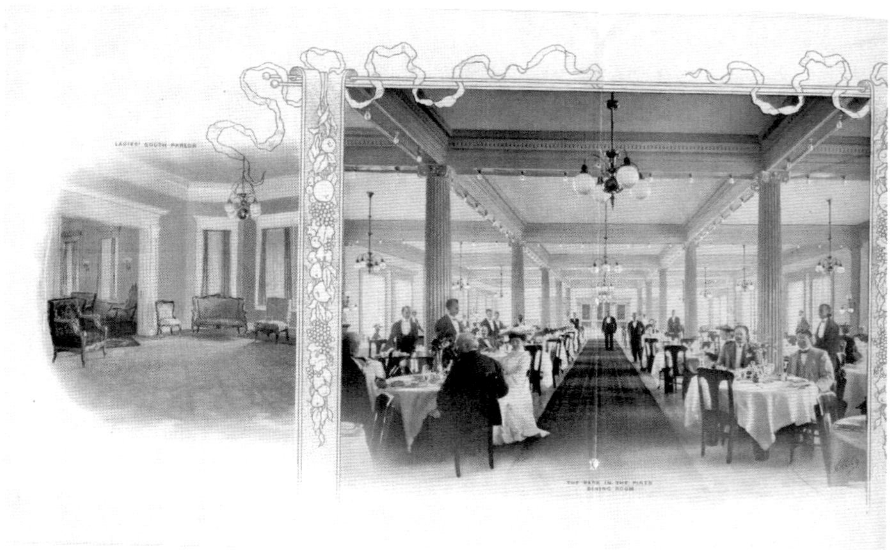

Dining room, Park-in-the-Pines Hotel. Promotional brochure. *Courtesy Allen Riddick Collection.*

The "spectacular" fire began in a storeroom in the basement that housed one thousand feet of lumber stored for a future renovation. Around 11:00 a.m., smoke rose through cracks in the floor. Manager A.F. Dick rushed to the basement but collapsed, overcome with smoke. The situation was dire, and only the quick action of his staff saved his life. Unfortunately, when they opened the door to the storeroom, the flames quickly shot up the adjacent elevator shaft. Flames engulfed the three-story frame structure. All forty-four guests escaped, but escape was perilous, especially for those in rooms on the upper floors. Most guests fled with little more than what they were wearing or could grab quickly.

Aiken firefighters were unable to extinguish the blaze. First, "the building proved to be a veritable fire trap," and second, water pressure was too low for the firehoses to work effectively. The hotel stood one mile from the center of Aiken. The rescued guests sat in the chill with their shawls and towels while perhaps one thousand Aiken residents watched the inferno. By 1:00 p.m., the hotel was a pile of smoking rubble. Ironically, as the last wing burned, Mrs. Dick, a group of new guests and twenty-five young women hired in New York to work in the hotel arrived.

Estimated losses for the "palatial" hotel exceeded $250,000. The fire moved so fast and burned so hot that firefighters were only able to salvage a few items

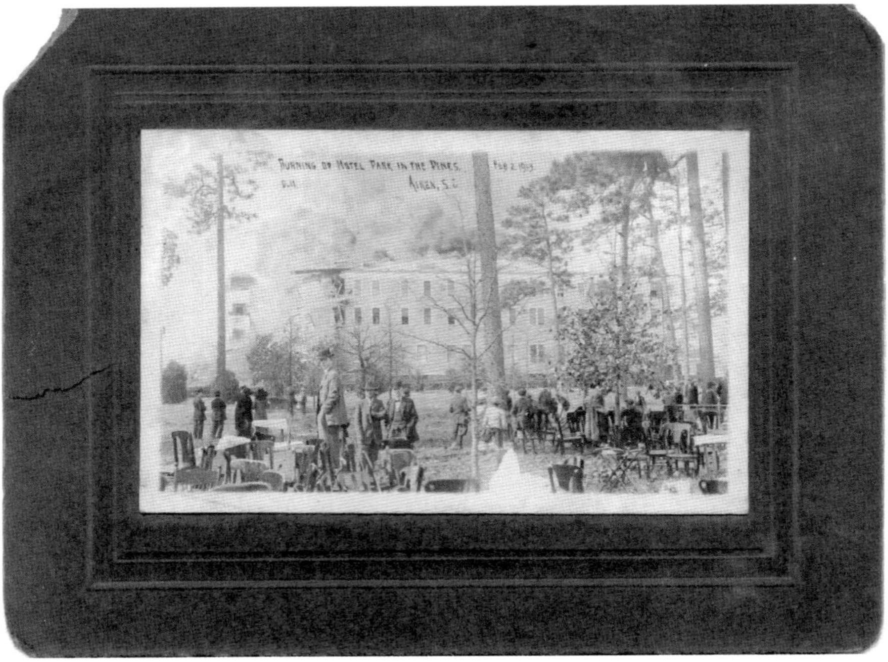

Park-in-the-Pines Hotel burns, February 2, 1913. *Courtesy Allen Riddick Collection.*

from the wing that housed the dining room. Many guests lost thousands of dollars in jewelry and the money deposited in the hotel's safe. Local residents housed some of the affected guests; others checked into other hotels, and a few left the area. The owner of the hotel was Mrs. Julia McArthur of Detroit, Michigan. When built, the initial phase of hotel construction required an investment of more than $100,000. The loss of the Park-in-the-Pines seriously limited accommodations for winter visitors to Aiken.[91]

HIGHLAND PARK REDUX

Nevertheless, construction the following year improved the Aiken accommodation scene. A second Highland Park Hotel opened on the site of the first one. In May 1914, developers awarded a contract to build a new hotel to W.R. Harbeck of Columbia. The initial contract of $45,369 included only the building. The builders expected the addition of plumbing and heating costs to add another $10,000 to the cost of construction. The developers were a stock company organized primarily by Aiken residents. Members of the building committee were H.M. Dibble, Henry Bush and I.W. Fowler. The new hotel had sixty-three "en suite" guestrooms and twelve servant rooms, a stucco exterior finish and metal roof shingles.

Great excitement greeted the news since Park-in-the-Pines burned in February 1913, "Aiken has been without a large and roomy hostelry." As a result, "It was practically impossible to accommodate the winter tourists." The new hotel sat on the site of the old Highland Park Hotel, "perhaps the most popular and best known tourist hostelry in the South." The site was optimum, as it was a block from the post office and business district and adjoined the popular Highland Park Golf Course.

According to Wilkins Byrd, McGhee and McGhee, African American contractors in Aiken, built the ornate Spanish Revival edifice. If this assertion is correct, perhaps the Columbia firm subcontracted with it or there was an issue with the original contract. The reborn Highland Park was the last of Aiken's grand hotels. An ad in 1928 guaranteed a "high-class... resort," "discriminating clientele," "delightful climate" and "18-hour golf grass greens." James J. Sweeney was the manager.[92]

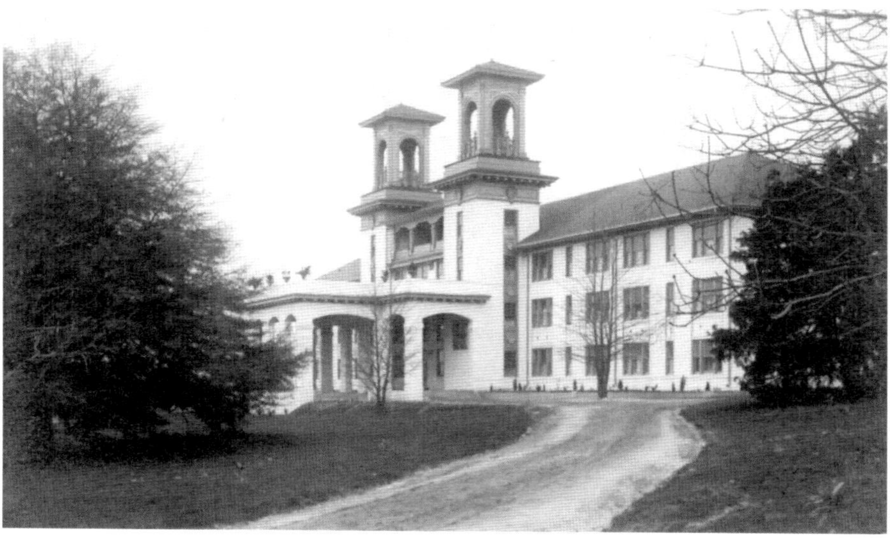

New Highland Park Hotel. The hotel partially burned in the 1940s, and the owners later tore it down. *Courtesy Allen Riddick Collection.*

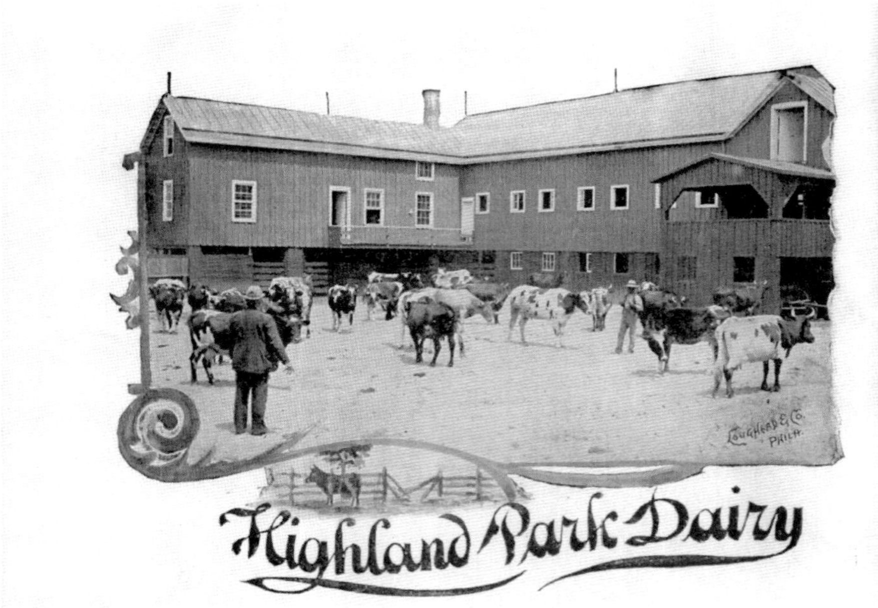

Highland Park Dairy. Promotional brochure. Art Press Loughead & Company, Philadelphia. *Courtesy Allen Riddick Collection.*

On March 6, 1927, the Highland Park Golf Club was at the center of a law enforcement showdown. Governor John G. Richards wanted South Carolina's blue laws enforced and consequently ordered Nollie Richardson, Aiken County sheriff, to "arrest every man or woman playing golf" on Sunday on either the Palmetto Club or Highland Park Club Golf Courses. The governor, in a gesture to encourage local action, also offered to send officers to support the sheriff in enforcing the law. In the interim, Judge Hayne F. Rice, according to Julian Salley,[93] an Aiken County lawyer, granted an injunction permitting play until March 19. Although Richards still wanted the arrests, legal advisors asserted that he would be liable for arrest himself if he persisted with the arrests. Several men—including Thomas Hitchcock, the largest taxpayer in Aiken, and Sweeney, part owner of the Highland Park Hotel—vowed to play on Sunday, March 7, regardless of the consequences. Both cited the serious economic consequences that loss of Sunday patronage would have for the golf clubs.[94]

The opening of the hotel signaled the beginning of the social season in Aiken. In 1939, the hotel ballroom was the site of the first of the weekly dances. Also, winter colonists looked forward that year to harness racing time trials, the Aiken Hunt and dove and quail shooting.[95] Again, a timber structure, the new Highland Park Hotel, burned in 1945.

Noted regional architect Willis Irvin designed two of Aiken's hotels: the Highland Park in 1922 and the Henderson in 1929. The Henderson Hotel stood on the corner of Richland Avenue and Chesterfield Street and officially opened on January 1, 1930.

In addition to the grand hotels, Aiken offered a wide-ranging choice of accommodations: hotels, inns and boardinghouses. In 1898, Henry Hahn built the Hotel Aiken on the corner of Richland Avenue and Laurens Street. In 1929, the owner extensively remodeled the building. An antebellum inn, perhaps known as the Ladson House, stood on the corner of Hayne Avenue and Florence Street. Another structure, erected circa 1860, but renovated in 1877, housed the Westview Inn, later known as the Palmetto Inn. Operating around the turn of the twentieth century, the Busch House on the corner of Richland Avenue and York Street epitomized the many private boardinghouses that catered to Aiken visitors.[96]

In addition to the Busch House, other boardinghouses that operated in Aiken were the Bell House, York House, West View, Pebble Ledge and Sunny Cliff. Mrs. H.R. Lawton operated Sunny Cliff, and Dr. B.H. Teague was very proud of Pebble Ledge, a new construction. According to his ad, the house was "finished in beautiful yellow pine." Each room had a bell to summon assistance. In addition, the establishment also had piazzas, a furnace and modern bathrooms. Some guestrooms even had private baths,

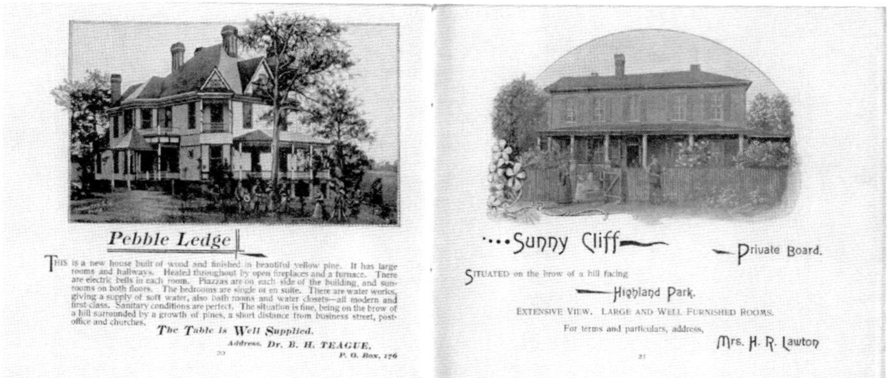

Advertisements for Pebble Ledge and Sunny Cliff, two of Aiken's turn-of-the-century boardinghouses. Promotional brochure of Highland Park Hotel. Most boardinghouses were larger, like Pebble Ledge. According to Allen Riddick, if Sunny Cliff "faced Highland Park Hotel, it sat on the other side of the Railroad Cut." *Courtesy Allen Riddick Collection.*

and Dr. Teague pointedly advertised, "The Table Is Well Supplied." Henry Bush was the proprietor of Busch House. He offered free transportation from the train depot to the boardinghouse. He listed his rates as two dollars per day. Mrs. P.G. Rockwell touted the "newly painted" West View, "located near 'Highland Park.'" Mrs. A. Holmes ran York House on the corner of York Street and Colleton Avenue, near the depot. Open through the year, Bell House was conveniently located near the post office and business district. Mrs. J.M. Bell was the manager. Aiken visitors also had access to "flowers, plants and vegetables." G.M. Wessels was the florist who operated Flora Villa Greenhouse and Garden, which stood on the corner of Richland Avenue and Newberry Street.[97]

Aiken offered rooming options that catered to the needs of a variety of visitors and different pocketbooks.

HAMPTON TERRACE HOTEL

Aiken was not the only city in the county to attract opulent hotels that catered to well-to-do clients. North Augusta was home to the spacious, well-appointed Hampton Terrace Hotel. The South Carolina legislature incorporated North Augusta, an early center of pottery production, on April 11, 1906. With the demise of Hamburg, new families moved into the area, and development followed, spurred by visionaries such as James Urquhart Jackson (1856–1925). A businessman and entrepreneur, Jackson dreamed of developing a city on the hills across the Savannah from Augusta. In pursuit of that dream, he was the moving force behind the founding of the planned city of North Augusta and the construction of the hotel in 1903.

In 1889, Jackson, a native of Augusta, began the serious pursuit of his long-held dream. He established the North Augusta Land Company. The company donated land for the town's first school in 1898, and Jackson's new company built a bridge (the Thirteenth Street Bridge) connecting Augusta and North Augusta. The bridge opened in 1891 and brought traffic and new economic opportunities for the area, as did Jackson's other endeavors. He invested in real estate and in the Augusta-Aiken Railway Company, which linked Aiken, North Augusta and Augusta. In 1897, North Augusta not only had a trolley line but also electricity. Consequently, North Augusta grew and prospered. In April 1902, Jackson and the North Augusta Hotel

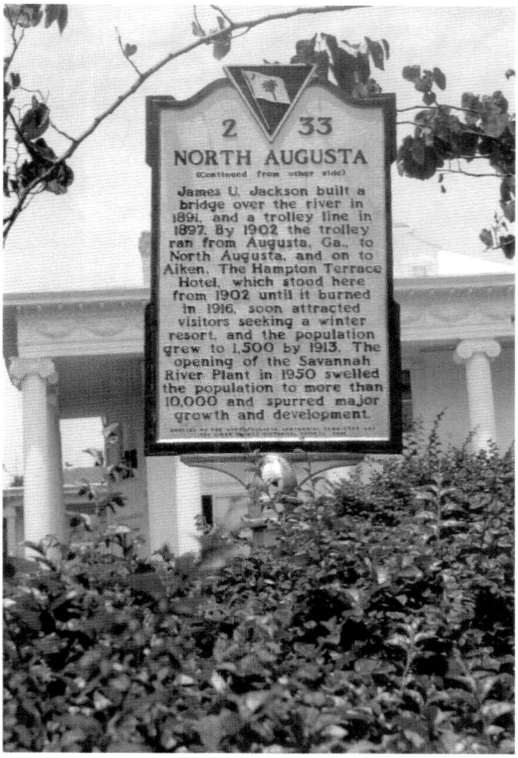

Right: North Augusta historical marker, North Augusta, 2018. *Photographer Terry L. Helsley.*

Below: Front entrance and grounds, Hampton Terrace Hotel, circa 1905. Detroit Publishing Company. LC-D4-18350 [P&P]. *Courtesy Library of Congress Prints and Photographs Division, Washington, D.C.*

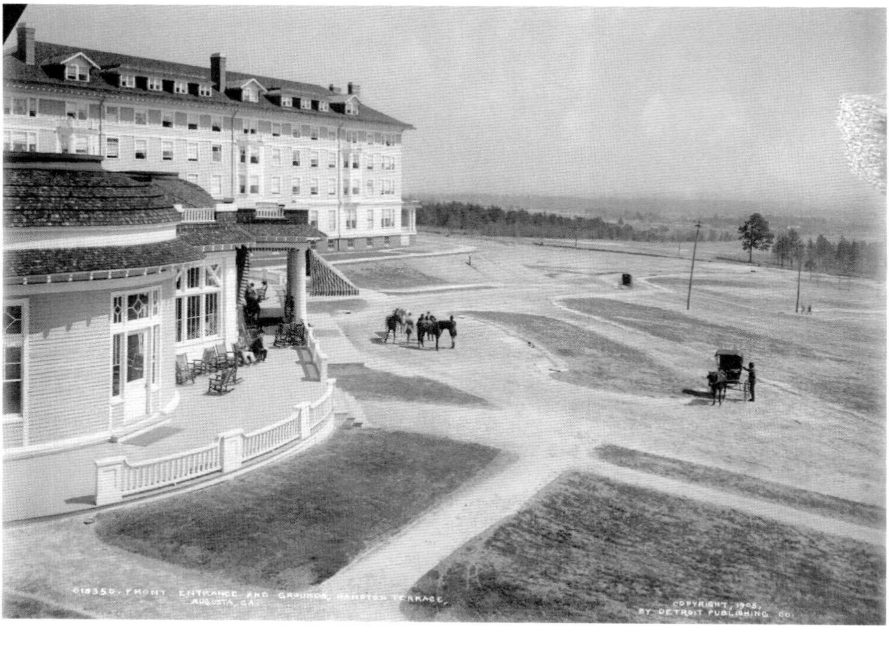

Company broke ground for a new hotel: the Hampton Terrace. The grand hotel opened for guests in late 1903.

The magnificent Hampton Terrace Hotel was located high on a hill. Hotel residents enjoyed a commanding view of the surrounding area, and visitors approaching the site were impressed.

With an initial investment of more than $500,000, the beautifully appointed hotel had five floors and three hundred rooms planned to accommodate five hundred visitors. A frame building, the hotel "was longer than two football fields." The hotel was an instant success and attracted such notables as mercantile magnate Marshal Field,[98] oil baron John D. Rockefeller,[99] manufacturer Harvey Firestone[100] and President-elect William Howard Taft.[101] Guests at the Hampton Terrace had a choice of numerous amenities and activities, as the hotel featured tennis courts, an eighteen-hole golf course, riding stables,[102] a ballroom, concerts, dances and access to a private hunting lodge and reserve. The hotel quickly became a destination for discriminating travelers. Guests to the luxurious hotel hailed from Boston, New York, Philadelphia and Chicago.

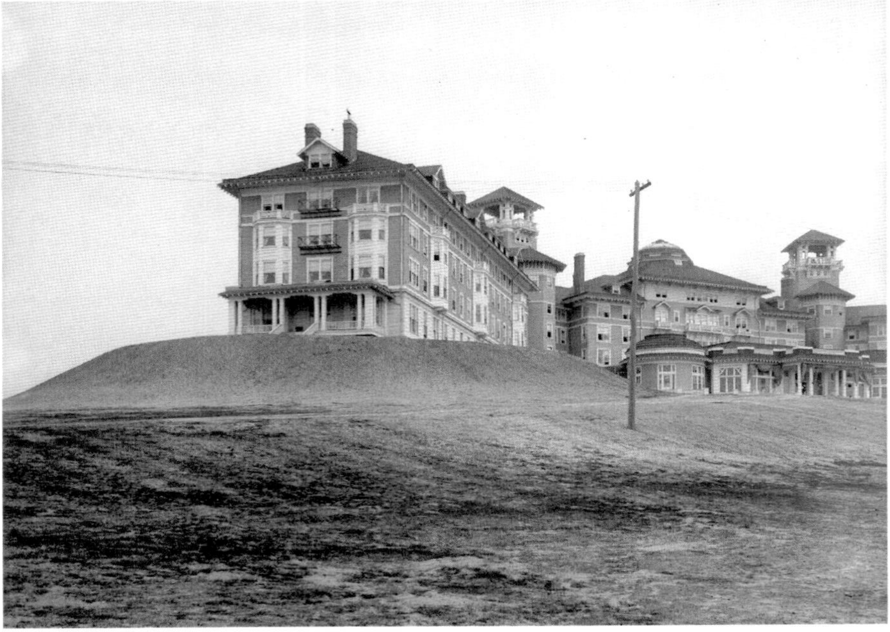

Hampton Terrace Hotel, circa 1905. The hotel stood on a commanding eminence. Detroit Publishing Company. LC-D4-3708 [P&P]. *Courtesy Library of Congress Prints and Photographs Division, Washington, D.C.*

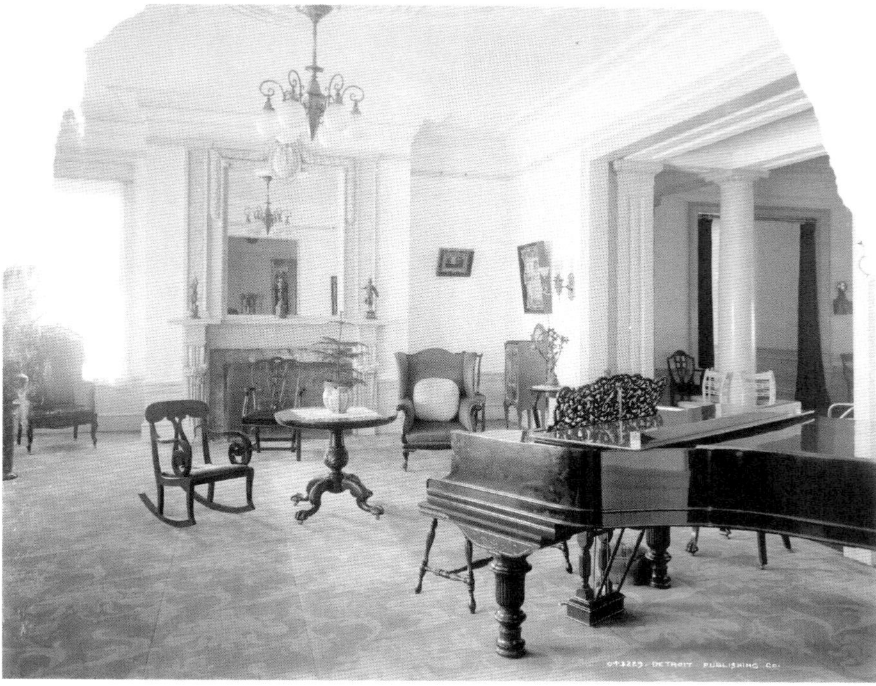

Green Parlor, Hampton Terrace Hotel, circa 1905. Detroit Publishing Company. LC-D4-43229 [P&P]. *Courtesy Library of Congress Prints and Photographs Division, Washington, D.C.*

Nevertheless, this promising era of growth and national attention ended abruptly. In January 1916, the recently renovated hotel unexpectedly burned to the ground. The fire broke out on the third floor. Despite the best efforts of Augusta firefighters, the fire destroyed the hotel. The Augusta fire chief, Frank G. Reynolds, later recalled a major challenge for the firefighters. Their hoses did not fit the hotel's hydrants. As a result, the firemen had to use adapters in order to access water to fight the blaze. According to eyewitness accounts, the fire burned for five hours, and some contend that the coal stored in the basement to fuel the furnace burned much longer.

Slated to open for the season on January 4, 1903, the hotel was completely booked for the new season. Those visitors never came, but the day after the fire, hundreds of spectators flocked to see the ruins of the great hotel. Some walked, and others traveled by trolley or automobile. According to the *Augusta Chronicle*, the demand was such that the Augusta-Aiken trolley line ran extra cars. Although the structure was underinsured, initially Jackson and the board of directors discussed rebuilding.[103] Nevertheless, despite their

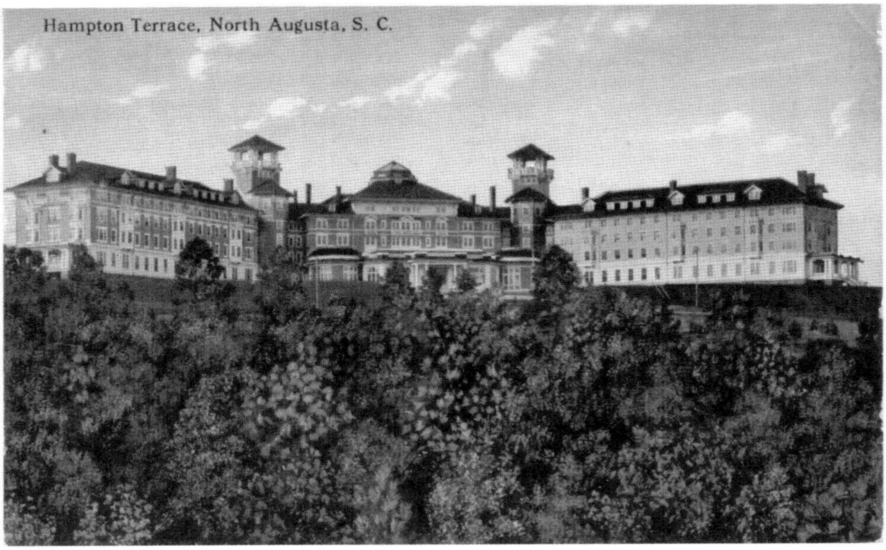

Hampton Terrace Hotel, North Augusta. *Courtesy Precious Memories, Collection of Bill Benton.*

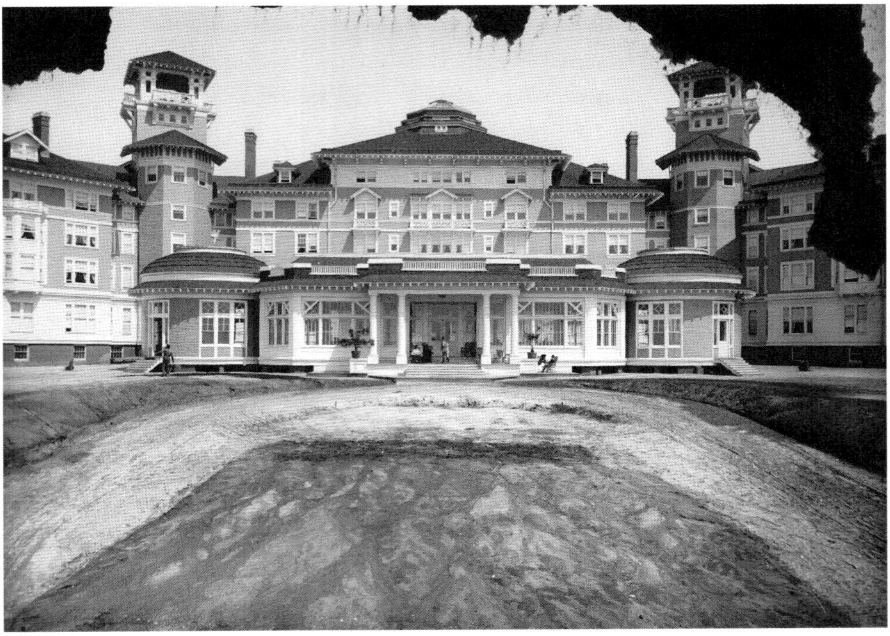

Hampton Terrace Hotel, front, North Augusta, circa 1905. Detroit Publishing Company. LC-D4-10766A [P&P]. *Courtesy Library of Congress Prints and Photographs Division, Washington, D.C.*

intentions, they were unable to rebuild the hotel, but its memory lives as an important chapter in North Augusta's rich history. In January 2018, the shadow of Hampton Terrace rose over the new Crowne Plaza Riverside Village at Hammond's Ferry, North Augusta. The new hotel, according to news reports by Stefany Bornman of WJBF, was supposed to have the feel of the historic hotel, but final plans did not reflect that inspiration.

Chapter 5
LOST HOME
Hamburg and Ellenton

In the course of Aiken's long history, a number of important towns have come and gone. The antebellum town of Hamburg and its Reconstruction reincarnation was one of the early casualties. Others disappeared in the 1950s, casualties of the Cold War and of the creation of the Savannah River Plant.

HAMBURG

Hamburg was an important antebellum river town located in the historic area that had included Savanna Town, Campbell Town and New Windsor. Located on the Savannah River, the town during its heyday was a major entrepôt for cotton, tobacco and other crops headed downriver to Savannah. The town owed its existence to Henry Schultz. German sources suggest that Henry Schultz was not the founder's name. Schultz was born Klaus Hinrich Klahn in Dahme, Duchy of Holstein, and fled the chaos and economic disruption of Napoleonic Europe for a new life in America.[104]

Columbian Edwin J. Scott described Schultz as an "extraordinary mechanical genius and financier." The self-proclaimed native of Hamburg began his American career as a laborer in Augusta. He invested in boats for the river trade with Savannah and spearheaded efforts to build a bridge over the Savannah River connecting Georgia and South Carolina.

In 1813, Henry Schultz and Lewis Cooper petitioned the South Carolina legislature for control of a bridge they planned to build over the Savannah River. The proposed bridge would connect Augusta, Georgia and South Carolina. Schultz and Cooper had acquired the existing ferry "with all the Right, Lands, Boats," that was formerly the property of Edward Rowell and Walter Leigh. Schultz and Cooper bought the ferry and its site because they planned to build a bridge, elevated thirty-four feet above the normal water level, across the river. They had begun construction by December 3, 1813, and expected to have the bridge built of cypress wood open within six months.

In the meantime, the entrepreneurs wanted to protect their investment. They wanted legal protection to "prevent any interfering Bridge or Ferry being erected or kept between Campelton[105] [Campbelltown] above and the Sandbar or Fort Moore below Augusta." Both principals and others had heavily invested in the project. To ensure that the bridge would be profitable, Schultz and Cooper wanted to adjust certain rates. For example, they wanted to assess "pleasure Carriages" the same rate as "wagons, carts and drays" and to charge bridge users the same rate for loaded and unloaded carriages.[106]

The company issued bank notes that functioned as local tender. Unfortunately, during the Panic of 1819, the Augusta bridge company failed, and the bank notes became worthless. With such great financial setbacks and pending bankruptcy, Schultz unsuccessfully attempted suicide. The Bank of Augusta ended up with Schultz's very profitable bridge and its annual revenues. Schultz launched legal challenges over control of the bridge and its assets until his death. Scott later described Schultz, whom he styled the "Autocrat of Hamburg," as a "tall, erect old man, wearing a heavy Waterloo coat that reached his heels."

While still trying to recoup his losses, Schultz moved his base of operations across the river and, in 1821, founded the town of Hamburg, reportedly named for his German home. The town, established to challenge Augusta's trade hegemony, was initially successful "enjoying an extensive trade."[107] Schultz, who discovered that the trajectory of success in Augusta was fleeting and felt mistreated by business leaders in Augusta, saw the new town as a commercial alternative to Augusta and perhaps an opportunity for revenge. Diverting trade from Augusta to Hamburg could damage the economic vitality of Augusta.

The South Carolina General Assembly granted Hamburg liberal tax incentives. For five years, "all land, negro slaves, stock in trade, and all other taxable property, within the town," were exempt from the payment of all taxes for five years.[108] Consequently, with such incentives, the new town flourished in the 1820s.

In 1821, the South Carolina legislature, at the request of Henry Schultz, approved "An Act to Establish an Inspection and Ware-house at Hamburg, in Edgefield District." The act also named Christian Breithaupt,[109] John Torrence, Benjamin Hightower Sr., John Wise and G.O. Wilkinson commissioners for the "inspection and warehouse" and empowered them to select an inspector or inspectors and develop appropriate regulations.[110]

Founder Schultz wasted no opportunity to promote his new town. For example, he established a mechanics society to celebrate the contributions of artisans, mechanics and others who worked in the mechanical trades. For Schultz, this was another way to develop a sense of community spirit and perhaps increase revenue for Hamburg.

The petition for incorporation stated several objectives for the proposed society. First, the society would encourage the "Mechanical Arts." Second, it would maintain the widows and children of members. Third, as the members wanted to erect a hall, they requested legislative permission for a $40,000 lottery. Signers of the petition included Joshua Mercer, president of the society; William B. Shivers, vice-president; William Robertson Jr., secretary and treasurer; and fourteen other members of the society. Although the South Carolina legislature granted the incorporation, it did not approve the lottery.[111]

Nevertheless, Schultz took his partial victory, and instead of raising money for a grand hall, he created a great spectacle. He celebrated the town of Hamburg's founding on July 2 in conjunction with the Mechanics' Festival. A newspaper article from Augusta described the festivities of 1827, offering a snapshot of similar annual celebrations. The day began with shots being fired—one for every year of the town's existence. Consequently, in 1827, there were six shots fired. Schultz then addressed the crowd of eight hundred or so and shared the history of Hamburg and his vision for the future. Afterward, all sat down to heavily laden tables. The president of the Mechanics' Society, Joshua Mercer, sat at the head of the table. All society members wore the insignia of their society, and a flag with the inscription *Nil desperandum* ("Do not despair") flew overhead. After dinner, a band played, and the participants drank thirteen toasts. Congressman George McDuffie was the principal speaker, and one thousand people attended the dinner.

Nevertheless, by August of that year, in a serious reversal of fortunes, Schultz was in the Edgefield jail. On July 30, 1827, two women arrived in

Hamburg with a complaint. Two men had stopped them outside Hamburg and stolen their trunk. Schultz and others investigated and apprehended the alleged culprits. As the women were content to "let bygones be bygones" if the trunk was recovered, Schultz tried various means of physical and moral persuasion on first one and then the other of the two men. Neither man would confess or reveal the location of the missing trunk. Exasperated by the "stubborn refusal" of the second man, Schultz whipped and tortured the man until he collapsed. At that point, Schultz sent for local doctors and cared for the man in his own home. Unfortunately, the suspect died several days later from his injuries. According to the attending physicians, the man died from fever as well as the beatings and ill-treatment.[112]

Consequently, Edgefield officials arrested Schultz. Officials there remanded him for trial, and a jury found him guilty of manslaughter. He served time in jail, but officials released him in December 1827. Meanwhile, Schultz's economic situation also deteriorated. Creditors forced the sale of much of his land in Hamburg to pay some, but not all, of his debts. With other claims still pending, officials jailed him again, but this time for debt. Schultz's financial difficulties persisted.[113] Then, in 1832, the South Carolina legislature included an interesting proviso in the revenue act of that year. According to the act, when Henry Schultz paid the state treasury $16,225, the solicitor of the western circuit would release him of "all pecuniary obligations to the State" and convey "for his own use and benefit, all the right and title which the State has in and to the Town of Hamburg."[114]

On December 19, 1827, the South Carolina General Assembly incorporated the town with the name Hamburg. The act stated that all United States citizens who had resided in the town for three months were part of the "Town corporate." In addition, the act set the town limits for the new town as follows: on the west side, the Savannah River was the line "for a half mile below and a half mile above the intersection of Mechanic and Market streets." The eastern boundary was also a mile long. The act appointed B.F. Whitner and Colonel Paul Fitzsimmons commissioners to have the town surveyed and the plat registered with the secretary of state. All white males who had lived in Hamburg for six months could vote in the first election to select an intendent and six wardens.[115]

Significantly, it became the western terminus of the South Carolina Canal and Railroad Company. The railroad was an attempt to divert trade from the port of Savannah to the port of Charleston by providing affordable land transportation. Railroad service began on December 25, 1830, with

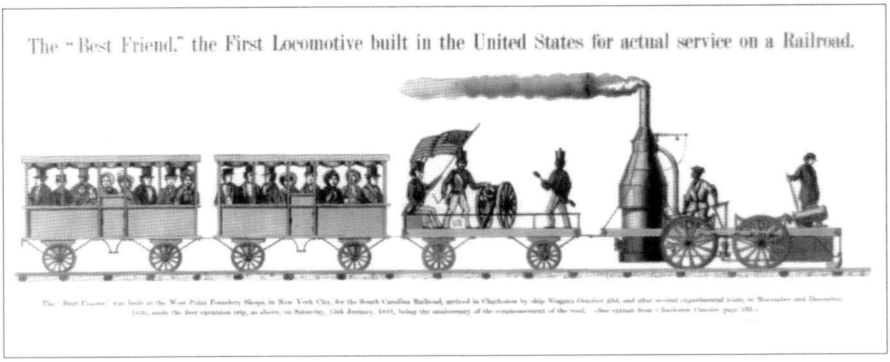

The "Best Friend," the first locomotive built for rail service in the United States. LC-US-Z62-90957. *Courtesy Library of Congress Prints and Photographs Division, Washington, D.C.*

the famous but short-lived "Best Friend." By 1833, the 136-mile track from Charleston to Hamburg had become the longest railroad in the world.[116]

The "Best Friend" of Charleston was the "first locomotive built in the United States for public service." It was a product of the West Point Foundry, and supporters launched the engine in Charleston on Christmas Day 1830. On its first run, the engine pulled a passenger car to Dorchester. Noted for its speed, in 1831 it carried passengers, freight and mail from Charleston to Hamburg, but its career was tragically short. In June 1831, a fireman blocked the safety valve, and as a result, the engine exploded. The results were frightful. The fireman died, and the engineer suffered serious burns. Others present at the time were also injured. Mechanics later rebuilt the engine, which operated under the name "Phoenix." A second engine named the "Best Friend" also ran on the same track but was not as fast as the original locomotive.[117]

By 1835, Hamburg not only had the railroad but also a bank (Schultz was the president). In 1835, the South Carolina General Assembly issued a charter for a bank in Hamburg. The act designated commissioners to receive subscriptions for the new bank at Hamburg, Charleston, Columbia, Edgefield, Barnwell, Abbeville, Anderson, Greenville, Laurens and Newberry. The commissioners could raise up to $300,000. Those who subscribed became stockholders of the Bank of Hamburg, South Carolina. The initial charter ran from 1835 to 1856.[118]

As Hamburg developed, it became the most successful inland port in South Carolina. With foresight, Schultz had constructed a large pier for the river trade. Wagons brought cotton from the rich agricultural

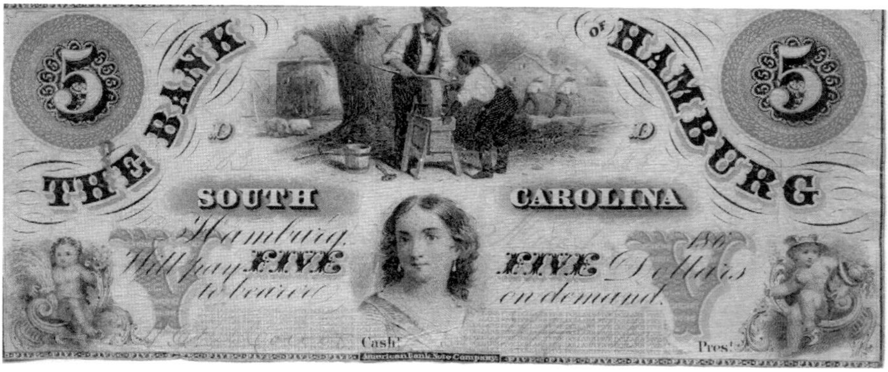

The Bank of Hamburg, five-dollar note. Note that the illustration of man sharpening an axe reflects Henry Shultz's focus on the mechanical trades in Hamburg. *Courtesy Gregg-Graniteville Photographic Archives, Gregg-Graniteville Library, USC Aiken.*

hinterlands, and boats and barges carried the bales downriver to Savannah or Charleston for shipment overseas. With the advent of the railroad, goods could also travel overland. On December 19, 1837, the South Carolina General Assembly incorporated the town.

The year 1837 brought another economic downturn for the United States. Hamburg persisted, and during the 1840s, the town had a population of 2,500. In 1841, the South Carolina legislature authorized three commissioners to "lay out and superintend the building of a Public road from Hamburg to Downers Red Beach [*sic*] Island." The named commissioners were M. Galphin, Jon T.M. Miller and Oliver Simpson. By 1848, the commissioners had not built the road. So, the Hamburg Town Council, with the consent of the commissioners, petitioned the legislature to assume the responsibility.[119] Nevertheless, by the 1850s, the town had floundered. The economic landscape had changed.

In 1850, though, 647 white inhabitants lived in the town. Schultz, the seventy-four-year-old founder, lived in Hamburg. In addition, the town boasted at least one hotel and several boardinghouses. Living in the town were a postmaster (Benjamin Harris), a jeweler, a watchmaker, a wheelwright, a wagon maker, a cooper, a printer, bookkeepers, clerks, merchants, a cabinetmaker, draymen, a schoolteacher, a lawyer (Matthew Gary), cotton buyers, slave traders, a physician (George Harris), a harness maker, a shoe and bootmaker, a magistrate (Robert Anderson) and Superintendent of the Railroad William V. Rains. Schultz's household included a thirty-year-old African American named Meriah Schultz. Of note, he listed his occupation as "Founder of Hamburg." As the decade opened, there was still considerable business in the town.[120]

Businessman J.L. Knight visited Hamburg in April 1851. On April 27, he wrote to James Evans in Fayetteville, North Carolina. In the letter, Knight commented on the rain and mentioned a "freshet in the Savannah" while he was still in Charleston. Most of the stores in Hamburg had flooded, but according to Knight, there was little damage to their stock in trade. In addition, Knight commented that money was "*remarkably* scarce in Hamburg." Then, in surprisingly poetic words that resonate (but likely not with a Hamburg Chamber of Commerce), Knight added that Hamburg was "one of the dullest paces on earth and looks like a country graveyard with leaning tombstones filled with bad epitaphs."[121]

Henry Schultz, the entrepreneur who dreamed and failed dramatically, died on October 13, 1851, at his home in Hamburg. Schultz died intestate and with few assets. On January 3, 1852, the probate judge issued letters of administration to James Jones and Joseph J. Kennedy to administer Schultz's estate.[122]

According to the 1860 census, Hamburg had a population of 404. The Bank of Hamburg had a president, bookkeeper and clerk. The town had a marshal, a druggist, a watchmaker, an artist, a wheelwright, a baker, a mason, a tailor, several merchants and three slave traders. There was still commercial activity, but as with the population, the commercial life was also in decline.[123]

Several factors contributed to the town's decline. For example, floods plagued the town, and in 1848, the new Augusta Canal diverted river traffic from Hamburg. The coup de grâce, however, was the continuation of the railroad over the Savannah River in 1854. With the railroad more widely available, Hamburg's trade moved to Augusta, and by the end of the Civil War, most of the town's white population had also moved elsewhere.[124]

POSTWAR HAMBURG

After the Civil War, Prince Rivers, a native of Beaufort, and other African American leaders revitalized Hamburg. Rivers and other freedmen moved into the town. Rivers was also instrumental in the creation of the county of Aiken in 1871. He represented the new county in the South Carolina legislature until 1874. After secession, Rivers, an Edgefield slave, fled his master, returned to Beaufort and enlisted in the First South Carolina Volunteers, the first African American regiment to receive its colors. The literate Rivers became color sergeant of the regiment, later known as the Thirty-Third U.S. Colored Troops. Recognized for his leadership ability, Rivers accompanied General David Hunter on a recruiting trip to New York City in 1862.

After his discharge, Prince Rivers moved to Edgefield, and voters elected him a delegate to the 1868 Constitutional Convention, which produced a progressive constitution that established South Carolina's first public school system. He also represented Edgefield District in the South Carolina House of Representatives (1868–72) and then became involved in the successful movement to create the new county. Rivers and South Carolina governor Robert K. Scott enjoyed a friendly relationship. Lacking funds to purchase a home in Hamburg and facing an imminent deadline, Rivers wrote to the governor seeking a short-term loan.[125] Following his service in the legislature, Scott named Rivers as a trial justice for Aiken County. Unfortunately, his efforts to mediate a volatile situation in Hamburg between aggressive paramilitary personnel and the resident African American militia were not successful, and his reputation suffered.[126]

After the Civil War ended, the town rebounded as a home for freedmen. In 1870, the census reflects a predominantly African American working-class settlement with a few white merchants and cotton buyers. Most of the residents were laborers, although some were carpenters, railroad workers, farmers, domestics and laundresses, with an occasional tailor, cooper, mason, bricklayer, minister, constable and schoolteacher.[127] The town continued to grow until 1876, when the Hamburg Massacre sounded its final death knell.

HAMBURG MASSACRE/RIOT

The Hamburg Massacre (or Riot) was a turning point in the gubernatorial election of 1876. Governor Daniel H. Chamberlain, the Republican incumbent, was running for reelection on a reform ticket and seeking Republican and Democratic support. Wade Hampton III, former Civil War general, headlined the Democratic ticket. Many white South Carolinians viewed the Hampton campaign as a serious, perhaps once-in-a-lifetime opportunity to overthrow Congressional Reconstruction and black political involvement in South Carolina. They considered Hampton as the man who could "redeem" the state. Many were willing to resort to violence in order to achieve that goal. Prior to the Hamburg Massacre, Chamberlain's Fusion approach had momentum. Nevertheless, on that hot July day in 1876, all that irrevocably changed.

In summary, on July 4, 1876, two white men, Henry Getsen and Thomas Butler, had words with African American militiamen in Hamburg. They wanted to drive through the town, but the militia were on parade and refused the white men's efforts to pass on the main roadway. After a standoff, the militia commander Doc Adams permitted the men to go on their way, but the situation continued to fester.

Getsen and Butler, seeing an opportunity to exploit the deep antagonism between whites and African Americans in the area, hired an Edgefield attorney. The attorney, Matthew C. Butler, a Confederate cavalryman under General Wade Hampton, then filed charges against Doc Adams, the militia commander, for blocking the street. He also demanded that the black militia disarm and disband. In return, Adams sued, alleging that the men had interfered with a military drill. Prince Rivers, the trial justice, set a hearing for July 8, but Butler appeared with large numbers of armed white men, including members of such paramilitary groups as the Sweetwater Sabre Club. Rivers, attempting to defuse the situation, volunteered to disarm the militia and return the weapons to Columbia. Butler refused Rivers's attempt at conciliation, and at Rivers's suggestion, the black militiamen retreated to a nearby warehouse for safety.

Two hundred armed, angry white men surrounded the warehouse, and a gunfight ensued. According to most sources, Butler did not participate in the violence. In the melee, shots wounded both black and white men, but the first casualty was a young white man, Thomas McKie Meriwether. The white attackers brought a cannon from Augusta and they fired into the warehouse. The militiamen then ran from the warehouse seeking safety. The attacking whites captured thirty or forty men and selected six for execution. They then fired on the remaining unarmed men as they ran into the woods.

The Red Shirts were paramilitary groups that organized in order to intimidate African American voters and guarantee Hampton's election. It was a coordinated campaign by the white elite to retake control of the state's government. Traditionally, the Sweetwater Sabre Club introduced red shirts as a response to the initial Hamburg confrontation. Among the members of the Sweetwater Sabre Club present in Hamburg on that fateful day was Benjamin R. Tillman of Edgefield. Tillman later justified his participation: "The leading white men of Edgefield" decided "to seize the first opportunity that the Negroes might offer them to provoke a riot and teach the negroes a lesson." Tillman used his participation and extreme racial positions to launch his later political career. Tillman served as both governor of South Carolina and in the United States Senate.[128]

The massacre confirmed Democratic intransigence and commitment to a "straight-out" ticket. That is, whites would unite and vote Democratic rather than consider a moderate or compromise ticket that included Democratic and Republican candidates. The ineffectiveness of the Republican regime was likewise on display.

Chamberlain railed about injustice and asked unsuccessfully for federal assistance. He also sent Attorney General William Stone to Hamburg to investigate. Stone interviewed Prince Rivers, the trial justice, studied the testimony submitted to the coroner's jury and spoke with the men who were seized and wounded during the conflict.

Stone's report provided historical background, as well as a non-participant's account of the incident. During the administration of Governor Robert K. Scott, the state organized a company of state militia, Company A, Ninth Regiment, South Carolina National Guard, in Hamburg. The governor named Rivers captain of the company, and the state issued arms and ammunition to the militiamen. Prior to May 1876, the company drilled little and had few members. Nevertheless, in May, much changed. The number of men increased to about eighty, and Doc Adams was named captain.

According to Stone's account of the incident, which includes more personal details, on July 4, the militia company was drilling on an overgrown, little-used street in Hamburg. While they were drilling, two brothers-in-law, Thomas Butler and Henry Getsen, drove up and demanded to pass through the soldiers rather than go around. Seeing their obduracy, Adams "opened ranks and allowed them to drive through." Yet Getsen and Butler filed a complaint accusing Captain Adams of "obstructing the highway." Trial Justice Rivers issued a warrant and summoned Adams. During the trial, Rivers and Adams had words, and Rivers had Adams arrested for contempt. He then continued the case until the afternoon of July 8.

In the interim, Robert J. Butler, the father of Thomas Butler, retained General M.C. Butler to represent the young men. The white men demanded that the black militia surrender their arms. Rivers learned that several hundred armed white men had assembled in Hamburg. The militiamen moved to the Sibley building on the bank of the river (home of their armory). Rivers asked M.C. Butler "if he would guaranty the safety of the town should the militia, surrender their arms." Butler reportedly replied, "That would depend on how the men behaved themselves afterward."

The surviving militiamen stated that the whites fired on the Sibley building and that Adams had ordered them not to fire unless so ordered, as the militia had little ammunition. After the firing began, Thomas McKie Meriwether, a young white man, was shot and killed. At that point, the white men obtained a cannon (possibly property of the Washington Artillery) from Augusta and fired on the armory. Although uninjured, the militiamen fled the building. Ironically, the first black casualty was James Cook, the town marshal, who was not a member of the militia company and had not been in the armory. The armed whites then rounded up "about twenty five" unarmed men and moved them near the railroad.

There, they took A.T. Attaway "out of the 'ring'" and, despite his and his mother's pleas, shot him. Then they killed David Phillips and Pompey Curry, who asked Henry Getsen and Dr. Pierce Butler to help him. Then they killed Albert Myniant (Miniant), Moses Parks and Hampton Stevens (not a member of the militia company). Three other black men reported injuries, alleging that the armed men wounded them as they ran away. One injured man, a corporal in Company A, said that two white men named Twiggs and Chafee saved his life. After he was wounded by gunfire, they rescued him and sent him to Augusta for treatment.

In addition to the deaths and injuries, the mob broke into stores, robbed black and white residents (including the U.S. postmaster), set some houses afire, cut the ropes for the town wells and robbed the home of Prince Rivers.[129]

In the end, neither state nor federal officials prosecuted any of those involved in the disturbance. The coroner's jury investigating the incident returned an indictment against ninety-four white men. Neither the accused nor their supporters considered the verdict a setback. Cheering supporters lined the route for the men who traveled to Aiken to surrender. They posted bail, and their supporters greeted them with more cheers and laughter. With the election of Hampton, South Carolina had new leadership, and officials never pursued justice for the victims of Hamburg. The state had entered a new era. After Hamburg, riots and armed conflicts continued and ended with the election of Democratic candidate Wade Hampton. In fact, General Mathew Butler, "the hero of Hamburg," nominated Hampton for governor.[130]

Following the Hamburg Massacre of July 8, 1876, the town once more declined, but this time there was no rebirth. Founded near the river in order to exploit the trade potential, the town lay on the floodplain. A few continued to live in the area, but as the O'Keefe family discovered, flooding continued to be a serious issue into the 1890s.[131] According to the 1900 census, John O'Keefe, a native of Germany, lived in Schultz Township with his wife, Catherine, and their children. O'Keefe and his eldest son were brick masons. In addition to skilled artisans—such as carpenters, a wheelwright and a potter—butchers, grocers and clerks lived in the township, as well as a number of railroad employees. Rail employees included John W. Boxx, a flagman; Charles M. Patrick, a mail agent; Ware Bullard, a fireman; Charles and Fred Wood, telegraph operators; John J. Mahoney, an apprentice at the railroad machine shop; and Robert A. Scott, an agent for the railroad. The railroad continued to be a factor in community life.

Years later, an excavation uncovered evidence of that railroad's past. In March 1944, S.H. Swint, president of the Graniteville Company, had a section of the original line of the South Carolina Railroad uncovered. Under the direction of Charles Foster, a company employee, laborers unearthed a "thirty three foot section of the timber sub-structure of the old railroad."

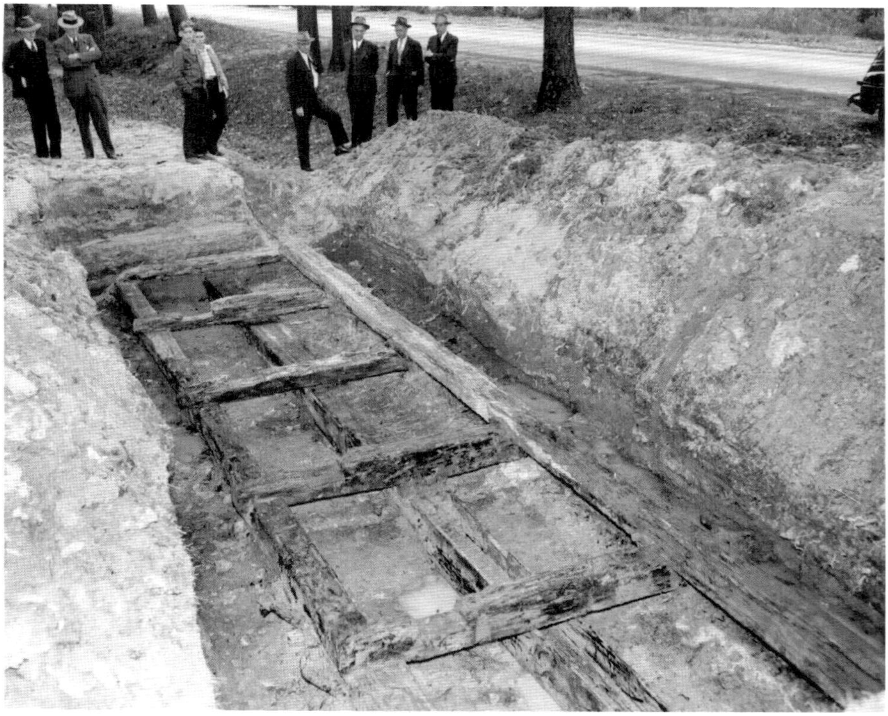

Site of original South Carolina Railroad. In 1944, Graniteville president S.H. Swint excavated a section of the original track that connected Hamburg and Charleston. The American Legion erected a sign marking the site. There are also remnants of the track in Hitchcock Woods. *Courtesy Gregg-Graniteville Photographic Archives, Gregg-Graniteville Library, USC Aiken.*

Although the rails were missing, the "6 x 9 timbers," many with spikes, were in excellent condition. The excavation provided new information about how the engineer laying out the rail lines innovatively addressed such issues as "soft ground."[132] Sometimes historical treasures lie hidden underground.

The site of Hamburg is now part of North Augusta—the area between the Fifth and Thirteenth Street bridges. The bluff still bears the name of the remarkable Henry Schultz. As his obituary noted: "There were few men of his day and time who possessed more of the high spirit of disinterested enterprise" and who "contended against adversity with the fortitude of a true hero."[133]

MONUMENTS

Controversy attends the monument honoring Thomas McKie Meriwether, the sole white man to die during the firefight. Meriwether was twenty-three years old at the time and accompanying his father, Joseph James Meriwether. In 1916, Meriwether supporters under an act of the General Assembly erected a monument to Thomas McKie Meriwether in the John C. Calhoun Park. According to the monument inscription, Meriwether exemplified the "highest

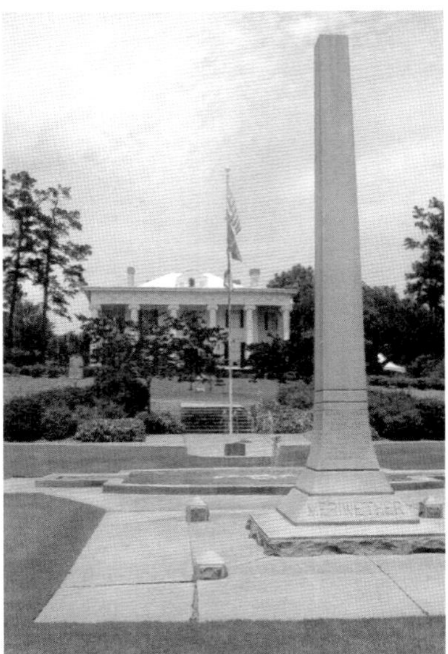

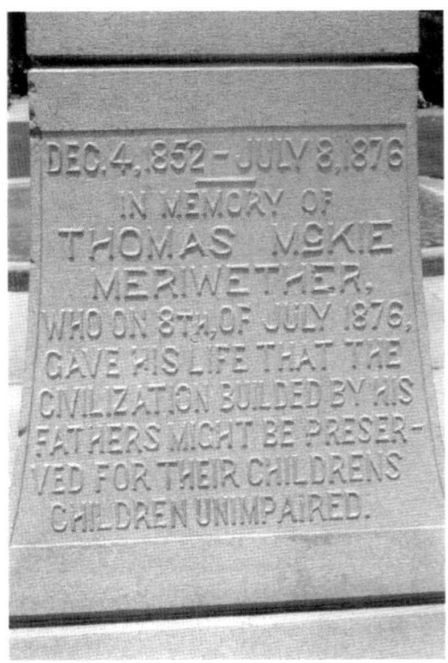

Left: Meriwether memorial, North Augusta, 2018. *Right*: Panel, Thomas McKie Meriwether memorial, North Augusta, 2018. *Photographer Terry L. Helsley.*

ideal of Anglo-Saxon Civilization." The monument does not mention the African Americans—James Cook, Allan Attaway, Albert Myniant (Miniant), Moses Parks, David Rivers (or Pompey Curry) and Hampton Stevens—who were murdered on that fateful day, July 8, 1876.

In 2011, the Heritage Council of North Augusta paid for a simple historical marker that recounted the history of the massacre. Supporters eventually placed the marker in Carrsville, near North Augusta. A granite stone near the marker lists the names of all the men, black and white, who died on that fateful day in a town that had begun with such promise as Schultz's dream of a great inland port.

ELLENTON

According to a historical marker near the Aiken-Barnwell County line, the lost town of Ellenton began as a post office in 1873. A story credits workers on the Port Royal & Augusta Railroad with the name. Some workers camped near the home of Robert Dunbar, who had given the railroad a right-of-way through his land. Others boarded in the Dunbar home and met his daughter Ellen. Consequently, as the story goes, when the railroad built the depot, officials named it Ellenton in her honor.

Ellenton also became the name of the town that grew up around the depot. In 1880, the town received its first charter. Its citizens lived and worked there until the 1950s, when the U.S. government acquired the town and surrounding area for the Savannah River Plant in the interest of national security.[134]

Ellenton Riot

In 1876, Ellenton was also the site of a major racial conflict. In a sense, the Ellenton incident was a follow-up to the unrest at Hamburg and part of a pattern of racial disturbances that spread across the state. The racially charged election of 1876 was a breeding ground for paramilitary actions, rumors and fear. The pre–Civil War elite were determined to limit black voting and undermine black confidence in the Republican government and its ability to protect them. Militant Democratic leaders such as former Confederate general Martin W. Gary advocated using all weapons available—including violence, intimidation and economic reprisals—in order to elect Wade Hampton III. His plan, known as the "Edgefield Plan," openly advocated violence to end black control of South Carolina. Consequently, hundreds of paramilitary rifle clubs, including the Sweetwater Sabres, organized. By late 1876, historians estimate that almost fifteen thousand white men belonged to these two hundred rifle clubs. Edgefield County had twenty-five rifle clubs and Aiken County more.[135] These clubs were not only paramilitary but also political in nature. The events at and around Ellenton had political and racial overtones.

In 1875, South Carolina's population included 74,199 adult white males and 110,744 adult black males. Aiken County had a total black population of 17,907 and total white population of 12,397. Mirroring the state figures, about 1,000 more adult black males lived in Aiken County than adult white males. Against this backdrop of population inequality, the events at Ellenton unfolded.

As historian Mark Smith noted, letters written to Governor Daniel Chamberlain suggest that racial tensions were high in Aiken County prior to the attack. As early as September 7, Probate Judge H.N. Boney wrote Chamberlain, "All is not quiet in our hellish county." Others wrote complaining about the proliferation of armed white rifle clubs. This was a serious issue that Chamberlain did not address until early October 1875.

Reportedly, the confrontation began on September 15 near Silverton on the Barnwell-Aiken County line. An elderly white woman, Mrs. Alonzo Harley, alleged that two African American men, Peter Williams and Fred Pope, tried to attack/rob her, but she grabbed a rifle and they fled. Armed white men pursued and seized Peter Williams and wounded him when he tried to escape. A few days later, Williams died of his wounds. On September 17, a posse of armed white men then attempted to arrest Williams's alleged accomplice, Fred Pope, at Rouse's bridge, where armed African Americans fired on the white posse.

During a subsequent ambush, a white man died. Shortly thereafter, hundreds of armed members of paramilitary organizations from South Carolina and Georgia converged on Ellenton. Ben Tillman and the Sweetwater Sabres were part of this armed force. A letter to Chamberlain dated September 18 alleged that more than five hundred armed men had crossed the Savannah River and camped at Hamburg. That same day, rioters proceeded to destroy rail tracks of the Port Royal Railroad and cause a derailment. Therefore, rail officials wanted armed guards on the rail lines until after the election.

Smith, citing the correspondence of F.E. Thomas, suggested that one reason details of the riot are scarce, contradictory and confusing is that the participants did not share information about their participation. Thomas managed a turpentine operation near Ellenton for an out-of-state owner. Therefore, his letters are contemporary reports of local happenings that he sent his employer. One of the more chilling quotations cited by Smith speaks to the issue of lives lost. Thomas wrote that no one knew how many African Americans died, as the ones doing the killing did not keep records. In Smith's assessment, the Ellenton Riot was deadly. Casualties included one white man killed and five or six wounded and "between twenty five and one hundred" African Americans dead.

The conflict in Ellenton lasted from September 15 to September 20, when the violence shifted from the Ellenton area into Barnwell County. For example, on September 28, in Blackville, Barnwell County, armed white men invaded a black worship service and shot a black Republican.

The disputed gubernatorial election of 1876 eventually ended Reconstruction in South Carolina and confirmed the election of former Confederate general Wade Hampton III. Hampton's election signaled the return of white control to South Carolina's government.[136]

In 1877, eleven of the white men from Aiken County appeared before Judge Waites in Charleston. Charged with political conspiracy, the prosecution accused them of interfering with the "political rights"—that is, the right to vote—of one African American, David Bush. White attackers killed Bush during several days of prolonged violence and "great excitement." Reportedly, authorities arrested between "50 and 300" other white men on similar charges, but the eleven were the only ones tried. Testimony in the case lasted from May 15 to May 21.

The prosecution attempted to prove that the events around Ellenton were part of a concerted conspiracy to deny black Republicans the right to vote. The defense argued that an attempt by a white posse to arrest an accused robber sparked an armed confrontation. From that spark, violence spread. Rioters killed a white man and tore up railroad tracks. Consequently, the white men of the area armed themselves to protect lives and property.

During days of testimony, the prosecution, on one hand, attempted to focus on the organized plan to deny African Americans, like Bush, the right to vote. On the other hand, the defense couched the charges in terms of "political persecution" by defeated Republicans. A jury of six black and six white jurors heard the case. George W. Williams, a prominent Charleston banker, was the foreman of the jury. According to press reports, no one expected the jury to agree on a verdict.[137]

The six black members of the jury found all but one of the eleven guilty of conspiracy. The six white jurymen considered all of the defendants innocent. They rejected a compromise to convict two and acquit the rest. Judge Waites questioned the jurors and acquitted Abner Watkinson of the charge. As the jury could not agree on the other ten, the judge discharged the jury. The accused posted appearance bonds, left the court[138] and returned home—a quiet end to the violence of September 1876.

As one report noted, "The murderers of Simon Coker, Warren Kellsey, John Kellsey, Samuel Brown, Oscar Brown, David Bush, George Turner, and scores of other Republican black men" will never face justice for their crimes. Simon Coker was a black state senator from Barnwell who boarded a train in order to investigate riot reports from Ellenton. He was not involved with the riots. Instead, a group of armed white Democrats, the Ellenton Rifles, commanded by A.P. Butler, forcibly removed him from the Port Royal Railroad Depot, took him to an open field and executed him. According to some reports, his executioners allowed Coker to kneel in prayer before they fired the fatal shot.[139] According to the 1870 census, the twenty-three-year-old Coker lived in Bennett Spring Township, Barnwell County, with his wife and three children.

Reconciliation

Concerned citizens sponsored several public meetings to address concerns in the aftermath of the violence. The first mass meeting convened in Ellenton on July 11, 1877. The audience was fairly equally divided between black and white. Major James E. Crosland presided, and W.W. Williams served as secretary. Crosland presented the object of the meeting: restoring order between "the citizens connected with the riots of last September, and the prosecutions arising therefrom." He appointed a biracial committee to draft and report resolutions toward that end. The committee unanimously reported resolutions that in order to restore harmonious relations, prosecutions of black or white rioters should end; all citizens, black and white, should be "protected in their homes"; officials should enforce the law without respect to race and stated, "It is wise and patriotic that the passions that have been engendered between the white and colored races during said riots and the trials that have resulted therefrom, be forgotten, and that we do again

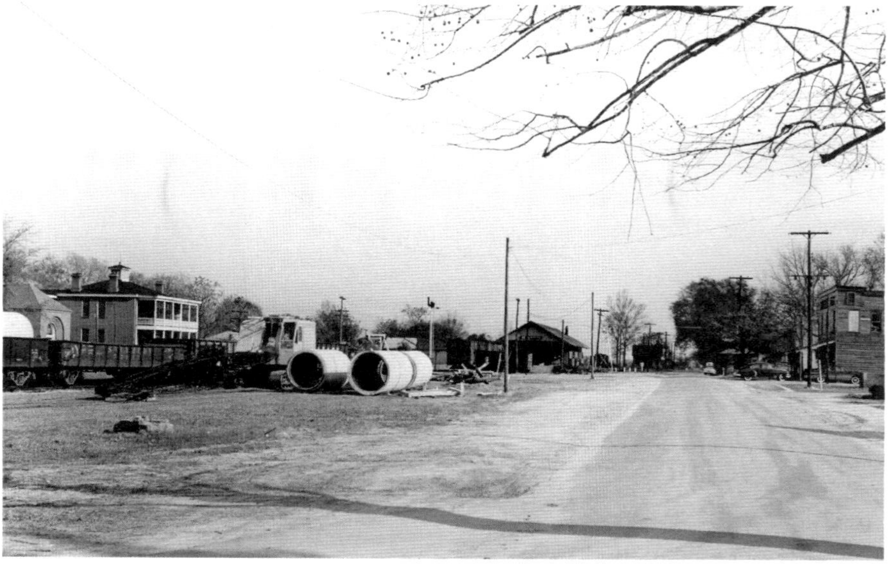

Train depot, Ellenton, March 15, 1951. S233002. Records of the Department of Transportation, Photographic Collection, 3.201, Highways: State Secondary, Barnwell County, Town Scenes, 1951, SC. 64 "Savannah River Plant Area." *Courtesy South Carolina Department of Archives and History.*

enter upon an era of good will and friendship." The two to three hundred individuals who attended unanimously adopted the resolutions.

When Aiken residents learned of the Ellenton meeting, they called a mass meeting on July 16. Only African Americans attended the Aiken meeting. Reverend H.D. Edwards presided, and the attendees read and adopted the Ellenton resolutions.[140] The wording of the resolutions focused heavily on ending the prosecutions on the state and federal level.

On April 4, 1878, J.C. Davant, an attorney of Barnwell, appeared in United States Circuit Court. Davant represented "a number of Gentlemen" arrested in October 1876 for "alleged conspiracy" during the Ellenton Riot. The men posted bond at the time, and officials released them. Given the lack of action, Davant asked the judge to order their discharge. The judge refused to grant the order.[141]

In 1880, the South Carolina legislature incorporated the town of Ellenton. According to the act of incorporation, the town limits of Ellenton formed a square with the Port Royal & Augusta Railroad Depot in the center. In 1909, the town received a new charter. Even before incorporation, in 1873, Ellenton had a post office. James Randolph Dunbar was the first postmaster.[142]

Vignettes from Ellenton in the 1880s

In 1883, Ellenton was the site of a grisly murder. Although details are scant, news reports, citing "private sources," suggest a murder-for-hire scheme that went wrong. Reportedly, a man named Wood employed a second individual named Carson to kill a third man named Rountree. While that situation sounds sufficiently complicated, Wood also hired two different men to kill Carson's brother-in-law named Sessions. Although Wood paid Carson, he did not kill Rountree. Nevertheless, someone killed Sessions, as searchers found his decapitated, mutilated body in the woods. Dogs and buzzards had attacked the corpse. Officials arrested Wood and Terry (one of the two men hired by Wood) and later captured the other man, Easley, in Thomson.[143]

An article in the *New York Times* recounted a strange story about old Ellenton. In 1885, a widow, Mrs. S.A. Snelling, lived alone in Ellenton. Following the death of her husband, she declined all overtures to live with her devoted son. Her son, Jerry, lived nearby and checked on his mother weekly. During one visit, she asked him to purchase a quantity of candles. Why? Mrs. Snelling assured her son that he would need them for her wake. Although his mother was in good health, despite her age, Jerry Snelling purchased the candles as requested. About one week later, an African American who lived nearby was passing the Snelling home during a hard rainstorm. Noticing the open windows and door, he called her name but heard no reply. He hastened to the home of Jerry Snelling. At the house, he found his mother, dressed in "her burial clothes," lying dead on her bed.[144]

A con artist also disturbed the calm of Ellenton in 1883. A local Campbellite[145] Baptist church called a new pastor. Reverend W.L. Mosley immediately impressed the congregation. In addition, he roomed with one of his church members, L.A. Ashley. Ashley was a well-to-do merchant and farmer.

As the two grew closer, Mosley began discussing with Ashley a possible business venture in Florida. The minister shared with Ashley a wonderful opportunity to mine a guano deposit on an island in Florida. The anticipated payout would be huge, but Mosley needed "capital" to take advantage of the opportunity. Intrigued, Ashley entered into a formal partnership agreement with Mosley to mine and market the fertilizer.

Once the men had signed the agreement, Mosley traveled to Washington, D.C., and returned with a "purported" license to mine the deposit. At that point, Mosley departed for Florida. Ostensibly, he had the island surveyed, purchased a "sloop" and then sailed back to South Carolina with samples.

En route, he encountered a terrible storm. He and his two-man crew valiantly struggled to survive until rescued. Unfortunately, the winds and waves destroyed the ship and its contents. Undeterred, Mosley reached out to his connections in Florida and secured a sample of guano. An analysis in Charleston valued the deposit at seventy-seven dollars per ton.

Ashley had been financing all of Mosley's travels and expenditures and, despite the setbacks, remained committed to the undertaking. Then, in true "the pen is mightier than the sword" tradition, fate intervened. Ashley read an announcement in a Christian (Campbellite) church paper. Numerous members of Mosley's previous church had taken out an ad warning others not to trust him. An investigation into Mosley and his background revealed that the erstwhile minister was an ex-convict from Iowa.

Even though Ashley had lost more than $900 in the scheme, he refused to prosecute the offender, who promptly left South Carolina for Augusta, Georgia.[146] The 1880 census schedule for Barnwell County lists L. (Laurence) A. Ashley, aged thirty-eight, who lived in the Four Mile Township. Ashley's household included his wife, six children, his mother and uncle, a housekeeper, three boarders and four servants. Ashley also owned fifty acres and a lumber or sawmill.[147]

Ellenton and the New County

The location of Ellenton was also key to defeating the last great effort to create a new county from Aiken. Consequently, the citizens of Aiken and Edgefield successfully defeated three well-organized and concerted efforts to create a new county from Aiken and Edgefield Counties. In 1902, the pro–new county faction proposed a new county named Hammond with a county seat at North Augusta. The secession effort failed by a slim margin.

James U. Jackson, founder of North Augusta, spearheaded the second effort. Organizers of the second effort, circa 1906, focused on addressing issues raised during the first campaign. Consequently, the proposed county had a different name, Heyward, and the proposed area for the new county specifically excluded areas, such as "several of the cotton mill villages of the Horse Creek valley." Such gerrymandering produced an oddly shaped "shoestring" area that was thirty miles long and, near North Augusta, only four miles wide! Again, the proposal failed by a close vote. Some protested the validity of the election, so the matter languished in the courts for several years before a court decision upheld the election results. Nevertheless, the

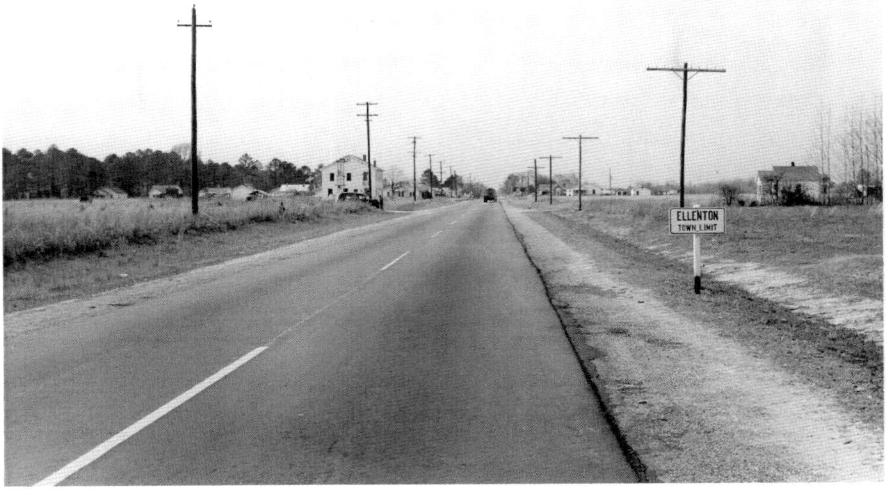

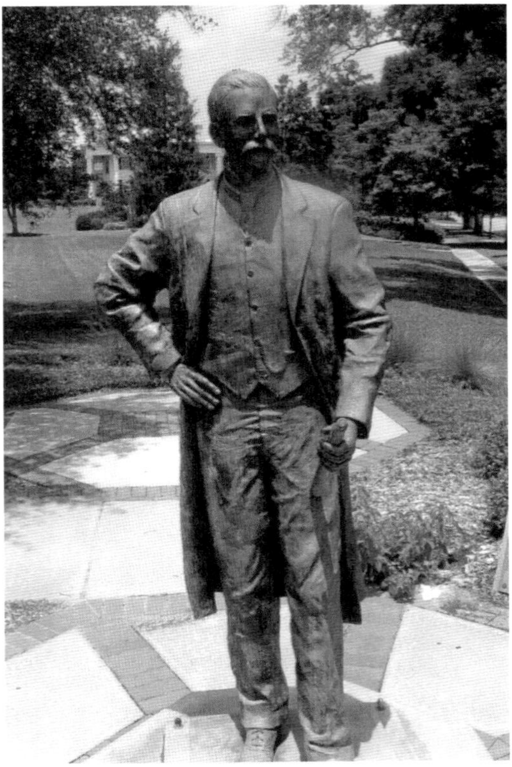

Above: City limits sign, Ellenton, March 15, 1951. S233002. Records of the Department of Transportation, Photographic Collection, 3.201, Highways: State Secondary, Barnwell County, Town Scenes, 1951, SC. 64 "Savannah River Plant Area." *Courtesy South Carolina Department of Archives and History.*

Left: Statue of James U. Jackson, father of North Augusta and builder of the Hampton Terrace Hotel, North Augusta, 2018. *Photographer Terry L. Helsley.*

court ruled that Jackson and the other planners had to wait four years from the time of the previous election before they could make another attempt.

The time was up in 1910, and once again, Jackson was the prime proponent of a new county. In 1910, he was a prominent man of business with major investments in the North Augusta Land Company and the Hampton Terrace Hotel. In addition, he served as vice-president of the Augusta-Aiken railroad. The third effort to form a new county featured a territory that was twenty miles long and ten miles wide. Members of the planning committee represented towns and communities interested in the possibility of a new county. Members of the planning committee included J.C. Gardner of Beech Island; James E. Green of Talatha; Winchester McDaniel of Modoc; William S. Middleton of Clarks Hill; W.R. Parks of Parksville; Luther W. Reese of Meriwether Township, Edgefield; William Turner of Ellenton; W. Scott Tyler of Silverton; and B.C. Wall, James U. Jackson, T.L. Foreman and W.T. Hite of North Augusta. North Augusta, given its prominence, had the largest representation. Anticipating success, the organizers hired R.H. Welch, a reputed "professional new county legal adviser," with considerable "experience with baby new county schemes."[148]

From hindsight, given the tax base needed to operate in the twenty-first century, such a move could have doomed the county of Aiken to an economic backwater. Despite several attempts, proponents of the new county were never able to capture the required two-thirds of votes cast. In the final foray, the issue came down to the legislatively intended boundaries for Ellenton, which sat astride the Aiken-Barnwell County line. One interpretation favored the new county party and the other those who wanted to keep Aiken County the way it was. The case worked its way to the South Carolina Supreme Court. There, the testimony of one of the original surveyors was key to a positive outcome for the Aiken County supporters.

Ellenton in the 1930s

A snapshot of Ellenton in 1930 shows a thriving town. Many residents worked for or in railroad jobs. Harold Buckingham and his wife, Myrtle, ran a boardinghouse. Their lodgers included Annette Dickinson, a bookkeeper, and John C. Watson, president of the bank. Allen B. Wise had a Ford dealership, and William E. McCurry was the superintendent of the public schools. Lodging with Jule and Jessie Smith were William H. Greene, a druggist. Willie A. Hayes was the Ellenton policeman. The town had two doctors in residence: Dr. Fred C. Brinkley and Dr. John G. Way. Jack D. Miller operated an automobile repair shop, and Earl Greene was an automobile mechanic. Theodore Rountree delivered ice. Wiley Mays was foreman of the highway department shop in Ellenton, and Glenn Franklin was a salesman for Standard Oil. Two ministers, Reverend Carl F. Outlaw (Christian church) and Reverend Hansel W. Stembridge (Baptist church), lived in town. Mary Foreman was the Ellenton postmistress, and Ralph D. Dunbar was the rural mail carrier. Ellenton had a barber, retail and grocery stores, a butcher and several restaurants. A number of residents worked in timber-related businesses—logging or in the veneer plant. Ellenton had all the necessary amenities and a thriving economy.[149]

In 1938–39, there were two cotton warehouses in Ellenton. M.B. Buckingham operated one of the warehouses and reported processing 509 bales of cotton. H.M. Cassels operated a smaller enterprise that processed 206 bales.[150] Cotton fields surrounded the town of Ellenton.

Another important local business was the Leigh Banana Case Company. Charles Q.C. Leigh of Paducah, Kentucky, founded the company in 1905 to manufacture wooden crates large enough to hold a bunch of bananas.

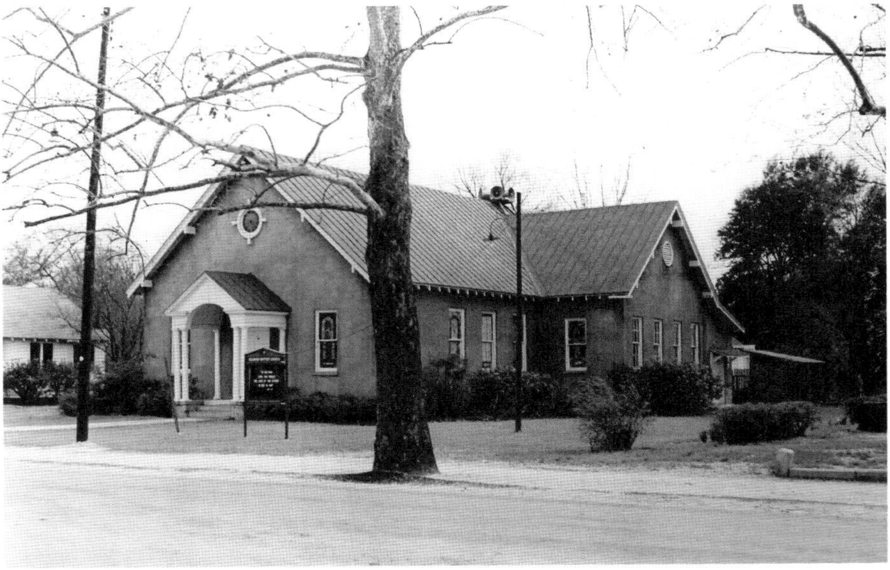

Ellenton Baptist Church, 1951. S233002. Records of the Department of Transportation, Photographic Collection, 3.201, Highways: State Secondary. Barnwell County, Town Scenes, 1951, SC. 64 "Savanna River Plant Area." *Courtesy South Carolina Department of Archives and History.*

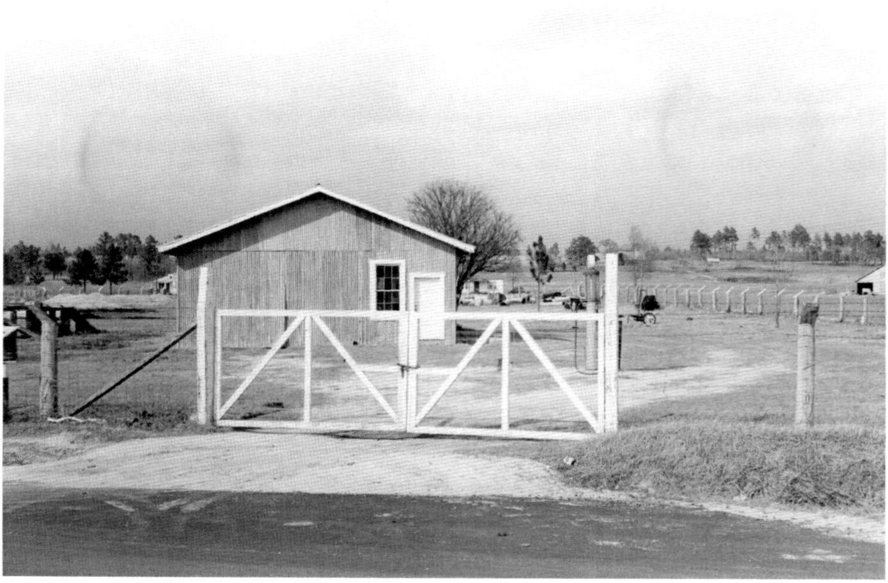

Highway Department Maintenance Shed, Ellenton, March 15, 1951. S233002. Records of the Department of Transportation, Photographic Collection, 3.201, Highways: State Secondary, Barnwell County, Town Scenes, 1951, SC. 64 "Savannah River Plant Area." *Courtesy South Carolina Department of Archives and History.*

For twenty-five years, the company had a virtual monopoly on banana crate production. In 1920, the company refocused its business to produce crates and containers for fruits and vegetables, and by the 1940s, the company was manufacturing baskets of differing sizes as well.

At one time, the company had more than fifty plants in the United States and needed large supplies of timber. Consequently, in 1926, the company relocated to the Savannah River Valley, about three miles from Ellenton. Built on the edge of a swamp, the company used two trains to haul the needed cypress and other wood from the swamp.

In the 1940s, the company diversified in order to produce wire crates and at times employed more than three hundred workers. Faced with the coming of the Savannah River Plant, the company closed.[151]

In 1940, according to the census, many Ellenton residents worked, either for the Leigh Banana Case Company or for Cassel's cotton warehouse or another Cassel's enterprise.

SAVANNAH RIVER PLANT

On November 28, 1950, the United States Atomic Energy Commission issued a press release that the AEC would build production plants in Aiken and Barnwell Counties. E.I. Nemours Company, Wilmington, Delaware, would build and manage the plant—a simple piece of paper and notice, but one with diverse and at times devastating results for thousands of unsuspecting South Carolinians. In response to the advent of the Cold War, the United States Atomic Energy Commission acquired three hundred square miles along the Savannah River in Aiken and Barnwell Counties and established the Savannah River Plant (later site). The plant would produce plutonium for the H-bomb. The plant purchased homes and businesses in Ellenton. Some residents relocated to the new town of New Ellenton. Others moved to communities nearby or to Columbia. With the relocation of Ellenton, the company had some of its buildings physically moved.[152]

In December 1950, Mike Cassels, "a leader among the families ordered evicted," said that the five thousand evacuees "feel just like they had a death in the family." At a mass meeting in Ellenton, Gordon Britton "assured the owners that their government would not cheat them." Britton was in charge of land acquisition for the Corps of Engineers. In addition to compensation and relocation possibilities, many were concerned about the fate of small farmers and tenant farmers. Amos Ward, of the Department of Agriculture, anticipated that many would prefer work at the Savannah River plant if jobs were available. On the other hand, county agricultural agents planned to set up a temporary office in Ellenton to aid displaced farmers and tenants locate new land.[153]

According to some accounts, in addition to Ellenton, the Savannah River Plant displaced another incorporated town, Dunbarton, and four unincorporated communities. Among the communities lost to the Savannah River Plant was Meyers Mill. Meyers Mill was small, and many of the early residents bore the name Meyers. Founded in the nineteenth century, at its heyday the community had a railroad depot, a post office and a few stores. A cotton gin opened in Meyers Mill, and the Atlantic Coastline Railroad ran through the community to service the gin. As a result, Meyers Mill gained a post office. Charlie Meyer was the first postmaster. At one point, a fire destroyed several stores and other buildings in Meyers Mill. Meyers Mill was south of Dunbarton and "about 10 miles southeast of Ellenton."[154]

The government purchased the homes of six thousand individuals but paid only $19 million for more than 200,000 acres. Everyone who lived

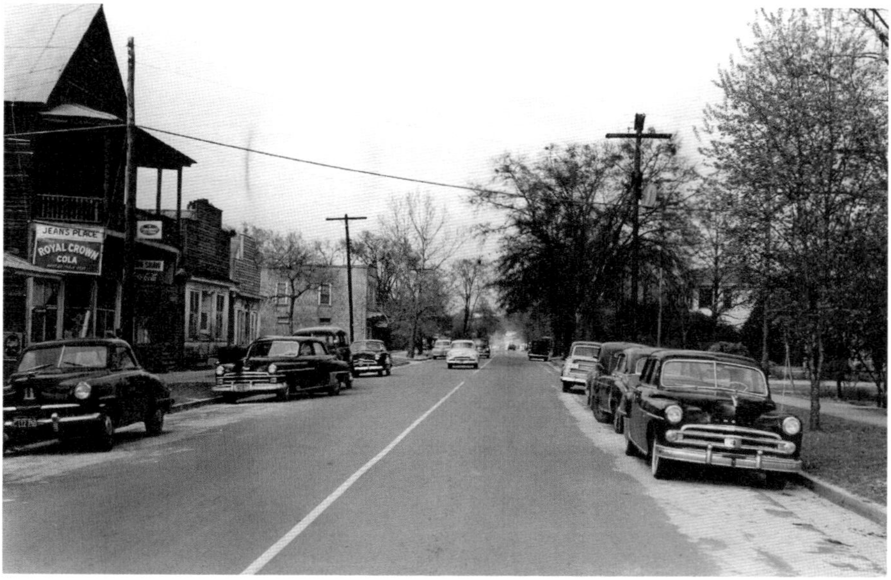

Main Street, Ellenton, March 15, 1951. Jean Shaw's store and pool room (*on left*). S233002. Records of the Department of Transportation, Photographic Collection, 3.201, Highways: State Secondary, Barnwell County, Town Scenes, 1951, SC. 64 "Savannah River Plant Area." *Courtesy South Carolina Department of Archives and History.*

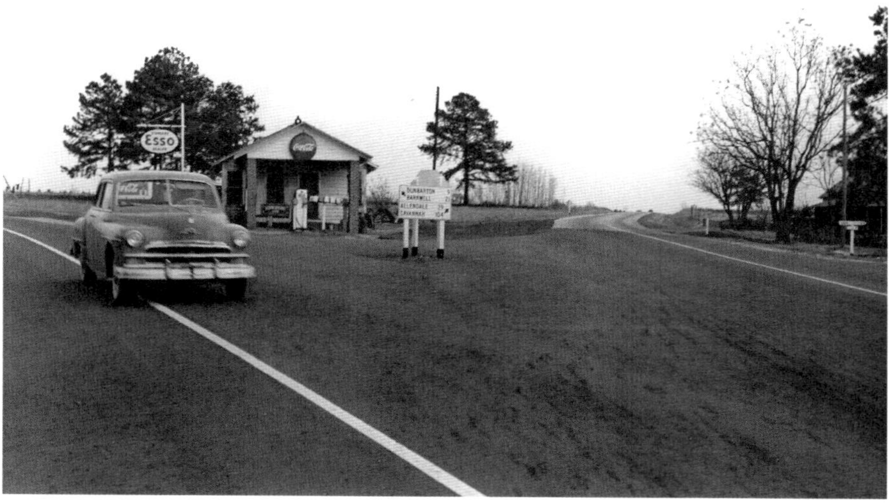

Route 64 between Dunbarton and Ellenton, 1951. S233002. Records of the Department of Transportation, Photographic Collection, 3.2, Highways: State Primary, Barnwell County, Town Scenes, 1951, SC. 64, SC 39, "Savannah River Plant Area." *Courtesy South Carolina Department of Archives and History.*

in the affected area had to move. Workers destroyed all structures that individuals had not moved. From a bustling little town, old Ellenton became a vast wasteland.[155]

Yet for some, time was a healer. For example, by October 1951, two-thirds of the displaced farmers and farm workers who had called themselves the "first displaced persons of World War III," and who ten months earlier had lamented loss of lifestyle and family farms, had new homes. Officials expected to resettle the remaining one-third within six months. Some of them were working in construction.

According to Arthur Foreman, a relocation consultant for the Clemson State College Extension Service, "Nobody has suffered, except for sentimental reasons." Mike Cassels, "Ellenton's general storekeeper and leading citizen," spoke for the six hundred former residents of Ellenton: "We've got over that first shock. People have adjusted. Some have nicked a slice off old Uncle Sugar, and nearly everybody is better off than before."[156]

Nevertheless, Bonner Lee Smith wrote in December 1950, "It is hard to understand why our town must be destroyed."[157]

Chapter 6

LOST DREAM

Textiles in Horse Valley

While the name of William Gregg is usually associated with the beginnings of the textile industry in Horse Valley, the honor actually belongs to Christian Breithaupt. A European immigrant who initially chose planting over mercantile pursuits as the path to success, Breithaupt remained open to other opportunities. Pursuing his initial dream, Breithaupt moved to rural Edgefield District. There he achieved remarkable success as a cotton planter and began to consider the possibility of enlarging his market share by processing that cotton at home rather than shipping the bales to the port cities of Charleston or Savannah for export and sale to other manufacturing venues.

VAUCLUSE

In 1822–23, Breithaupt and other investors built Vaucluse, a four-story factory in then Edgefield District. Powered by Horse Creek, Breithaupt's mill was the first textile mill erected in Horse Creek. The mill sat "among the rolling hills of the upper Horse Creek Valley," about twenty-five miles from the Savannah River. He used granite for the first floor and purchased looms, spindles and carding machines in order to produce cotton bagging. He also built housing for his workers, Horse Creek's first mill village. By 1828, the mill was producing cloth for the market. Breithaupt's fledgling enterprise was successfully underway. Nevertheless, in 1831, the original investors sold the mill to Thomas Higginbottom and Daniel P. Merriam of North Adams, Massachusetts. The purchasers paid $15,000 for the mill and 1,200 acres. Not long after the sale, the mill burned. Challenged by this dramatic change of events, in 1833 the Massachusetts owners resold the factory to Breithaupt for $7,000.

A more aggressive Breithaupt then sought state incorporation for the enterprise. He also raised substantial capital and began constructing a larger, more advanced facility.[158]

In 1833,[159] the South Carolina legislature incorporated the Vaucluse Manufacturing Company. The act authorized the company to select officers, adopt bylaws and "enjoy every right incident to incorporations." In addition, the act also empowered the Vaucluse Manufacturing Company to hold property valued at up to $100,000.[160]

This interest of Breithaupt and his associates produced an early, unique approach to textile manufacturing. Breithaupt and his fellow investors were planters. Theirs was an agricultural focus, so the early mill worked to produce cotton bagging for the local market. Their marketing plan did

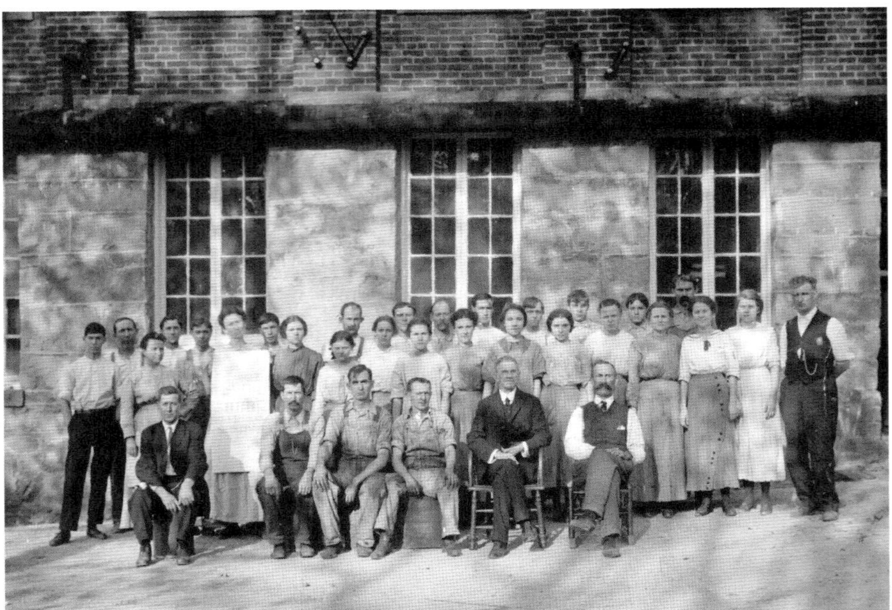

Millworkers outside the Vaucluse Mill, Vaucluse, South Carolina, 1910. *Courtesy Gregg-Graniteville Photographic Archives, Gregg-Graniteville Library, USC Aiken.*

not extend beyond Hamburg, Aiken, Edgefield and Augusta. In fact, at times they seemed more interested in local South Carolina outlets rather than looking for outlets across the Savannah River in Augusta. As successful planters, these early adventurers into the world of textile manufacturing also relied heavily on slave labor. For example, in 1837, George McDuffie wrote concerning the pay he wanted for the six slaves he had hired out to the mill.

With a second chance at Vaucluse, Breithaupt not only rebuilt the factory but also added manufacturing capacity. Among the investors in Vaucluse were George McDuffie (governor of South Carolina, 1834–36), Christian Breithaupt, Richard Cunningham, Mitchell King (Charleston attorney and developer of Flat Rock, North Carolina) and Paul Fitzsimons (perhaps the brother of Catherine Fitzsimons Hammond). The new Vaucluse employed fifty workers, including twenty probably enslaved African Americans. Nevertheless, the isolated location of the mill presented labor challenges. As one Vaucluse worker noted, the site was "in the midst of woods 16 miles from any Town." With labor more expensive, the new mill soon encountered financial difficulties. As an added complication, Breithaupt, the textile pioneer, died in 1835. With his death, his associates proved either unwilling or unable to give the mill the attention and management needed. Consequently, the mill suffered, and by 1837, the Vaucluse Company was heavily in debt. It owed $6,000.[161]

In a drama, the playwright would note "enter stage right": one William Gregg. The interjection of Gregg into the Vaucluse textile challenge was a moment of great drama with long-term consequences.

WILLIAM GREGG AND VAUCLUSE

William Gregg (1800–1867) was a dreamer, a visionary, and his dream cast a long shadow not only in Horse Creek but also across the state of South Carolina. He saw a new future for the South—one with a diversified economy that coupled agriculture with industrialization—in essence, a "New South" long before Henry Grady made his famous speech in December 1889.

Born in Virginia, William Gregg at age ten began his education in textile manufacturing. He went to work for his uncle Jacob Gregg, a watchmaker, who also manufactured spinning equipment. The young man moved with his uncle to Georgia. There, Jacob Gregg established a textile mill that enjoyed commercial success until the end of the War of 1812. The loss of the embargo on imports made it difficult for American manufacturing to survive and thrive in the postwar years.

With the closing of Jacob Gregg's mill, Jacob apprenticed William to a watchmaker in Kentucky. Mastering that trade, he moved to Columbia, South Carolina. There, William Gregg built a successful business with luxury goods. He produced watches and silver items and imported specialty goods for well-to-do customers. In addition, he made and sold military items. While in Columbia, Gregg married Marina Jones from Edgefield District, South Carolina. William and Marina were the parents of four children.

With the demise of Breithaupt and the disarray of Vaucluse, the company's directors turned day-to-day management of the mill over to William Gregg. Vaucluse Mill was in serious economic difficulties, and Gregg had just closed a highly profitable business in Columbia. Though young, Gregg could afford to retire and pursue other interests. One of those interests was textile manufacturing. His early experiences with his uncle in Georgia had sparked a deep fascination with the possibilities. Gregg became a stockholder in and manager of the Vaucluse Mill. Gregg also had the necessary understanding of market forces, labor issues and technology to be successful.

Consequently, in less than a year after Gregg assumed management of the mill, Vaucluse Mill executed a dramatic about-face. Production increased tremendously, and the company not only retired its debt but also recorded a significant profit. Nevertheless, the company's stockholders were nervous about the company prospects and sold the enterprise to George McDuffie and John Bauskett.[162] Shortly, Bauskett became the sole owner of Vaucluse. Bauskett, a native of Edgefield, was a successful planter and attorney and served in the South Carolina Senate.

Under Bauskett's management, the mill continued to be highly profitable. He increased production and spindle capacity and at one point employed almost seventy millworkers, mainly white. The mill produced much more income for Bauskett than his plantation. To meet labor needs, he even employed several of his slaves in the mill.

Fearing that the mill was consuming too much of his time and energy, to the detriment of both his legal and legislative careers, in 1841 Bauskett sold half his interest in the mill. General James Jones, brother of Marina Gregg,[163] purchased a half-interest in Vaucluse and agreed to live on site and oversee daily mill operations. In 1843, Bauskett sold his remaining interest in Vaucluse to William Gregg. Jones and Gregg together managed the mill for several years until January 1848. Then with his own dream, Graniteville, on the horizon, three miles south of Vaucluse, Gregg sold his interest to

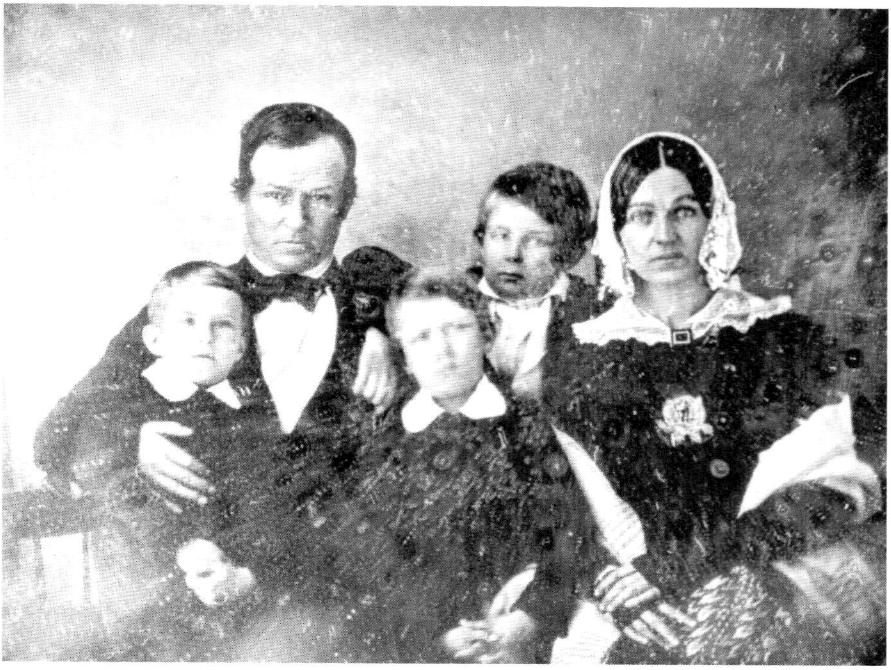

William Gregg and family, circa 1845. *Left to right*: William Gregg, Marina Gregg and their sons, William Jr. (born in 1834), James J. Gregg (born in 1836) and John (born in 1838). *Courtesy Gregg-Graniteville Photographic Archives, Gregg-Graniteville Library, USC Aiken.*

Jones. Jones oversaw the mill alone until other business interests intervened. Given the challenge of overseeing the construction of the new statehouse in Columbia, Jones sold Vaucluse to William Gregg. So, Gregg in 1856 found himself owner of Vaucluse and Graniteville. He named his son James J. Gregg manager of Vaucluse.

For several years after the sale, the two Greggs did little but renovate and modernize the factory and its equipment. In June 1859, the Vaucluse Mill reopened. Following his father's example, James J. (J.J.) Gregg implemented the strict policies pioneered at Graniteville at the newly refurbished Vaucluse. The fifty-person workforce was all white. The mill operated twelve hours a day. According to mill policy, millworkers could not purchase or consume alcoholic beverages in the mill village. Children aged six through eleven attended school, and all mill employees had to be over twelve years of age.[164]

Meanwhile, after his first sale of Vaucluse, Gregg took the profits and established Hayden, Gregg & Company in Charleston. Gregg, with his partners, Nathaniel and Hezekiah Hayden, built the company into the leading importer and producer of luxury items and jewelry in the port city. The success of the new company increased Gregg's status among Charleston's commercial class and provided Gregg with adequate capital for additional investments.

GRANITEVILLE

Not content with his success, Gregg toured the major textile mills in the Northeast in order to improve his understanding of manufacturing processes. Enthusiastic about his findings, Gregg became an outspoken advocate for manufacturing in the South. He wrote and published a series of articles in a Charleston newspaper extolling the virtues and necessity of the South embracing textile manufacturing and ending its long dependence on agriculture, specifically the cultivation of cotton. In his first essay, Gregg articulated his position that the future of South Carolina "lies in a change of our industrial pursuits" because the United States was "destined to be a great manufacturing country." In support of his position, Gregg cited the progress of neighboring Georgia and North Carolina in textile manufacturing. In other words, if they could do it, South Carolina could do it better.[165]

As a result, Gregg and fellow investors petitioned the South Carolina legislature for a charter for the Graniteville Manufacturing Company. Initial investors in the company were Wit O. Mills, William Gregg, Hiram Hutchison (president of the Bank of Hamburg) and Joel Smith. In December 1845, the South Carolina legislature incorporated the company with an initial capitalization of $300,000. Gregg purchased 7,952 acres on Horse Creek near Aiken.

William Gregg not only was the founder of Graniteville but also the first president of the Graniteville Manufacturing Company. He served from March 7, 1846, until his death. Gregg personally recruited and trained personnel and oversaw construction of the mill, dams, canal, sawmill and housing for the mill operatives, The process from clearing the site to operative mill took several years to complete.

In 1846, the company dug the canal connecting the factory with Horse and Bridge Creeks, and the mill village gained Baptist and Methodist churches. Later, the minister of St. Thaddeus Episcopal Church in Aiken would also hold services in Graniteville. In 1847, the company erected the Graniteville Academy and the first five mill cottages. Known as the "Blue

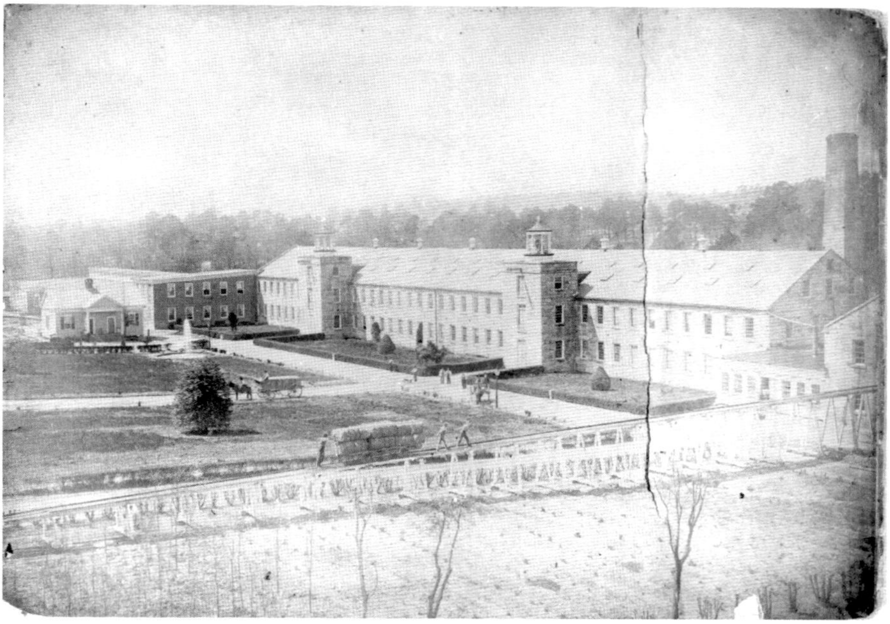

Early photograph, original granite mill, Graniteville Manufacturing Company. *Courtesy Gregg-Graniteville Photographic Archives, Gregg-Graniteville Library, USC Aiken.*

Row," the blue-washed cottages featured Gothic architecture, and each cost $400. By 1848, Graniteville was a town. It had forty cottages for the mill hands and additional housing for supervisors, as well as a post office, a hotel, stores, churches, boardinghouses, streets and fences.

Built on the banks of Horse Creek in Edgefield District, the massive granite factory at Graniteville mill opened in 1849. In May 1849, the company shipped 176 bales of cloth to New York by mule, train, rail and ship. The new enterprise was up and running. Graniteville quickly became "one of the most successful textile factories in the entire South." That fall, Gregg reported that the mill employed 325, and 900 people lived in the village.[166]

Graniteville was different from most antebellum textile mills. Unlike most southern mills, Gregg did not use slave labor in his mill. Instead, he employed white labor, often women and teenaged children. He installed modern machinery, constructed well-designed mill villages for his workers, mandated education for children under twelve and promulgated rules for Graniteville employees. In creating this prototype mill village with housing, churches, schools and retail, Gregg developed a model that dozens if not

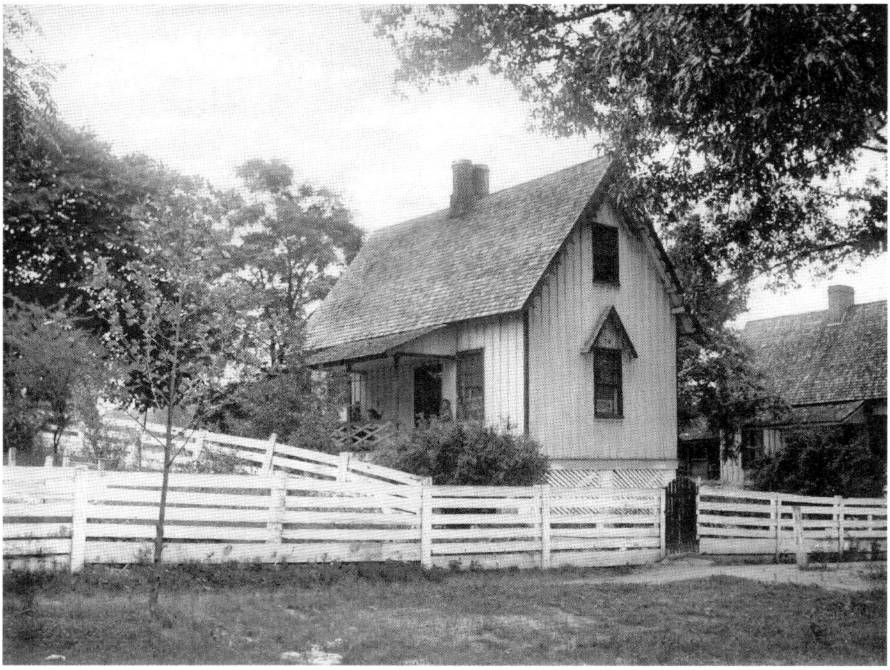

Early photograph of one of the "Blue Row Houses" on Gregg Street in Graniteville, a section of company housing built by Graniteville Manufacturing Company. *Courtesy Gregg-Graniteville Photographic Archives, Gregg-Graniteville Library, USC Aiken.*

hundreds of mills would follow. According to Broadus Mitchell, Gregg's biographer, Gregg built "the first typical Southern cotton-mill village."[167]

In addition, he never ceased to advocate for textile manufacturing in the South. In 1849, Gregg wrote to James H. Hammond that South Carolina mills had advantages over eastern ones. They had ready access to raw materials and abundant water to power the mills. In addition, owners in South Carolina could purchase machinery inexpensively and by bidding a little higher could "obtain their most skillful artisans."[168]

Possibly related to Gregg's views on acquiring talented textile workers from New England, the 1850 census for Barnwell District lists two possible New England millworkers living in the Aiken area. The census includes Benjamin Kimball, a native of Rhode Island, as a twenty-five-year-old millwright, and Newton Caperson, another native of Rhode Island and a member of Kimball's household, appears as a weaver. Perhaps Gregg or other mill personnel had recruited these New England millworkers

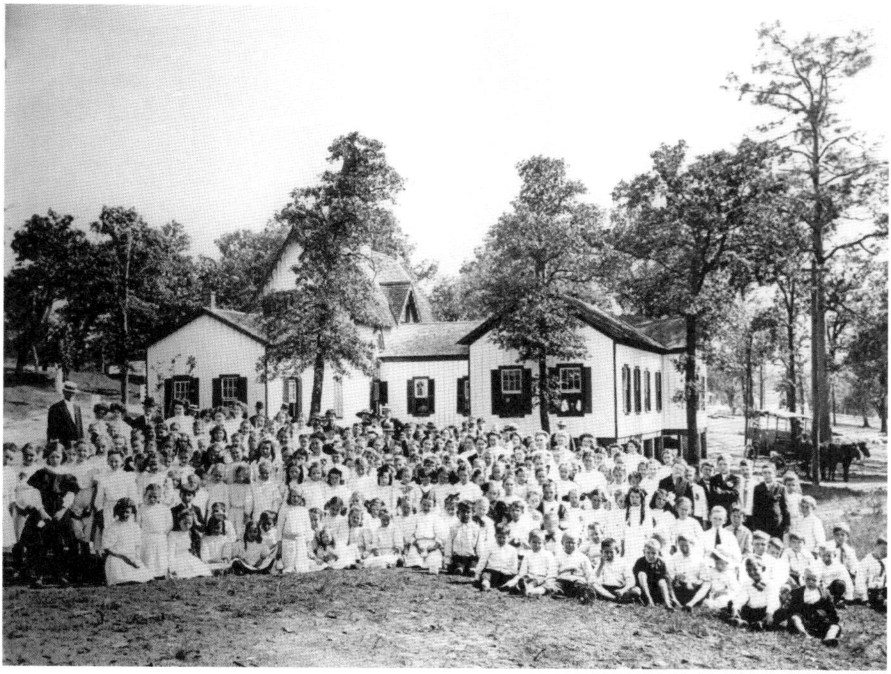

Students, Graniteville Academy, circa 1900. This was the school for millworkers' children, Graniteville Manufacturing Company. William Gregg pioneered compulsory education for the children who lived in his mill villages. *Courtesy Gregg-Graniteville Photographic Archives, Gregg-Graniteville Library, USC Aiken.*

either to work in the Horse Valley mills or to aid in the instruction of local textile workers.

In 1850, Gregg wrote to a Massachusetts colleague, Amos A. Lawrence, describing the Graniteville operation. Concerning labor, Gregg wrote that all the overseers were "Eastern men" (that is, trained in New England mills) and "nearly all of our hands live under parental care: in 85 cottages built by the company. Each cottage has between an acre and an acre and a half of land. Employee turnover is low. Gregg shared the rules governing Graniteville life: no alcohol; free, compulsory education for all children between six and twelve; no child labor." Gregg continued his overview and wrote of the "airy and commodious" factory buildings with four acres of "grass lawns and broad handsomely graded walks."

Gregg continued with information about the mill village. Graniteville, he wrote, "has a hotel, two churches, five mercantile establishments, besides smiths, shoe & hat makers" and so forth. He also stated that "no one can visit

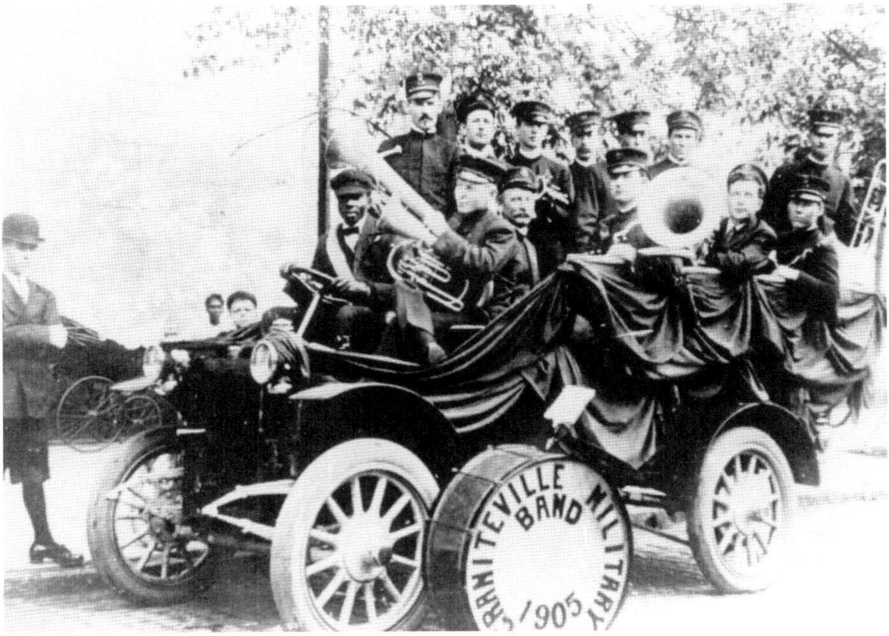

Graniteville Military Band, Gregg Park Civic Center, 1905. On special occasions, the band gave concerts. *Courtesy Gregg-Graniteville Photographic Archives, Gregg-Graniteville Library, USC Aiken.*

the place without being struck with the air of neatness and comfort which meets the eye in every direction." In conclusion, to Gregg, Graniteville was "a town of industry."[169]

Gregg continued to write in favor of the necessity of economic diversification and the incalculable benefits of textile manufacturing for South Carolina and the South. In 1856, the voters in Edgefield elected him to the South Carolina House of Representatives. On April 12, 1858, as an unsuccessful candidate for the South Carolina Senate, Gregg reflected on his role in Edgefield District: "I think I have some claims on the District. I have been working here on Horse Creek for 15 years, to develop a new and important branch of industry. I have educated the poor, given comfortable homes to the Widows & indigent families of the District, such as would be a God-send to the people of any District in the state."[170]

Still, Gregg was an important figure in Edgefield and the state. In 1860, Edgefield voters elected him as a delegate to the Secession Convention, and he signed the Ordinance of Secession. Supporting the war effort, without interruption, the Graniteville mill produced cloth for Confederate

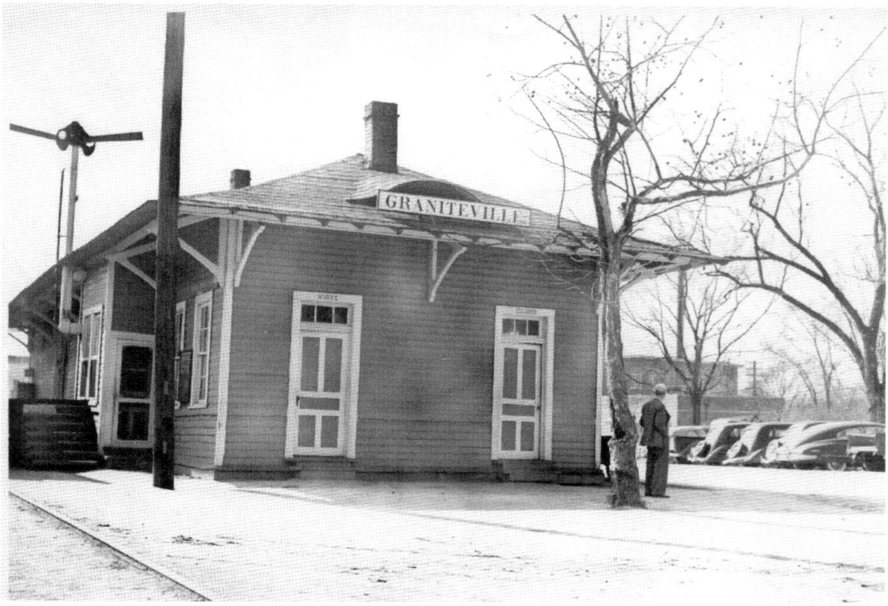

Graniteville Freight Depot, 1945. J.G. McKay, agent, is standing at right front. *Courtesy Gregg-Graniteville Photographic Archives, Gregg-Graniteville Library, USC Aiken.*

uniforms. While the mill escaped the war years unscathed, perhaps thanks to the Battle of Aiken, the war years had their challenges. There were health issues and labor shortages, and in 1864, work began on a new railroad. The war ended in a Union victory, and Gregg began replacing worn-out and outdated mill equipment. As part of this effort, Gregg traveled to Europe to secure needed machinery.

Work on the Columbia-Hamburg railroad ended in 1867. Nevertheless, in the midst of progress and Gregg's recovery efforts, disaster struck. In September 1867, a dam broke at the Graniteville mill. The hands-on Gregg stood in waist-deep water with others trying to repair the damage. Unfortunately, Gregg became ill and died on September 12, 1867.[171] To historian Clement Eaton, Gregg was the "most significant figure in the development of cotton mills in the South."[172]

On April 23, 1868, stockholders elected Hamilton H. Hickman president. Under its second president, Graniteville entered a new phase of its long existence. Hickman served as company president until 1898, the longest tenure of any Graniteville president.[173]

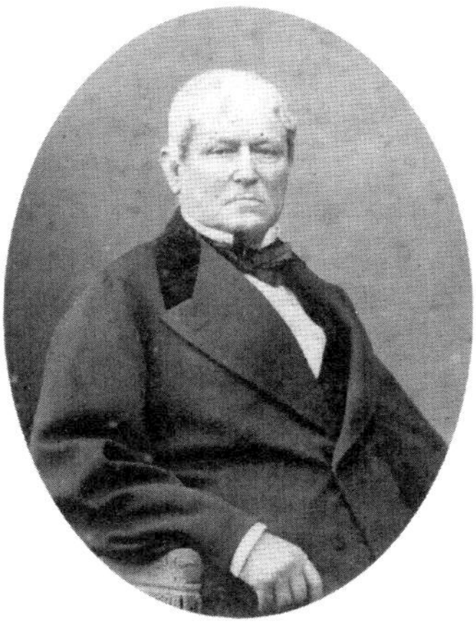

William Gregg (1800–1867), visionary founder of Graniteville Manufacturing Company. Carte de visite, taken in Paris, circa 1866. *Courtesy Gregg-Graniteville Photographic Archives, Gregg-Graniteville Library, USC Aiken.*

The mill at Vaucluse also survived the Civil War. The postwar years were difficult ones. On January 3, 1867, fire destroyed the mill under murky circumstances. A few suspected that James J. Gregg, superintendent of the Graniteville Manufacturing Company, had purposefully set the fire in order to collect the insurance money. With no hard evidence, the insurance company settled the claim, but Gregg did not use the money to rebuild or reopen the mill.

Meanwhile, Graniteville reached full capacity and enjoyed remarkable success in the post–Civil War years. Graniteville was one of the few southern mills that survived the war without serious damage. Consequently, Graniteville quickly switched to domestic production when the war ended and, in effect, beat the competition to market. So successful was the Graniteville Manufacturing Company that President H.H. Hickman urged the stockholders to expand. Under Hickman's leadership, Graniteville expanded in South Carolina and in Georgia.[174]

In April 1877, Hickman passionately lobbied the Graniteville stockholders either to build a new factory on the Vaucluse property or to sell the land. According to Hickman's argument, labor was cheap and construction and equipment costs well within the company's reach. He also pushed the advantages of new textile technologies and the necessity for Graniteville to stay abreast of such changes in order to remain competitive and profitable. Following Hickman's plea, the stockholders agreed and building began for a new factory at Vaucluse.

The new Vaucluse Mill, built of brick and stone, incorporated the latest architectural innovations from New England mills. The company constructed a dam to power the mill, and within one two-week period in 1880, the Vaucluse Mill generated "197,000 yards of cloth." The company also renovated old millhouses and added new ones to house the increased number of mill operatives. In addition, the mill provided housing for mill supervisors and the mill superintendent.

To Hickman, the Vaucluse Mill village was a positive influence on the workers in the mill and their families. For example, each cottage had a

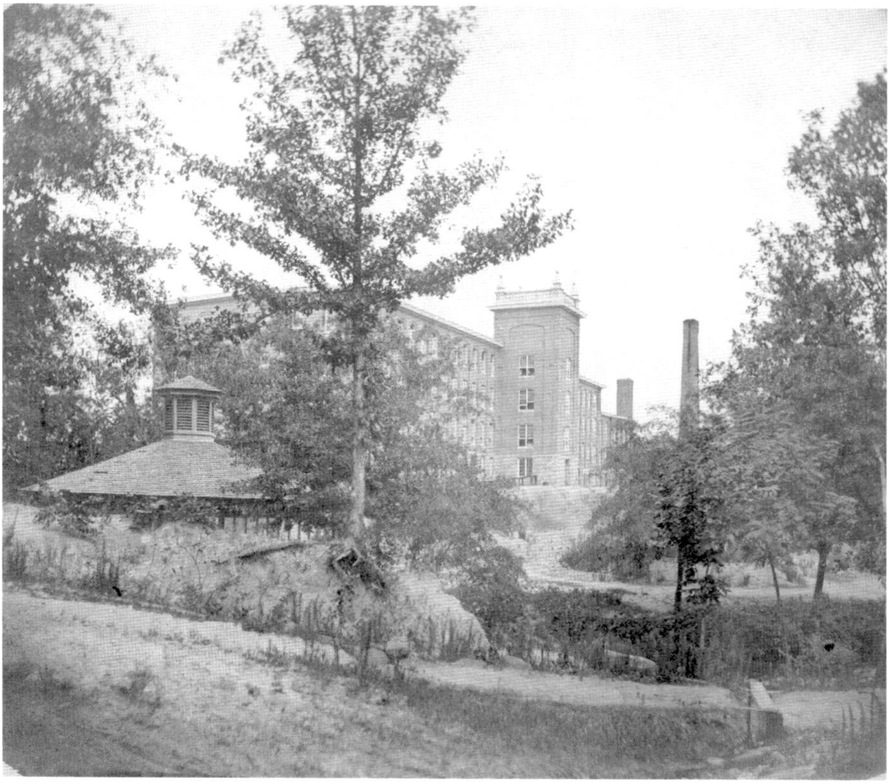

Vaucluse Division Mill, Graniteville Manufacturing Company, Graniteville, South Carolina. *Courtesy Gregg-Graniteville Photographic Archives, Gregg-Graniteville Library, USC Aiken.*

garden where workers could cultivate vegetables. In addition, perhaps similarly to medieval manors, the operatives could own chicken and hogs and cut timber from the company-owned woods. Mill owners also encouraged churches to organize in the mill village. The village at Vaucluse had both Baptist and Methodist congregations. In addition, several stores catered to the mill families.

Yet Hickman faced numerous obstacles in keeping Vaucluse and Graniteville operating efficiently and effectively. First, despite company paternalism, there were labor issues and unrest. In 1876, a disgruntled employee killed James J. Gregg. Earlier in 1875, a wage cut had led Graniteville workers to launch one of the first southern textile labor strikes. The company held firm, but feelings ran high and workers fired at the house of a mill overseer and shot a mill superintendent. In 1886, an overseer at Vaucluse encouraged the workers to demand a pay increase. The company

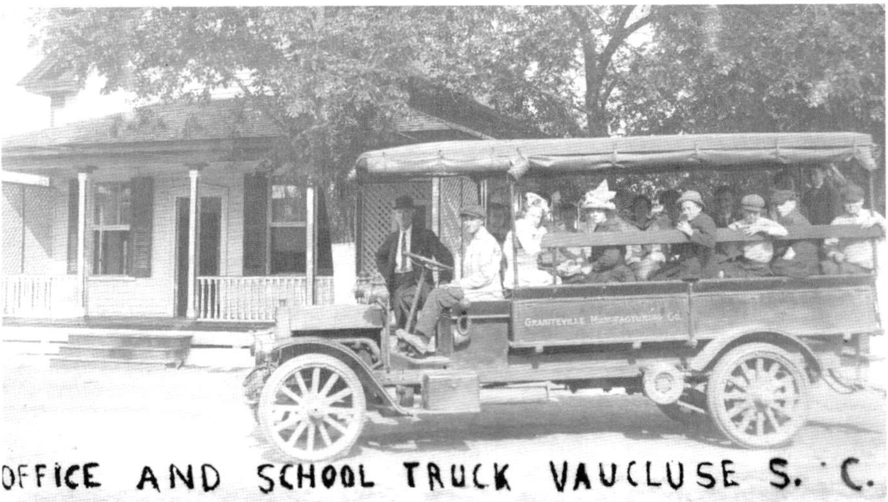

School truck, Vaucluse Mill, 1910. All Graniteville Company mills required mill village children to attend school until age eleven. Officials even provided transportation. This Federal Motor Truck served as a school bus and company truck. *Courtesy Gregg-Graniteville Photographic Archives, Gregg-Graniteville Library, USC Aiken.*

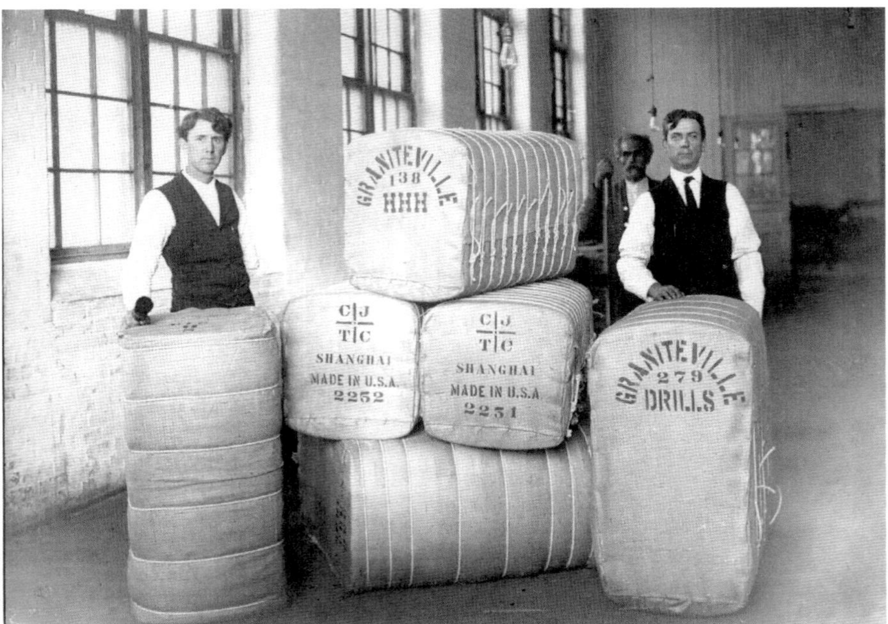

Mill employees with Graniteville Manufacturing Company output bundled for shipment, circa 1900. *Courtesy Gregg-Graniteville Photographic Archives, Gregg-Graniteville Library, USC Aiken.*

replaced him with a more malleable person, but due to threats from the workforce, the new man went to work armed for several weeks.

Hickman also had power supply issues and felt the constant pressure to renovate and update mill equipment. The water supply was not always sufficient to power the giant turbines that operated the mill equipment. Any interruption in the power source interfered with production and employees' work schedules. To address this issue, Hickman installed steam engines so the mill was no longer dependent on a water source for operating power.

Historically, Vaucluse's dependency on Horse Creek brought times of feast or famine. High water levels flooded dams, and low ones, either from lack of rain or from too many other mills using the creek, were inadequate for the mill to operate. To mitigate the situation, Graniteville Mill built ponds to provide extra water for mill operation.

In addition, Hickman focused on updating plant equipment. Increased competition made modernization a key to maintaining a competitive advantage. Throughout the late nineteenth and early twentieth centuries, plant management improved equipment and expanded capacity and the workforce.[175]

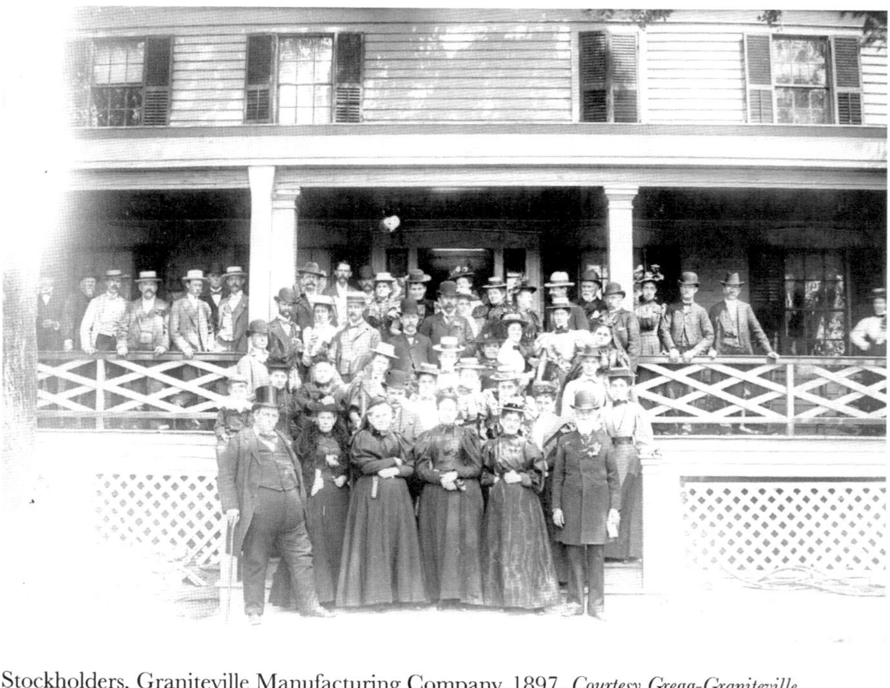

Stockholders, Graniteville Manufacturing Company, 1897. *Courtesy Gregg-Graniteville Photographic Archives, Gregg-Graniteville Library, USC Aiken.*

In 1882, the South Carolina Department of Agriculture listed two cotton mills in Aiken County: Langley on Horse Creek and the Graniteville & Vaucluse factory on Horse Creek.[176] The nucleus for the future was in place, and Graniteville led the way. In 1891, Graniteville workers had electric lights, a first for the state of South Carolina, and in 1899, Tracy I. Hickman succeeded his father as president of the Graniteville Company.

The twentieth century was one of expansion for the textile industry in South Carolina. With two world wars and a burgeoning middle class, the textile world expanded dramatically. Every city or town in South Carolina wanted its own mill. Town boosters saw textile mills as economic engines that could address employment and revenue issues.

The new century opened with a new mill at Graniteville. The company later named the steam-powered state-of-the-art mill Hickman Mill in honor of Hamilton H. Hickman, the company's second president and Tracy Hickman's father. Trolley service connected Graniteville with Aiken and Augusta. Then, in 1907, Graniteville build a community building, Hickman Hall, also named in honor of the second president. Hickman Hall had a swimming pool, a bowling center, a library and a gym.

Yet the path was not always easy. For example, in the early nineteenth century, Graniteville's profits flat-lined. As a result, in 1915 the company entered receivership. The buildup for World War I brought large government orders, and the company exited receivership within seventeen months.[177]

Factory success also brought labor issues. For example, during the World War I boom, mill operatives wanted more pay and shorter working hours. The American Federation of Labor tried to organize the Horse Creek workers and, in 1918, even secured a small pay increase for them. Unfortunately, when the workers sought additional pay and an eight-hour workday, the company closed the affected mills and destroyed the union.

In the early twentieth century, between four hundred and five hundred individuals lived in the Vaucluse Mill village. In time, the mill had a barber, a post office and, with the coming of the railroad, a depot. In addition, the village had a movie theater and, by 1920, a school. The mill village at Graniteville was larger, with similar amenities, as well as Hickman Hall and other recreational options.

The postwar years brought more economic difficulties. Yet in 1919, the Graniteville Company purchased Warren Mill in Warrenville. Nevertheless, with more manufacturing, there was more competition. When the stock market crashed and the Great Depression settled over the United States, there was less business and orders declined.

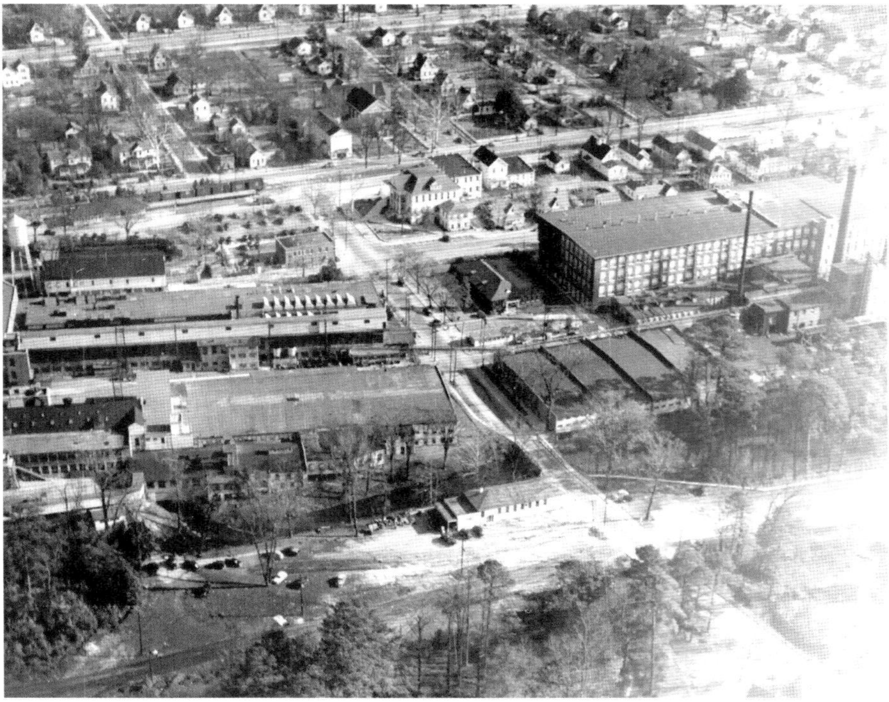

Aerial view, Graniteville, South Carolina, with Granite Division Mill, Hickman Mill and Hickman Hall visible. *Courtesy Gregg-Graniteville Photographic Archives, Gregg-Graniteville Library, USC Aiken.*

During the Depression years, the 1920s and 1930s, profits were low, and the company not only reduced wages but also at times closed the mills. In the 1920s, flooding was also an issue, as several bad floods damaged homes and other structures in Graniteville, but in 1938, Graniteville Company acquired Enterprise Mill in Augusta. Despite economic challenges, the company sought competitive opportunities. While many textile companies began to move away from providing housing for millworkers in the 1930s, the Graniteville Company continued to own the Vaucluse village.

In 1939, the Graniteville Company elected Samuel H. Swint Sr. president. Swint's twenty-three-year tenure in many respects was a golden age for the company. Under his leadership, the Graniteville Company created the Gregg-Graniteville Foundation, the first major textile-based philanthropic foundation. His son Samuel Swint Jr. also worked for the Graniteville Company from 1960 to 1994 and retired as executive vice-president.[178]

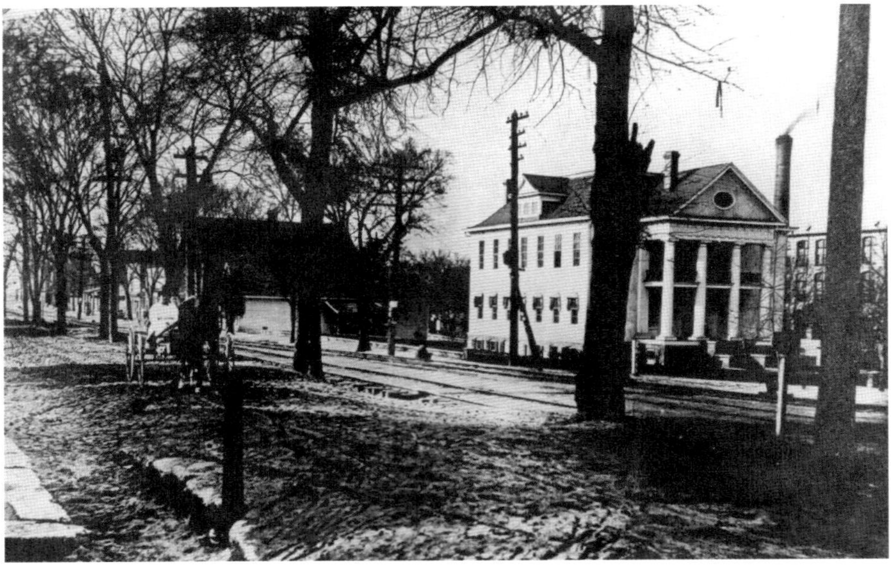

Hickman Hall, community center, Graniteville Manufacturing Company. *Courtesy Gregg-Graniteville Photographic Archives, Gregg-Graniteville Library, USC Aiken.*

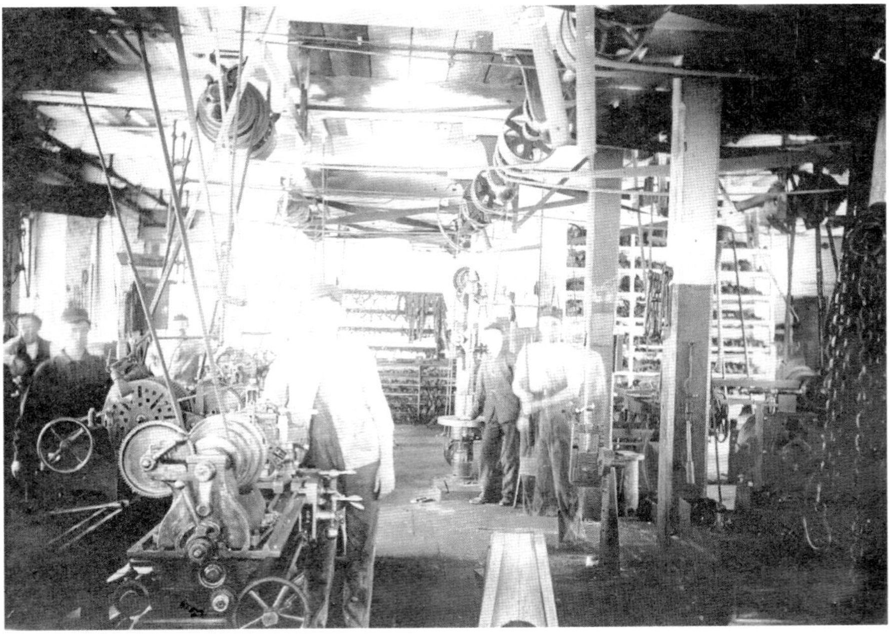

Machine shop of the Graniteville Manufacturing Company, 1908. *Left to right*: Charlie Beaufort (foreman), Jim Snelling, Mike Beaufort, Pierce Ward, Hugh May and John Feaster. *Courtesy Gregg-Graniteville Photographic Archives, Gregg-Graniteville Library, USC Aiken.*

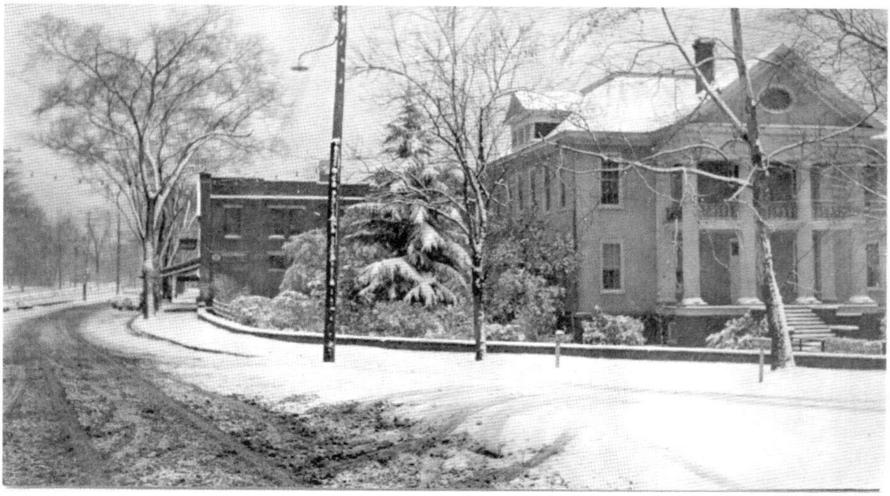

Hickman Hall, Community Center in the snow, Graniteville Manufacturing Company, built in 1907. Named in honor of H.H. Hickman, second president, Graniteville Manufacturing Company. *Courtesy Gregg-Graniteville Photographic Archives, Gregg-Graniteville Library, USC Aiken.*

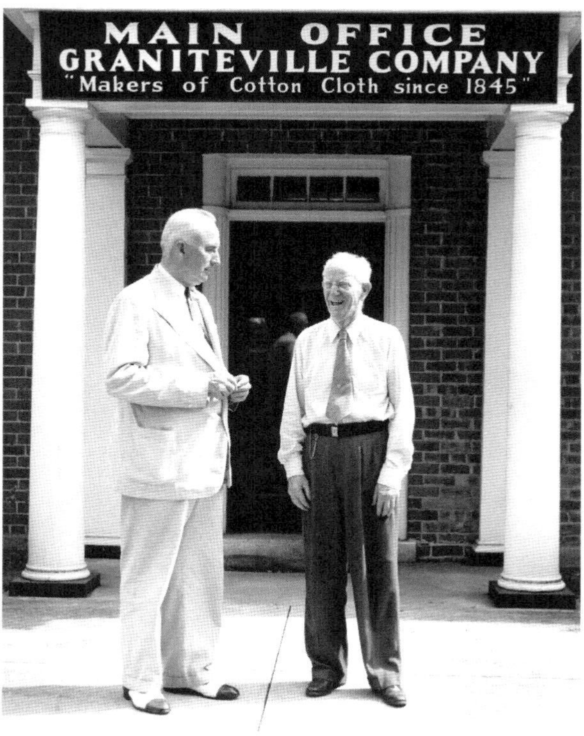

President Samuel H. Swint, seventh president, Graniteville Manufacturing Company (1939–1962) and James Wesley Reardon (1861–1959), outside main office, Graniteville Manufacturing Company. Reardon worked continuously for Graniteville Manufacturing Company for eighty-seven years. His first day of work was May 10, 1872. Graniteville Manufacturing Company. *Courtesy Gregg-Graniteville Photographic Archives, Gregg-Graniteville Library, USC Aiken.*

World War II brought good economic times for Vaucluse and the Graniteville Company. The company retired its indebtedness and raised employee pay. For example, to meet war demand, Vaucluse ran three shifts. The company added new houses, renovated existing ones and added amenities, such as a swimming pavilion and, in the immediate postwar years, new electric lighting and sewer and water systems. By the end of 1947, the village had 108 dwellings.

While the Graniteville Company began divesting itself of mill housing in 1941, the company continued to own the Vaucluse Mill village into the 1960s. In 1959, the Gregg-Graniteville pool opened, and in 1978, the U.S. Department of the Interior added the Graniteville Historic District to the National Register and designated the site a National Historic Landmark and, in 1996, the Vaucluse Mill became the Vaucluse Mill Village Historic District. These designations reflect the significant historic value of the antebellum mills of Horse Creek, but change was in the wind.

In the 1980s, the workforce was desegregated. In the second half of the twentieth century, following the national trend, textile manufacturing

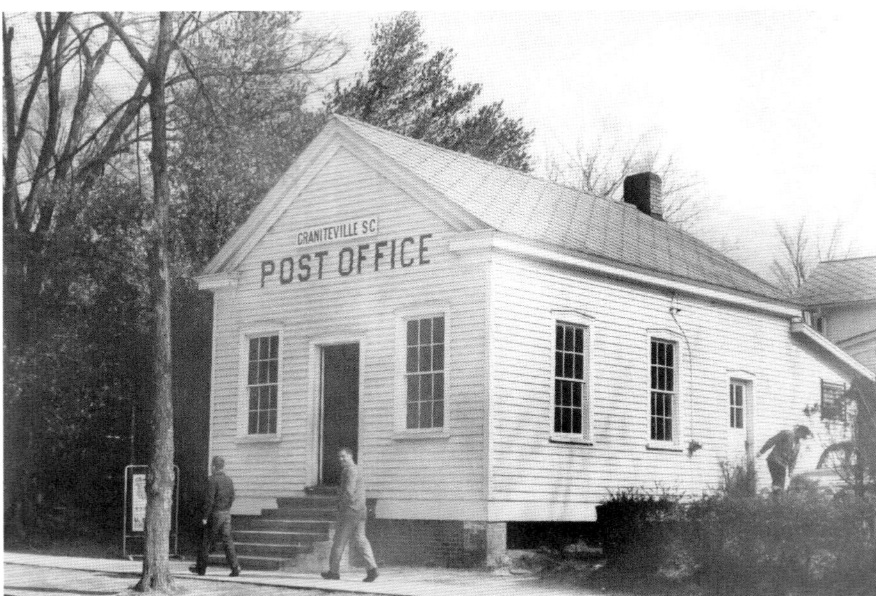

United States Post Office, Graniteville, South Carolina, 1948. Graniteville Company mill villages had all the amenities the millworkers needed. *Courtesy Gregg-Graniteville Photographic Archives, Gregg-Graniteville Library, USC Aiken.*

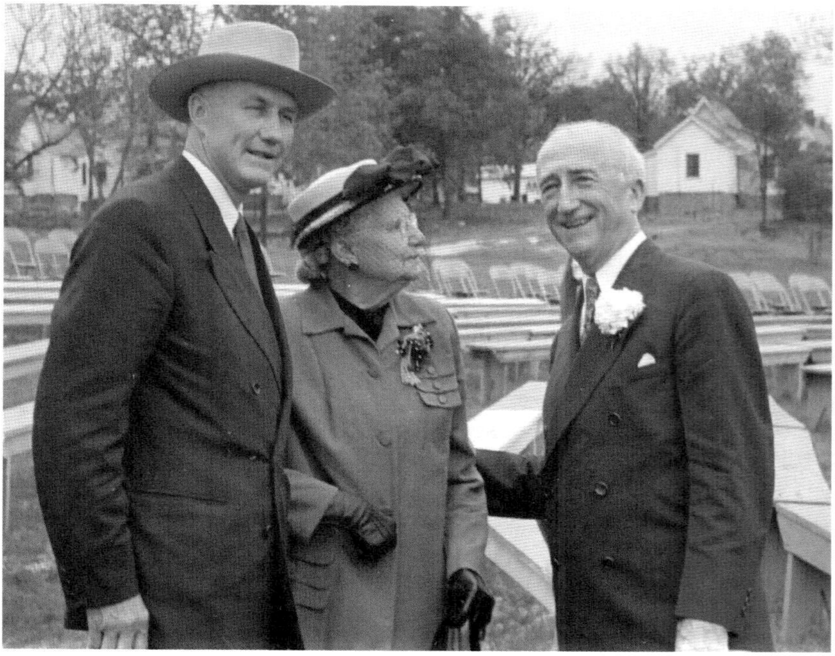

Governor J. Strom Thurmond and James F. Byrnes, governor-elect, at dedication of new Gregg Division, Graniteville Manufacturing Company, 1950. *Courtesy Gregg-Graniteville Photographic Archives, Gregg-Graniteville Library, USC Aiken.*

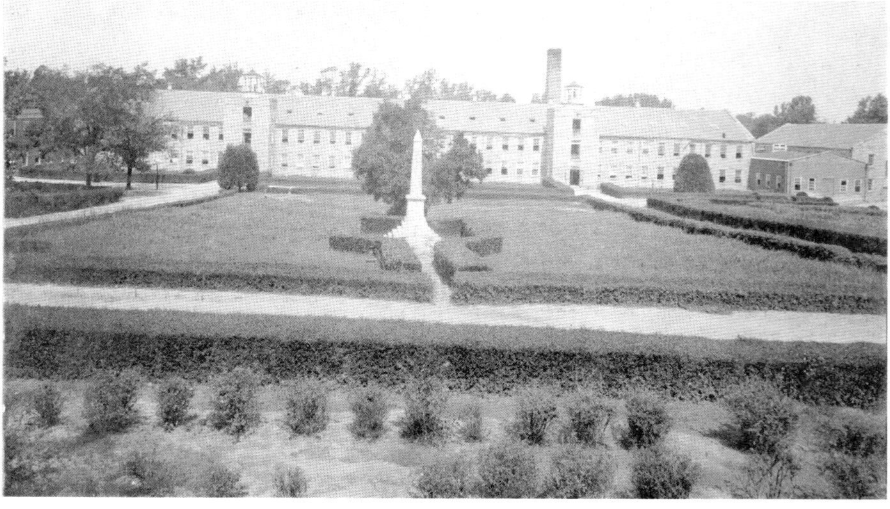

Graniteville Division Mill, Graniteville Manufacturing Company, Graniteville, South Carolina. Gregg Monument stands in the center. *Courtesy Gregg-Graniteville Photographic Archives, Gregg-Graniteville Library, USC Aiken.*

in South Carolina began to decline. Textile factory employment fell from roughly 200,000 in 1975 to 137,000 in 1993. The Warren Mill closed in the 1980s. Yet the Vaucluse Mill survived into the 1990s. Eventually, the mill's ancient wooden floors proved inadequate to support the vibrations of ever-faster and more technologically advanced equipment. In 1991, the Graniteville Company shut down production at the Vaucluse Mill, ending the mill's historic run as a Horse Creek textile pioneer, and also closed Granite Mill.[179] Nevertheless, other Graniteville Company mills continued to operate in the Horse Creek Valley.

By the 1980s, ownership of the Graniteville Company had changed and operations contracted. In 1996, Avondale Mills Inc., a Georgia-based textile company, acquired the Graniteville Company.[180] Then, in 2005, disaster struck.

A CHLORINE FOG

In the wee hours of a cold January morning in 2005, two Norfolk Southern freight trains collided in Graniteville with deadly results. Norfolk Southern Train 192 derailed and hit a parked locomotive on a spur. The resulting collision on January 6 derailed thirteen rail cars and damaged one of three tank cars carrying ninety tons of pressurized chlorine gas—liquid chlorine spewed high into the air. At that point, the liquid changed into a yellowish-green gas, and because it is heavier than air, the gas began to sink.

Unfortunately, the area near the train wreck was a depression, "perfect for funneling a deadly, ground-hugging fog of chlorine gas." The area was also the center of the Avondale Mills Graniteville complex. The complex included seven textile mills, offices and warehouses—the center of old Graniteville. The gas killed the locomotive's engineer and "rolled" over the Stevens Steam Plant, killed a resident in his home, chased "graveyard shift" workers to the roof, killed a man on the loading dock, killed three employees at Woodhead plant and then followed the Horse Creek valley behind the plant. Gas also killed two workers at the Gregg Division plant as the plant's ventilation system sucked in the deadly chlorine. In addition, a truck driver died sleeping in his parked truck.

Nine died in the deadly nightmare, and the gas release forced 5,400 individuals who lived in a one-mile radius to evacuate. Residents and workers flooded hospitals in Aiken and Augusta, and emergency workers quickly established a decontamination site at USC Aiken. The January

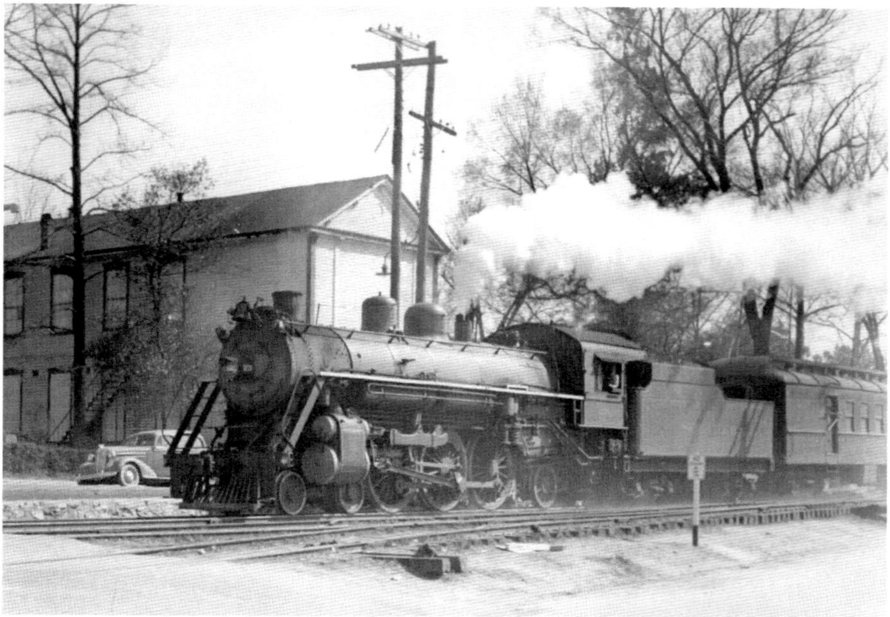

Steam locomotive, Graniteville, 1947, near Graniteville Manufacturing Company. *Courtesy Gregg-Graniteville Photographic Archives, Gregg-Graniteville Library, USC Aiken.*

wreck followed a November incident when five Avondale employees died in a car/train collision.[181]

With four of seven mills damaged and the mills' computers destroyed, Avondale closed the mills with the promise that they would reopen.[182]

In October 2005, Stephen Felker Jr., an Avondale Mills executive, announced layoffs in Graniteville. As Felker noted, the release of chlorine gas "heavily damaged some of our plants." Chlorine is not only toxic to breathe but also corrosive. Consequently, Avondale Mills, which operated seven plants in Graniteville, had "no choice but to take the equipment off-line." In order to resume operations at the affected facilities, staff would need to restore or replace damaged equipment. Escaping chlorine damaged at least two Avondale Mills, but the layoffs would affect the entire Graniteville workforce. Although the company only projected 350 layoffs, affected employees, depending on tenure, might have been able to "bid on jobs" at other mills in the area. In 2005, Avondale Mills, based in Georgia, controlled twenty plants in Alabama, the Carolinas and Georgia.[183]

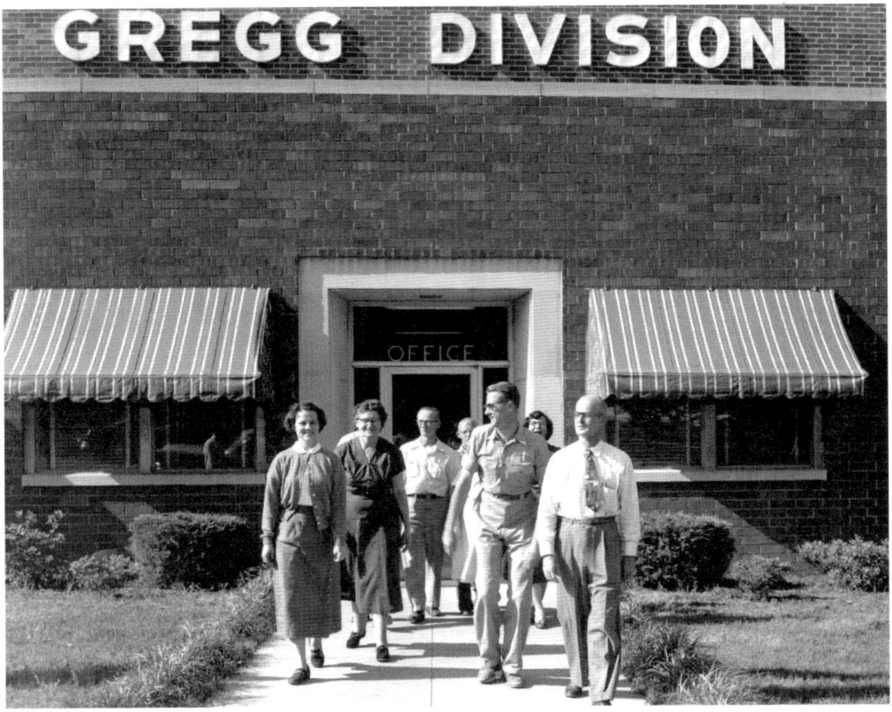

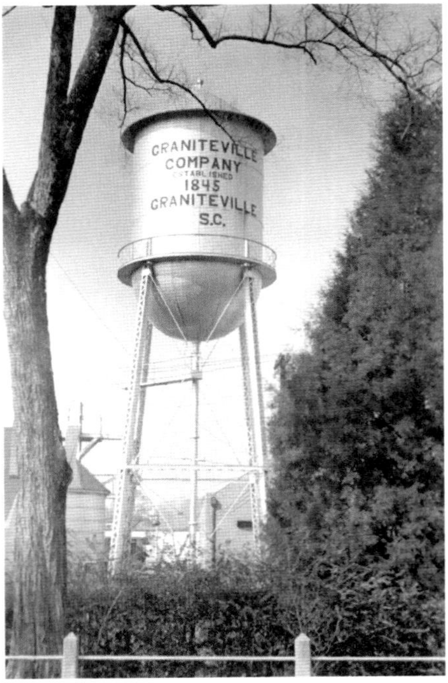

Above: Mill employees leaving Gregg Division, Graniteville Manufacturing Company, circa 1950. *Left*: Iconic Graniteville Water Tower. *Courtesy Gregg-Graniteville Photographic Archives, Gregg-Graniteville Library, USC Aiken.*

DENOUEMENT

The last chapter of this story is a sad one. The Graniteville mills did not reopen. As Stephen Felker Jr., president and CEO of Avondale Mills, summed up the situation, "Without the train derailment and chemical spill we were challenged [by overseas competition], with it we were destroyed." After 161 years, Avondale Mills, based in Monroe, Georgia, closed. The closings affected four thousand employers, some of whom were second-, third-, fourth- or even fifth-generation employees of the Avondale Mills in Georgia, South Carolina and Alabama. Felker also commented, "Events occurred that have taken our future from us. I regret that I could not prevent them."[184]

Breithaupt opened the pioneering Vaucluse in 1832, and Gregg built the textile game–changing Graniteville in 1849, but human error and a yellowish-green chlorine fog destroyed those 150-plus years of dreams in a few short hours.

Chapter 7

LOST BEGINNINGS

USC Aiken at Banksia

Dreams come in many shapes and sizes. One of them became the University of South Carolina Aiken. USC Aiken began in the historic Winter Colony mansion. Banksia, now the home of the Aiken County Historical Museum, features a unique serpentine wall. Noted southern architect Willis Irvin designed the mansion, which Richard Flint Howe had built circa 1931. The United States Department of the Interior approved listing the building, located on the corner of South Boundary and Newberry Street, in the National Register of Historic Places. Willis Irvin, a native of Washington, Georgia, was a prominent southern architect in the early twentieth century. His active career stretched from the 1910s to the 1940s. He designed public, commercial and residential buildings. He is particularly famous for his "Old South" residential designs for well-to-do clients in the Lowcountry of South Carolina and Georgia.[185]

Irvin's client for Banksia was a noted businessman, Richard Flint Howe. Howe, born in Green Bay Wisconsin, graduated from Harvard University, entered the banking business and married Abbey Deering. Mrs. Howe's grandfather was William Deering, who began building harvesters in the 1870s and in 1900 manufactured the first self-propelled harvester. In 1902, Deering merged Deering Manufacturing Company with Cyrus McCormick's McCormick Harvester Company. The merger produced a new company, International Harvester. Richard Flint Howe became secretary/treasurer and director of the new company. In 1911, he retired and moved his family to New York. There he built Linden House near Jericho on Long Island and

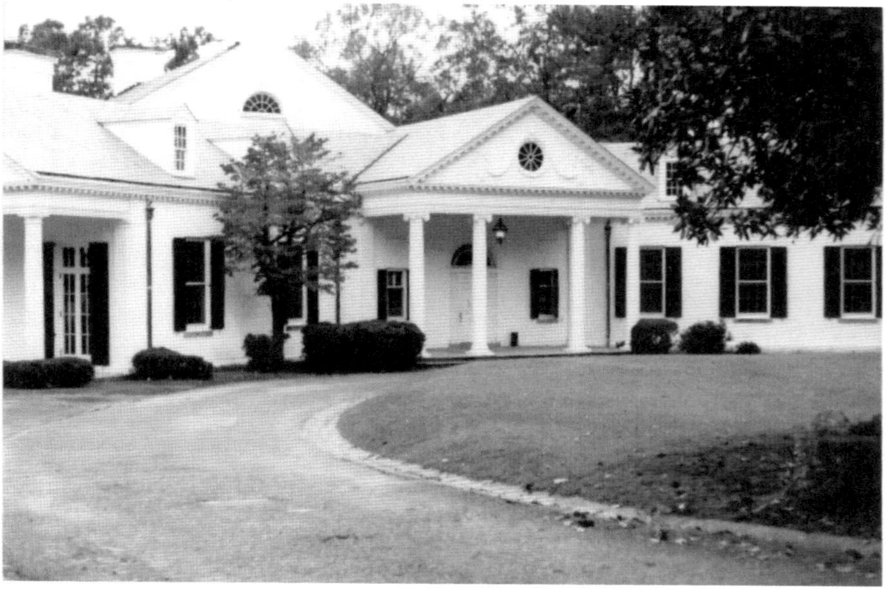

"Banksia," home of USC Aiken branch. *Courtesy Photographic Archives, USCA Institutional Archives, USC Aiken.*

later constructed a winter home in Aiken, South Carolina. He called his Aiken home Banksia after the *Rosa banksia*, or "Lady Banksia," a member of the climbing rose family that is native to China.[186]

In 1917, President Woodrow Wilson named Howe to the aircraft board. Howe was also interested in equestrian pursuits. He and his son, William Deering Howe, for many years owned the largest stable at Belmont Park, home of the third race of Thoroughbred Racing's Triple Crown. On January 26, 1943, during a visit to Aiken, the seventy-nine-year-old Richard Flint Howe fell and died in Aiken County Hospital. His death notice attributed his death to injuries resulting from a fall from a horse, but his death certificate states that he fell at home. Perhaps he accidentally fell from a horse he was riding on his estate.

His family held Howe's funeral at Episcopal Church of the Transfiguration. Among the honorary pallbearers was at least one with a South Carolina connection, Bernard Baruch. Baruch, a native of Camden, was a highly successful New York financier and noted presidential advisor who acquired Hobcaw Barony in Georgetown County.[187]

Ironically, both of Howe's final homes have an educational connection. His New York estate now houses the Long Island Lutheran Middle and High

School, and his Aiken estate not only was the home of Southern Methodist College but also was the first home of USC Aiken. Today, the historic mansion houses the Aiken County Historical Museum. After Howe's death, the ownership of the Aiken property passed to his heirs, and at one point, Banksia was a boardinghouse for Savannah River Plant construction workers. According to Mary White of the Aiken County Historical Museum, during Howe's tenure the Howes entertained many distinguished guests at Banksia, such as the Duke and Duchess of Windsor.[188]

Today, the University of South Carolina Aiken is a highly regarded, four-year, coeducational liberal arts school with a beautiful campus and modern facilities. In 2016, there were 3,548 students enrolled. In 2018, for the thirteenth time, *U.S. News & World Report* ranked USC Aiken as no. 1 among Regional Colleges in the South.

The germ of the idea that would flower into this institution of higher learning began in 1960. In May, Governor Ernest F. Hollings, committed to educating South Carolinians, appointed a study committee to "consider the problems of college level education for the increasing number of college age students." Between 1945 and 1958, the number of students in South Carolina high schools more than doubled, jumping from 53,783 to 118,251. The six-member gubernatorial study group included Representative Edward C. Cushman Jr. of Aiken. Cushman favored increasing the number of state institutions, so that more South Carolina students could have access to a college education.

After six terms of service in the South Carolina House of Representatives, Aiken voters elected Edward Cushman to the South Carolina Senate. There, as chair of the Aiken County legislative delegation, he continued his pursuit of a two-year state college for Aiken. In the meantime, the University of South Carolina moved ahead with its plan to add "extension centers" by creating branch campuses in Beaufort, Florence, Horry and Lancaster Counties. Under newly elected Senator Cushman's leadership, the Aiken legislative delegation proposed a "need program" that included the creation of a two-year state college in Aiken. Aiken City Council, the Aiken Branch of the American Association of University Women, the Aiken High School Parent Teachers Association, the Aiken County Board of Education and many other residents backed the proposal.

Nevertheless, support for the new venture was not universal. Recruited by the Aiken Chamber of Commerce in 1958, Southern Methodist College, a private two-year college, relocated from Greenville to Aiken. Ads and op-ed pieces in the *Aiken Standard* supported the status quo: "Aiken has a college."

In 1956, the Southern Methodist Church had founded Southern Methodist College in Greenville. Prior to moving to Aiken, the private college purchased the Banksia property for $64,000 and renovated it for educational purposes. In 1961, Southern Methodist College had about sixty students enrolled.

Despite these objections, the Aiken County Legislative Delegation introduced bills in the House and Senate to establish a University of South Carolina Extension in Aiken. According to press coverage, the annual tuition at the University of South Carolina–Columbia was $980 per year. Advocates for the Aiken branch estimated that a year of study in Aiken would cost $328, a significant annual savings for local students and a major argument for the new campus.

As proposed, the new school would offer standard liberal arts courses such as English, mathematics (algebra, trigonometry and calculus), foreign languages, government, history, science (chemistry and biology), psychology, composition and grammar. Students at the new center would have the same standing as university students at the main campus and would be able to transfer their credits.

Senator Cushman, the senior member of the four-man delegation, led the push for the USC center at Aiken. Representative John May, the only returning representative, had served as an instructor in history and political science at Southern Methodist College. He supported the project "100 per cent." Simultaneously, Cushman presented the bill in the South Carolina Senate, and Representatives Charles Simons, John A. May and B.W. Baker, Aiken's House members, presented the bill in the South Carolina House of Representatives.

Cushman also introduced legislation establishing an Aiken County Commission for Higher Education. The commission would be responsible for furnishing facilities for the students at the new center and would be empowered to make contracts and raise the funds needed to make the dream a reality. According to the proposal, the governor would appoint members of the board with the consent of a majority of the Aiken County legislative delegation.

In February 1961, the South Carolina General Assembly approved legislation creating the USC Branch Campus at Aiken, administered by the Aiken County Commission for Higher Education, Aiken County. According to the legislation, the commission was responsible for providing needed physical facilities and salaries for a full-time director and a secretary. For its contribution, USC would appoint the director. The dream was becoming a reality.

On March 28, 1961, Governor Ernest Hollings named individuals to serve on the Aiken County Commission for Higher Education. At the first meeting of the commission, the members elected Francis A. Townsend, chair; Julian D. Ellet, vice-chair; John Kennedy, treasurer; and Charles Kneece, secretary. Other commission members were Elden Jones, George Parks, Eugene Sawyer and Raymond Warner. The commission's first and most pressing need was to locate an appropriate location for the new institution.

On May 24, 1961, F.A. Townsend, vice-president and later president of Graniteville Company and chair of the Aiken County Commission on Higher Education, signed a contract with the University of South Carolina to establish a branch campus in Aiken. Present at the signing were Dr. Nicholas P. Mitchell, head of USC Extension; Senator Edward Cushman; Dr. R.L. Sumwalt, president of USC; and county representatives, B.W. Baker, Charles Simons and John May.

As momentum grew for the new USC campus, Dr. Wallace R. Terry, president of Southern Methodist, announced that the college's administrators were monitoring the situation and considering the possibility of relocating the

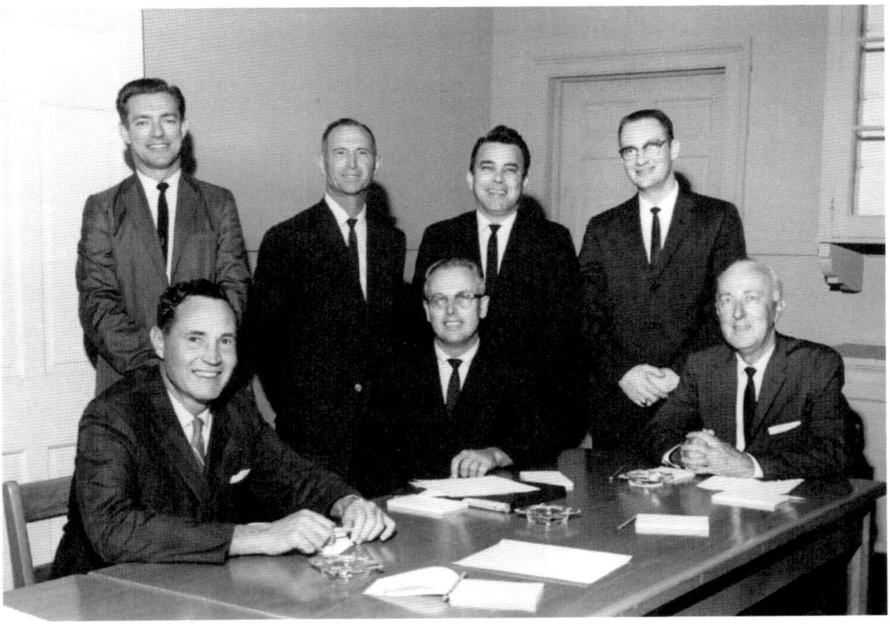

Christopher Sharp, first director, USC Aiken, with the Aiken County Commission for Higher Education. Sharp stands at rear far left, and Francis A. Townsend, commission chair, is seated far right. *Courtesy Photographic Archives, USCA Institutional Archives, USC Aiken.*

campus. Eventually, when plans for a USC branch in Aiken became final, Southern Methodist decided to move to Orangeburg, where a supporter had donated a suitable tract of land. Consequently, Southern Methodist leaders offered the Banksia property for sale. Perhaps somewhat ironically, the Aiken County Commission for Higher Education seized the opportunity and purchased the mansion, including the college's biology laboratory equipment, furnishings, lighting and new furnace, for $66,000. As Commission Chair Townsend noted, members of the commission had considered several sites, but the Southern Methodist property was in better repair than other options and "would cost less money to renovate and maintain."

After the sale, Dr. Terry graciously commented, "We [staff and faculty of Southern Methodist College] are particularly happy that the property is… to be used for educational purposes," and "we sincerely wish the University Extension in Aiken every possible success." Southern Methodist's move to Orangeburg brought stability to the college.

BEGINNINGS

From the records of the Aiken County Commission on Higher Education and the records of the chancellor (resident director), when classes began in the fall of 1961, the commission and the Aiken County Delegation were responsible for providing facilities and for reimbursing USC for certain expenses. Included in those expenses were between $7,200 and $7,600 for the salary of the resident director and between $3,000 and $3,600 for the salary of the secretary to the resident director. Both positions were twelve-month positions. The records indicate that Christopher Samuel Sharp was the resident director in the fall of 1961 and Jessie C. Lybrand the secretary. The commission also employed several custodians. At least by 1963, the center also employed Ernestine Law to handle "Publicity & Student Activities." According to the budget for 1964–65, members of the custodial staff were Dewey Drayton and Pearl Chavous.

The school initially opened with three full-time faculty (one of whom was the director) and a secretary. Director Christopher Samuel Sharp, a native of North Augusta and graduate of Wofford College, held a master's degree in biology from the University of North Carolina. Therefore, he served as chief administrator and taught science.

Many attended an open house at Banksia on September 10, 1961. Mrs. Paul Dahleen was the interior designer for the renovated mansion. Visitors

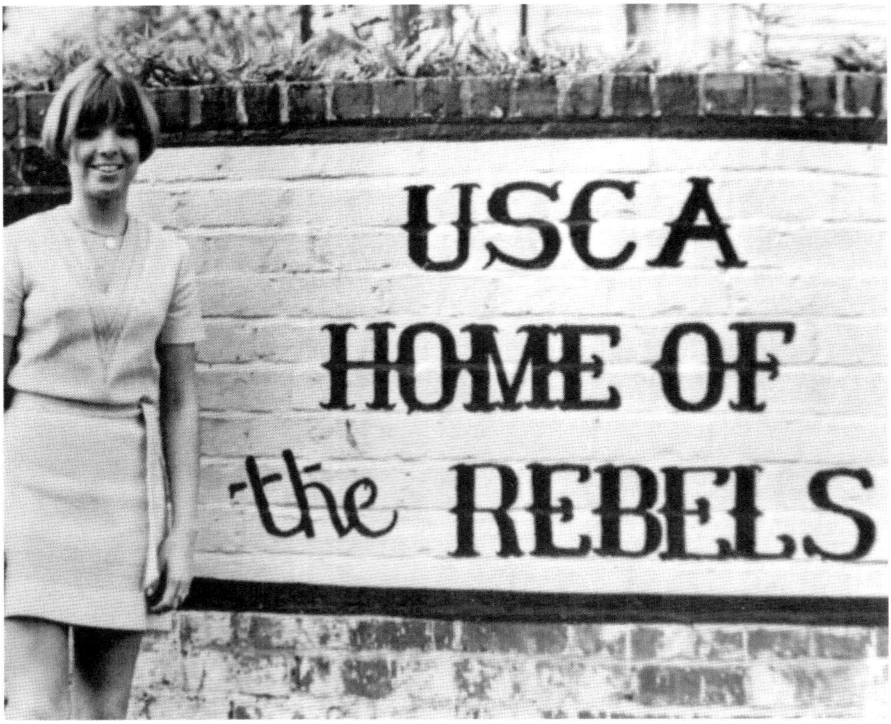

"USCA Home of the Rebels." *Courtesy Photographic Archives, USCA Institutional Archives, USC Aiken.*

especially noted the "lovely" floral arrangements and commented favorably on the well-equipped library and the student center with vending machines.

On September 13, 1961, the first students to enroll in the newly established University of South Carolina Aiken Branch gathered for registration. They completed paperwork, bought textbooks and, on Friday, attended their first orientation. Director Sharp discussed student government, athletics, student life and the new student newspaper. Professor Roy Wilson addressed academics and the grading system and presented a history of the university. Sharp then introduced Nancy Hester, first editor of the USC Aiken Branch newspaper. She introduced the paper staff and presented the students with their first paper. According to Gary Barton, sports editor, bowling would be the school's first team sport. Classes officially began on September 18, 1961.[189]

By the time the paper staff had published the third issue in October, the paper had a name, *Rebelaire*. Mary Coffey won the "Name the Paper" contest. The newspaper staff liked her suggestion, as they thought the title "appropriate." On October 4, the student body elected its first slate of officers. The newly elected student body officers were John Knox, president; George Alexander, vice-president; Jane Sanderson, secretary; and Bill Brockington, treasurer. In addition, the students selected class officers. Members of the freshman class chose Paul Hyer, president; Ronnie Aull, vice-president; Charwin Harmstad, secretary; and Bill Langley, treasurer. Sophomore class officers were Joe Hamilton, president; Charles Copley, vice-president, Linda Sampson, secretary; and Peter McKenna, treasurer. Even with such obvious progress, Editor Hester ran two editorials—one about students "defacing" and "abusing" their newly renovated space and the other about the poor voter turnout for student elections—just 40 percent had voted.[190]

DEDICATION

On October 22, 1961, the Aiken County Commission for Higher Education dedicated the building for the new University of South Carolina Aiken Branch. Speakers for the dedication on the beautiful grounds of Banksia were Francis A. Townsend, chair of the Aiken County Commission for Higher Education; Dr. Robert L. Sumwalt, president of USC, 1959–62; and Dr. Nicholas P. Mitchell, director of the USC Extension system. Senator Edward Cushman, a member of the Aiken County delegation, presided and introduced the speakers. His "untiring work" had come to fruition.

Ceremonies began with the national anthem, played by the Aiken High School Band under the direction of William T. Slaughter. Reverend Clyde Rhinehart gave the invocation.

USC president Sumwalt spoke first. According to Sumwalt, the early success of the Aiken branch greatly exceeded expectations. For example, the initial enrollment far surpassed enrollments at the other branches. Sumwalt also recognized those who had made the USCA Branch possible. Commenting on the need for higher education to "meet the needs of social and scientific progress in the world today," Sumwalt stressed the need for "quality education." To him, quality education was the result of "quality teachers, quality physical facilities, quality students of ability and preparation." In conclusion, the USC president reminded the students that they "are regular students at USC" and invited them to continue their

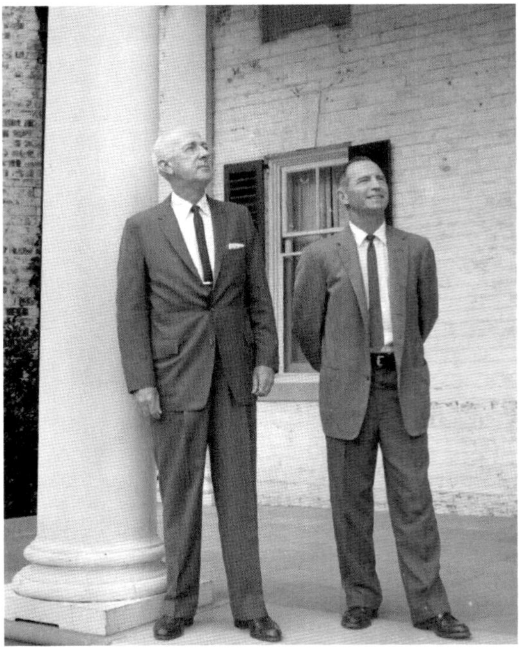

Francis A. Townsend, chair, Aiken County Commission for Higher Education, and Charles Kneece, superintendent of schools, Aiken County outside Banksia. *Courtesy Gregg-Graniteville Photographic Archives, Gregg-Graniteville Library, USC Aiken.*

education at USC in Columbia and use their talents after graduation to improve the state of South Carolina.

Francis A. Townsend Sr., chair of the Aiken County Commission for Higher Education, acknowledged the great contribution of Senator Cushman and thanked Gilbert H. VanderVoort, the supervisor of Banksia renovations, and Christopher Sharp, the first director of the Aiken branch, for their contributions. Townsend stated, "Now we have the building renovated…with a student body of 196 [136 regular students]…the largest enrollment of any Branch of the University in South Carolina in its first year, even though some of the others have been in operation for four years." Townsend confidently predicted continued success for the branch and anticipated an enrollment of 250 for the academic year 1962–63.

Dr. Nicholas Mitchell, director of USC Extensions, stressed that USC Aiken was not a junior college but rather a branch of the University of South Carolina. He continued, noting that the branch campuses offer "top grade" programs to "meet the need of financial economy" and provide the basic courses needed for students' "first two years of college." Mitchell also invited Aiken civic groups to use the school's facilities.

All the speakers praised the leadership and assistance of Director Sharp. Cushman also thanked the American Association of University Women

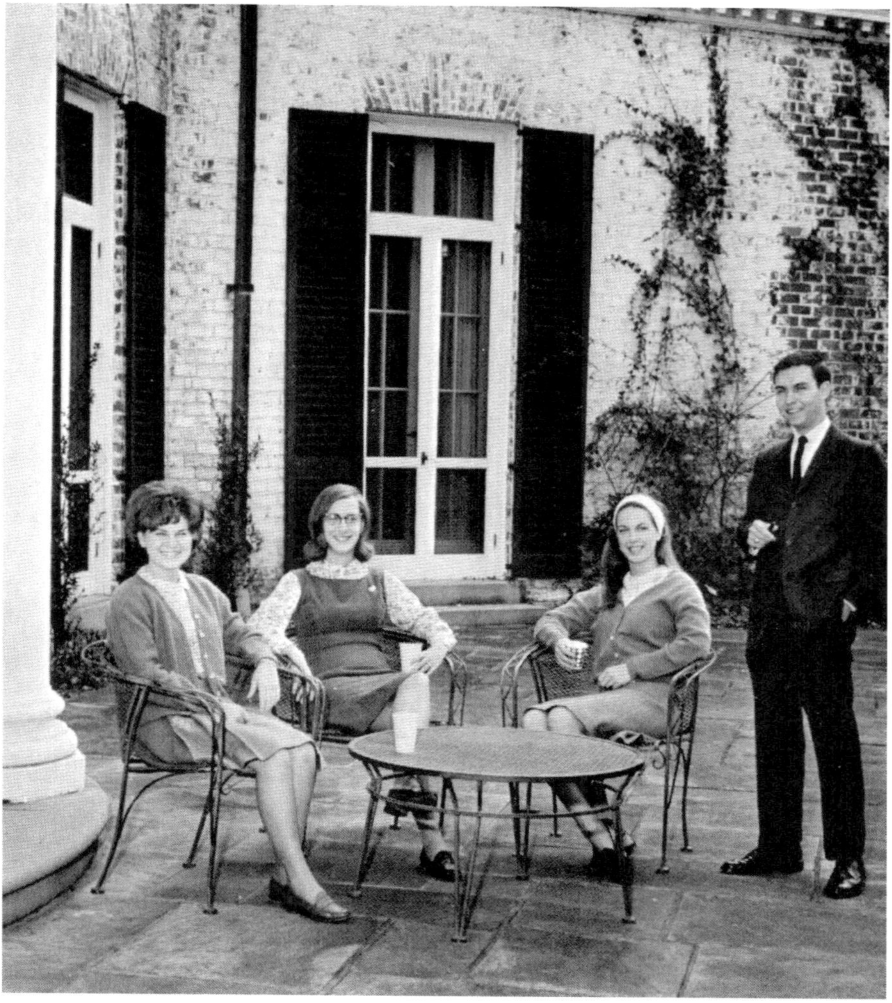

Students relaxing outside Banksia. *Courtesy Photographic Archives, USCA Institutional Archives, USC Aiken.*

(AAUW) for its assistance with the dedication ceremony. Also attending the dedication was G.L. Toole, acknowledged as the "oldest living" USC alumnus; the Aiken County legislative delegation; Mayor H. Odell Weeks; the Aiken City Council; and the members of the Advisory Committee.[191] Many wanted to be part of the history-making event.

The Aiken branch grew and continued to exceed expectations. After ably working to establish the new college, Sharp resigned effective June 15, 1963, to enter Candler School of Theology, Emory University, Atlanta, and become a Methodist minister. Later in life, he earned a doctorate in education from the University of South Carolina and served as dean at Lander College, director of graduate studies at Valdosta State University and head of the Education Department at North Georgia University. Thus, former director Sharp had a long and productive career in higher education.[192]

William Christopher Casper succeeded Sharp as director and later became the first chancellor of USC Aiken. Casper, a graduate of the University of North Carolina, was director of USC Coastal Junior College, 1960–63. During his tenure at USC Coastal, Casper was instrumental in directing the school's transition from a two-year to a four-year institution. In 1962, he also oversaw groundbreaking for the school's first building on its new campus. In 1963, he moved to Aiken and similarly managed the school's transition from a two-year to a four-year college and the branch's move from Banksia to a new campus. His work accomplished, Casper retired as chancellor in 1982.[193]

Paul J. Hyer Jr. was there when the new Aiken branch opened its doors in 1961. He also served as the first freshman class president of those inaugural students. In an interview published in the 1968 *USCA Magazine*, Hyer had many fond memories of his year and a half at Aiken and the quality of his education there. As he stated, "I wanted to stay in the state, so at the time USCA was my best choice." He also commented that USCA "has provided a lot of opportunities for local students who would otherwise not be able to attend college."[194]

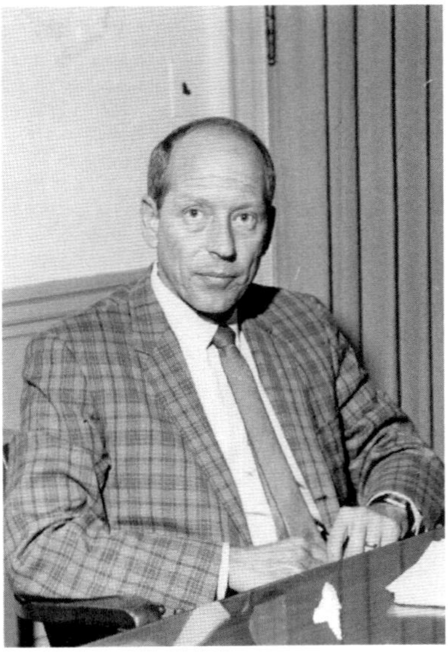

William C. Casper, second director and first chancellor, USC Aiken. *Courtesy Photographic Archives, USCA Institutional Archives, USC Aiken.*

Students celebrated in March 1963 when the USC Aiken basketball team claimed its second consecutive N.P. Mitchell Championship trophy. In addition, the Carolina League named three USCA basketball players—Glen DeHart, Finley Garvin and Steve Carter—to the All-Tournament Team. DeHart and Carter played guard, and Garvin was a forward. In 1963, the five USC branch campuses formed the Carolina League.[195]

In 1968, after an intensive institutional self-study, the Southern Association of Colleges and Schools (SACS) accredited the Aiken institution. Consequently, Aiken awarded its first associate degrees in June 1968. Accreditation was a major milestone and affirmation for the quality of the new institution's academics and faculty.

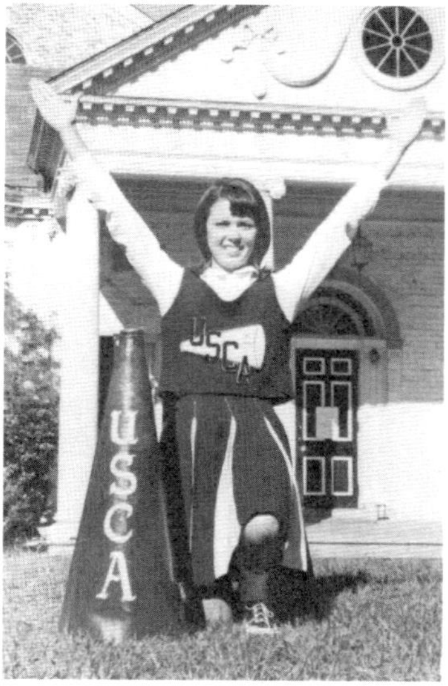

Happy cheerleader. USC Aiken won back-to-back basketball championships in 1962 and 1963. *Courtesy Photographic Archives, USCA Institutional Archives, USC Aiken.*

For some, attending USC Aiken at Banksia was "culture shock." Carol McKay remembered her first sight of the renovated mansion. "We had moved to Aiken from California where I expected to attend the University of California–San Diego." Instead, she found herself in Aiken and attending a much different institution. Nevertheless, McKay had two good years at the branch campus before completing her degree at the University of South Carolina–Columbia. As an added bonus, on her first day on the Aiken campus, she met her future husband. Aiken became more appealing.[196]

Nevertheless, the years at Banksia had their challenges. Space was a critical one. As the student population grew, there was increased demand for more laboratories and a gym, as well as increased space for the student union and library. Students also wanted more course offerings and access to a four-year degree.

In addition, there were security concerns. During 1970, the *Aiken Standard* carried two accounts of thefts at the USC Aiken regional campus. On a Friday afternoon in July, a person or persons broke into the biology lab. Staff discovered that a key ring, a vacuum cleaner, a blanket, a pillow and a wall clock were missing. One might surmise that someone needed bedding and valued a clean living environment!

Later, on September 11, 1970, an alarm summoned the Aiken police to investigate another theft on the campus. While on night patrol to check one of the college's doors responding officers found "no sign of forced entry," but the thief or thieves had absconded with three television sets, a couch and an electric fan. One can only wonder if there was a connection between the thefts. Perhaps the first thief/thieves not only found the

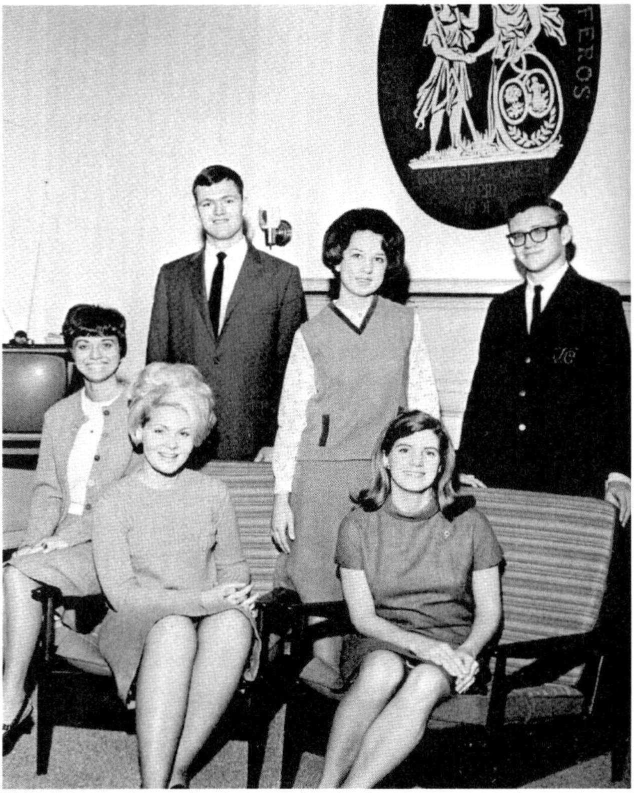

Left: Students inside "Banksia." *Below*: Storm damage at "Banksia." *Courtesy Photographic Archives, USCA Institutional Archives, USC Aiken.*

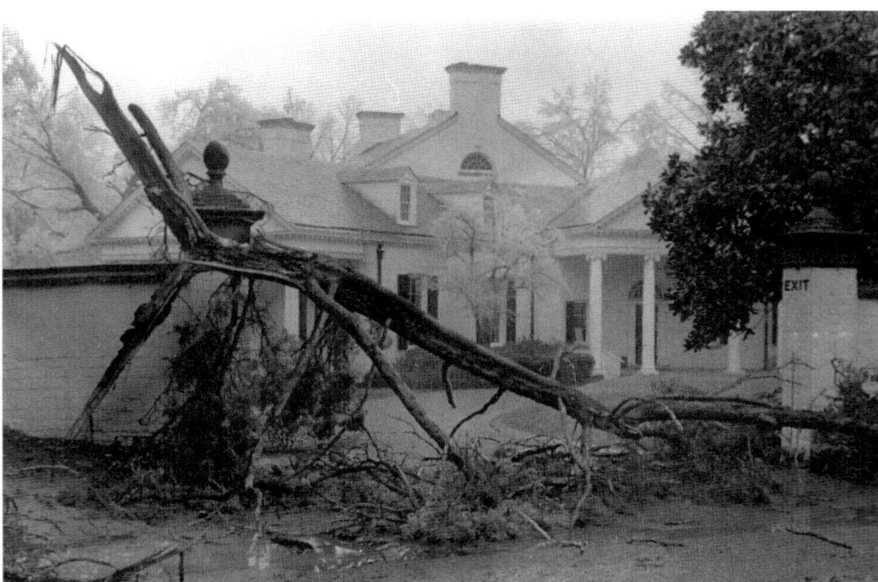

summer too hot but also wanted facilities and equipment for entertaining. Of course, the truly disheartening part was that no sign of forced entry clearly pointed to an "inside job."[197]

Later that September, students received good news. USC Aiken had acquired a new student activities bus. According to Coach Lew Perkins, school officials determined that it was too expensive to rent a bus to transport the basketball team to games. Consequently, the school bought a bus not only for athletic events but also for community projects. To launch the new amenity's first official use of the bus, fifty students and faculty members boarded and visited the Fort Gordon hospital to deliver presents to the patients.[198]

The year 1970 was also noteworthy for another reason. Interstate Highway 20 opened, and the Aiken campus became a feasible educational possibility for hundreds of Midland students. Viewed historically, the interstate joins the river and the railroad as agents of accessibility. Accessibility is essential for economic and population growth.

ANOTHER NEW BEGINNING

In 1968, the South Carolina General Assembly, at the request of the Aiken legislative delegation, approved a bond issue to purchase land for a new USCA campus. In 1970, the Aiken County Commission for Higher Education purchased land for the new campus from the Graniteville Company.

On July 1, 1970, Robert E. Penland, chair of the Aiken County Commission for Higher Education, revealed preliminary plans for phase one of the new campus for the USC Aiken Branch. Phase I as presented would be a $1,550,000 "all-purpose building" of fifty-one thousand square feet. The modern glass and brick two-story building would adequately meet the needs of six hundred full-time students. The new building would feature an unusual "square doughnut shape" with an open courtyard as the hole in the doughnut. Around that courtyard would be offices, classrooms, a library, a student center and laboratories. The multipurpose building, athletic field and three-hundred-car parking lot would occupy about ten of the one hundred acres recently acquired for the new campus.

Once the commission approved the preliminary drawings, architectural firm Lyles, Bissett, Carlisle and Wolf would proceed to develop "working drawings" and a "master plan." In addition, the Department of Health,

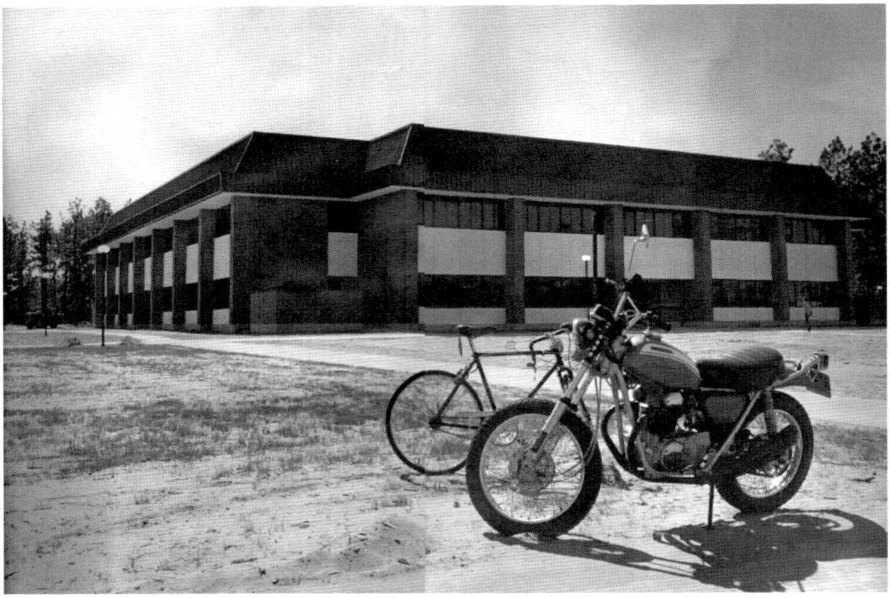

First building on USCA campus, now Penland Administration Building, with bikes. Note the unpaved parking area. *Courtesy Photographic Archives, USCA Institutional Archives, USC Aiken.*

Education and Welfare had approved a grant of $256,274 to assist with financing the new building. With financing coming together, Penland expected construction to begin in December 1970.

As planned, the 23,100-square-foot first floor would contain faculty and administrative offices; 4,000 square feet of student union space for recreation and other purposes; a large two-hundred-person lecture room that could function as an auditorium; and a music and art center. The 27,900-square-foot second floor would house a 5,000-square-foot library; ten similarly sized classrooms; adequate laboratories for science, chemistry, physics and biology, as well as foreign languages; and space for necessary office equipment. The building would also have an elevator and "portable" inner walls. The architects designed the latter feature so that the school could reconfigure the space as needed. According to Penland, Phase II would probably focus on a library and Phase III would include a student union.[199]

For the academic year 1971–72, USC Aiken fielded basketball, tennis and golf teams. Lew Perkins coached the basketball team, and Randy Clark coached the golf team. Gene Heath of Aiken was president of the student body.[200]

The year 1972 was one of transition. USC Aiken left its beginnings in Banksia and moved to its present campus: a 144-acre site on the outskirts of Aiken, with room to grow and develop. That same year, the Gregg-Graniteville Foundation and the Swint Foundation donated $400,000 to establish a library on the new campus. At that time, the gift to fund the Gregg-Graniteville Library was the largest ever given to a library in South Carolina.

Yet for Aiken students during those formative years, Banksia was home. The "old house," as one alumna commented later, was the college. Interviewed in 1986, Bunny Smith Richardson admitted that she had not visited the new campus. "Part of that is the nostalgia thing, because I want to remember it the way it was."[201]

The Graniteville Company, a leitmotif in this story of loss and change, was critical in that move. The new campus sits on Graniteville company land. Gregg-Graniteville and the Swint Foundations helped finance construction of the university library, and officials donated the company's archives to the new library. Consequently, the campus of USC Aiken today is part of the legacy of William Gregg and his antebellum dream. History is about connections, and connections transcend lifetimes and loss.

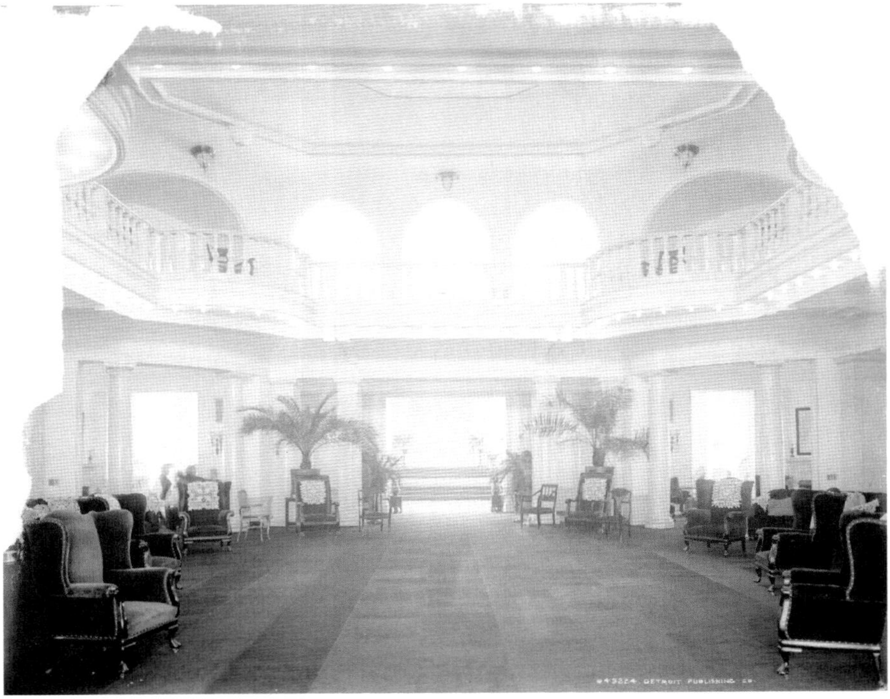

Lobby, Hampton Terrace Hotel, circa 1905. Detroit Publishing Company. LC-D4-43224 [P&P]. *Courtesy Library of Congress Prints and Photographs Division, Washington, D.C.*

EPILOGUE

Aiken is a place of endless attraction and deep memories. Despite the county's small size, as these stories show, giants walked the land. Few places in South Carolina can boast of the longest railroad track in the world or the first steam locomotive. Few can approach the grandeur of Aiken County's grand hotels or demonstrate the resilient streetscape of downtown Aiken. Few attracted the larger-than-life men, such as George Galphin, Henry Schultz, William Gregg, James U. Jackson and Edward C. Cushman, who despite great challenges dreamed big dreams and, with those dreams, altered the landscape and the history of Aiken and South Carolina.

Read the stories and ponder the exigencies of fate, the variegated strands that form the fabric of Aiken today.

NOTES

Preface

1. Frontispiece in Toole, *Ninety Years in Aiken County.*

Chapter 1

2. Morris, "Westos," *South Carolina Encyclopedia*, 1,017–18; Gillam, Cobb, DePratter and Herron, "Exploring the Native American Colonial Landscape," 24; Morris, "Henry Woodward," *South Carolina Encyclopedia*, 1,045.
3. Gillam, Cobb, DePratter and Herron, "Exploring the Native American Colonial Landscape," 24.
4. Morris, "Yamasse War," *South Carolina Encyclopedia*, 1,055; Helsley, *Beaufort, South Carolina.*
5. Groover and Leader, "Exploring Fort Moore," 17.
6. Cashin, "Fanni Mingo."
7. Meriwether, *Expansion of South Carolina*, 70–71.
8. Caldwell, "Southern Frontier during King George's War," 43–44.
9. Vandervelde, *Aiken County*, 27.
10. Calmes, "Lyttleton Expedition of 1759," 12.
11. U.S. Department of the Interior, National Register of Historic Places, Abbeville County, Long Cane Massacre Nomination, South Carolina Department of Archives and History.

12. Hamer, "Fort Moore," *South Carolina Encyclopedia*, 335.
13. Records of the Secretary of State, Miscellaneous Records, 2G, 29–30, South Carolina Department of Archives and History.
14. Meriwether, *Expansion of South Carolina*, 71.
15. Records of the South Carolina General Assembly, Petitions, 1824, no. 107, South Carolina Department of Archives and History.
16. Cashin, *Guardians of the Valley*, 139–40.
17. Elliott and Barnwell, "Bernard Elliott's Recruiting Journal," 98.
18. Van Ruymbeke, "Purrysburg," 764.
19. Alexia Jones Helsley, "New Windsor," unpublished manuscript; Voigt, "Swiss Notes on South Carolina," 93–94.
20. Meriwether, *Expansion of South Carolina*, 690–70; Cashin and McGillivray, *Indian Trader*, 48–49.
21. Meriwether, *Expansion of South Carolina*, 66–67.
22. Robbins and Tobler, "John Tobler's Description of South Carolina," 141, 149–51.
23. Calmes, "Lyttleton Expedition of 1759," 16.
24. Salley, "Calhoun Family of South Carolina," 6.

Chapter 2

25. Records of the Secretary of State, Surveyor General, Colonial Plats, vol. 2, 27.
26. Morris, "Indian Trade," *South Carolina Encyclopedia*, 476–77.
27. *Georgia Historical Quarterly* 4, "Oglethorpe's Treaty with the Lower Creek Indians," 9; Helsley, *Unsung Heroines*, 19.
28. Groover, "George Galphin," *South Carolina Encyclopedia*, 356; Meriwether, *Expansion of South Carolina*, 70.
29. Meriwether, *Expansion of South Carolina*, 194.
30. Swan, "Present Defenceless State of the Country," 303; *South Carolina Historical Magazine* 2, "Papers of the First Council of Safety," 99–100.
31. Swan, "Present Defenceless State of the Country," 303–4.
32. Ibid., 306–7.
33. Ibid., 312–13.
34. *South Carolina Historical Magazine* 2, "Papers of the First Council of Safety," 88–89.
35. Elliott and Barnwell, "Bernard Elliott's Recruiting Journal," 98–99. According to Galphin's will, dated April 6, 1776, Galphin fathered

numerous multiracial children, including three mulatto daughters and two daughters and a son of Native American descent. Young, *Abstracts of Old Ninety-Six and Abbeville*, 128–29.

36. Gervais and Starr, "Letters from John Lewis Gervais to Henry Laurens," 21–22; Olson, "Loyalists and the American Revolution," 55; Vandervelde, *Aiken County*, 21; Cashin, "Thomas Brown."
37. Gervais and Starr, "Letters from John Lewis Gervais to Henry Laurens," 22.
38. Morris, *George Galphin*, 118.
39. Rindfleisch, "George Galphin and the War in the South."
40. Robert W. Gibbes, printer, "Stuart, John, Letter to David Taitt, concerning Relations with the Cherokees and Gunpowder," Documentary History, 1764–76, 158–59, South Carolina Department of Archives and History.
41. Morris, *George Galphin*, 146.
42. Ibid., 128.
43. Ibid., 148.
44. Cashin, *Guardians of the Valley*, 139.
45. Young, *Abstracts of Old Ninety-Six and Abbeville*, 128–29.
46. South Carolina Deed Abstracts, 1783–1788, abstracted by Brent Holcomb, *South Carolina Magazine of Ancestral Research*, Columbia, 1996, 434–35.
47. Helsley, "Roadside Guide to the Revolutionary War."
48. South Carolina Records of the General Assembly, Petitions, 1794, no. 155, South Carolina Department of Archives and History.

Chapter 3

49. Towles, "William Aiken, Sr.," *South Carolina Encyclopedia*, 12.
50. *Journal of the Aiken County Historical Society*, "American Railroad Journal," 3–4.
51. Thomas Jefferson from Felix Pascalis, August 18, 1803, Founders Online Home, http://founders.archives.gov/Jefferson/01-41-02-0172.
52. For marriage, please see Pennsylvania Compiled Marriage Records, 1700–1821, Christ Church, Philadelphia, ancestry.com.
53. See also Rey, *Priest and the Prophetess*, chapter 8.
54. Farmer, "Aiken," 10; Alexia Jones Helsley, "Andrew Alfred Dexter," unpublished manuscript.
55. Records of the South Carolina General Assembly, Petitions, ND, no. 3905, South Carolina Department of Archives and History.

56. Vandervelde, *Aiken County*, 242; Records of the General Assembly, Petitions, 1839, no. 80, South Carolina Department of Archives and History.
57. Anonymous Travel Diary, October 1837–August 1838, no. 3000, South Caroliniana Library, University Libraries, University of South Carolina.
58. Records of the South Carolina General Assembly, Petitions, 1838, no. 19, South Carolina Department of Archives and History.
59. Ibid., 1839, no. 86, and 1840, no. 126, South Carolina Department of Archives and History.
60. Ibid., 1841, no. 36, South Carolina Department of Archives and History.
61. Ibid., 1840, no. 126, South Carolina Department of Archives and History.
62. John Hamilton Cornish Papers, 1833–1966, Abstract, Wilson Library, University of North Carolina–Chapel Hill; "Aiken County, South Carolina Cemetery Inscriptions," ancestry.com.
63. Records of the South Carolina General Assembly, Petitions, 1854, no. 42, South Carolina Department of Archives and History.
64. Find-a-Grave Memorial, "Marion Washington Sams," https://www.findagrave.com/memorial/77898848/sams.
65. Charleston, South Carolina City Directory, 1859, lists Nicholas N. Darrell as a foreman for the South Carolina Railroad.
66. Charleston, South Carolina City Directory, 1809, lists Julius Petsch as a machinist.
67. Possibly the John F. Schmidt who owned six slaves in Barnwell District in 1830.
68. Brown, *History of the First Locomotive in America*, 159–65; *Locomotive Fireman's Magazine* 12 (October 1888): 732; *Railway Age* (August 24, 1888): 546.
69. *(Aiken, SC) Journal & Review*, November 30, 1887.
70. Peters, "Earthquakes," *South Carolina Encyclopedia*, 280–81.
71. Coker, *World War II Prisoners of War in Georgia*, 1–4, 13–15; *Aiken Standard*, June 7, 2017; HD News 12, "Remembering German POW Camp in Aiken," September 21, 2008, www.twin-citynews.com/community/German-family-visits-site-world-war-ii-pow-camp-aiken-county.
72. McDonald and Miles, *Aiken*, 124.
73. Press clipping, February 12, 1953, collection of Allen Riddick.
74. Press clipping, undated, collection of Allen Riddick; U.S. Department of Commerce, Population Schedules, 1940, Aiken County.
75. Allen Riddick, "The 1953 Gas Explosion," collection of Allen Riddick.
76. *Aiken Standard*, October 15, 1953.
77. Ira Henry Freeman, "Atomic Neighbors Foresee Rich Era," *New York Times*, December 10, 1950.

Chapter 4

78. Thomas H. Williamson, "Aiken County," in Toole, *Ninety Years in Aiken County*.
79. Anonymous Travel Diary, October 1837–August 1838, no. 3000, South Caroliniana Library, University Libraries, University of South Carolina.
80. U.S. Department of Commerce, Census Schedules, Population, 1850; Vandervelde, *Aiken County*, 375; Charlotte Hixon, "A Trip to Aiken," no. 12135, South Caroliniana Library, University Libraries, University of South Carolina.
81. Letter of Joshua Hathaway, March 15, 1855, South Caroliniana Library, University Libraries, University of South Carolina.
82. *New York Times*, "Days of Sunshine for Aiken Gayety," December 13, 1914, xxi.
83. Winter Colony Thematic Resources, Aiken County, South Carolina, National Register of Historic Places, South Carolina Department of Archives and History; *New York Times*, "Pines of 'Ole Car'line': Aiken on the Hilltop, and the Country Around," February 28, 1892, 20.
84. McDonald and Miles, *Aiken*, 37.
85. *The (Columbia, SC) State*, April 8, 1892.
86. B.P. Chatfield to R.L. Barstow, January 21, 1879; Highland Park Hotel ad, undated, collection of Allen Riddick.
87. *The (Columbia, SC) State*, December 17, 1897.
88. Ibid., November 30, 1897; June 26, 1897.
89. Spar, *New Haven's Civil War Hospital*, 221; *Aiken Standard*, "At 75 Feet, Hotel Project Would Harken Back to Aiken's History," June 13, 2015; *New York Times*, "Hotel Burned at Aiken, S.C.: All the Guests Escape with Their Baggage—Boston Man Shot," February 7, 1898, 1.
90. *Official Gazette of the United States Patent Office* 15, 269; Find-a-Grave, https://findagrave.com/memorial/19201656.
91. *The (Columbia, SC) State*, February 3, 1913; *New York Times*, "Days of Sunshine for Aiken Gayety."
92. *The (Columbia, SC) State*, May 9, 1914; *New York Times*, "Highland Park Hotel, Aiken, S.C.," January 11, 1928, 26; McDonald and Miles, *Aiken*, 38; for Sherrard's career, please see Gloucester, Massachusetts City Directories, 1907 and 1909.
93. Julian B. Salley Sr. of the Henderson & Salley law firm. He was also the husband of Eulalie Chaffee.
94. *New York Times*, "To Arrest Golfers Despite Court Rule," March 6, 1927, 23.

95. Ibid., "Activities at Aiken," January 15, 1939, 4.
96. Byrd, *Splendid Time*, 69–78. Unless otherwise noted, this is the basic source for Aiken material in this section.
97. Undated brochure, collection of Allen Riddick.
98. Marshall Field founded Marshall Field & Company, Chicago department stores.
99. John D. Rockefeller was an oil magnate and industrialist, as well as one of America's richest men.
100. Harvey Firestone was the founder of Firestone Tire & Rubber Company.
101. In 1909, the Augusta Chamber of Commerce entertained President-elect William Howard Taft with a banquet at the Hampton Terrace Hotel in North Augusta. *Augusta Chronicle*, January 9, 2009.
102. Former North Augusta mayor Robert B. Mealing, as a young man, worked as a stable hand for the hotel. *History of North Augusta*, 189; Vandervelde, *Aiken County*, 204.
103. Helsley, "North Augusta," *South Carolina Encyclopedia*, 674; *History of North Augusta*, 19–25, 185–87, 211–12.

Chapter 5

104. Ostseebad Dahme, "Die Wundersame Geschichte des Stadtebaurers Henry Schultz alias Klaus Hinrich Klahn," https://www.wirliebendahme.de/dahmer-profile/stadtebauer-klaus-hinrich-klahn.
105. Campbelltown was an earlier town near the site of Hamburg.
106. Records of the General Assembly, Petitions, 1813, no. 96, South Carolina Department of Archives and History.
107. Scott, *Random Recollections of a Long Life*, 25–28. For more information and comments on Scott's account and posts about Schultz's origins, see *Henry Shultz and His Town of Hamburg, SC*, "Economic War to the Death in the Antebellum South," https://henryshultz.wordpress.com/2015/shultzs-the-story-by-edwin-j-scott.
108. Act no. 2274, *South Carolina Statutes at Large*, vol. 6, 172.
109. Christian Breithaupt, a wealthy planter, was the founder of the Vaucluse Manufacturing Company.
110. "An Act to Establish an Inspection and Ware-house at Hamburg, in Edgefield District," Act no. 2255, *South Carolina Statutes at Large*, vol. 6, 159.
111. Records of the South Carolina General Assembly, Petitions, ND, no. 5708, South Carolina Department of Archives and History.

112. A.B. Williams, "Hamburg Beside the Savannah," *The (Columbia, SC) State*, November 20, 1927.
113. Peter Hughes, "The Sixth Hamburg Mechanic's Festival," *Carolina Herald and Newsletter* 38 (2010), posted on *Henry Shultz and His Town of Hamburg, SC.*
114. *South Carolina Statutes at Large*, vol. 6, 477.
115. Ibid., 326–27.
116. *Guide to Historical Markers*, 4–5.
117. Poole, "Best Friend of Charleston," *South Carolina Encyclopedia*, 69.
118. *South Carolina Statutes at Large*, vol. 8, 85–90.
119. South Carolina General Assembly, Petitions, 1849, no. 133, South Carolina Department of Archives and History.
120. United States Department of Commerce, Population Schedules, Edgefield County, Town of Hamburg, 1850.
121. J.L. Knight to James Evans, Fayetteville, North Carolina, April 27, 1851, no. 10539, South Caroliniana Library, University Libraries, University of South Carolina.
122. Edgefield District, Letters of Administration, Guardianship and Testamentary, 1839–1861, 102.
123. United States Department of Commerce, Population Schedules, Edgefield County, Town of Hamburg, 1860.
124. Downey, "Hamburg," *South Carolina Encyclopedia*, 415.
125. Prince Rivers to Robert K. Scott, 1871, S518004, Letters Received in Governors' Papers for Robert K. Scott, South Carolina Department of Archives and History.
126. Poole, "Prince Rivers," *South Carolina Encyclopedia*, 808; Copp, *South Carolina African Americans in the Civil War.*
127. United States Department of Commerce, Population Schedules, Aiken County, Hamburg, 1870.
128. Kantrowitz, "Benjamin Ryan Tillman," *South Carolina Encyclopedia*, 961–62.
129. William Stone to Daniel H. Chamberlain, July 12, 1876, S518004, Letters Received in Governors' Papers for Daniel H. Chamberlain, South Carolina Department of Archives and History.
130. Zucek, "Hamburg Massacre," *South Carolina Encyclopedia*, 415–16.
131. *History of North Augusta*, 211.
132. David Duncan Wallace, "Uncovering South Carolina's First Railroad," unpublished manuscript, Gregg-Graniteville Archives, Gregg-Graniteville Library, University of South Carolina Aiken.

133. *History of North Augusta*, 15.
134. Henderson, "Some Aiken County Names," 16; *Guide to Historical Markers*, 8.
135. Simkins and Woody, *South Carolina during Reconstruction*, 499–501.
136. Smith, "All Is Not Quiet in Our Hellish County," 142–55; Zucek, "Ellenton Riot," *South Carolina Encyclopedia*, 295.
137. *(Augusta, GA) Daily Constitution*, June 1, 1877.
138. Ibid., June 5, 1877.
139. *New York Times*, June 5, 1877.
140. Ibid., August 4, 1877; *(Augusta, GA) Daily Constitution*, July 13, 1977.
141. *New York Times*, April 7, 1878.
142. Browder and Brooks, *Memories of Home*, Series 2, 6.
143. *Atlanta Constitution*, July 13, 1884.
144. *New York Times*, June 30, 1885.
145. Alexander Campbell had visited Ellenton in 1839 and preached in the Union Baptist Church (1805). His preaching split the church, and his followers ousted the regular Baptists. Browder and Brooks, *Memories of Home*, Series 2, 81–83.
146. *New York Times*, August 17, 1883.
147. U.S. Department of Commerce, Population, Industry and Agriculture Schedules, Barnwell County, 1880.
148. *The (Columbia, SC) State*, March 27, 1910.
149. U.S. Department of Commerce, Population Schedules, Aiken County, 1930.
150. South Carolina Department of Agriculture, Commerce and Industries of the State of South Carolina, 1938–39, 256–57.
151. Savannah River Archaeological Research Program, "The Leigh Banana Case Company," 2010, http://www.srarp.org/leigh-banana-case-company.
152. Ibid.
153. Freeman, "Atomic Neighbors Foresee Rich Era."
154. Savannah River Archaeological Research Program, "Meyers Mill," 1913, http://www.srarp.org/myers-mill.
155. *An Atomic History 08*, Chapter 8, "Changing Identity," https://srs.gov/general/about/50anniv/Chapter%2008.pdf.
156. Ira Henry Freeman, "Atom Plant 'D.P.S.' Escape Unscathed," *New York Times*, October 4, 1951.
157. *An Atomic History 08*, Chapter 8, "Changing Identity."

Chapter 6

158. U.S. Department of the Interior, National Register of Historic Places, Vaucluse Mill Village Historic District, South Carolina Department of Archives and History; David Duncan Wallace, "A Hundred Years of William Gregg and Graniteville," unpublished manuscript, Gregg-Graniteville Archives, Gregg-Graniteville Library, University of South Carolina Aiken.
159. By Act no. 2631, the South Carolina legislature also incorporated the Saluda Manufacturing Company, another textile pioneer, in 1834. *South Carolina Statutes at Large*, vol. 8, 394.
160. "An Act to Incorporate Certain Societies," 1833, Act no. 2593, *South Carolina Statutes at Large*, vol. 8, 381–82.
161. Vaucluse Mill Historic District; Wallace, "Hundred Years," 9; George McDuffie to John Bauskett, February 25, 1837, in "The Advent of William Gregg and the Graniteville Co.," ed. Thomas P. Martin, reprinted from the *Journal of Southern History* 11 (1945): 402–3.
162. Wallace, "Hundred Years," 10.
163. Interview with Deborah Tritt Harmon, Gregg-Graniteville Archives, June 12, 2018.
164. Vaucluse Mill Village Historic District; Wallace, "Hundred Years," 11.
165. Gregg, *Essays on Domestic Industry*, 11.
166. Downey, "William Gregg," *South Carolina Encyclopedia*, 405; Ker Boyce to James H. Hammond, December 12, 1845, in "Advent of William Gregg," 403–4; *Pictorial Timeline of Graniteville.*
167. Mitchell, "William Gregg," *Dictionary of American Biography*, 600.
168. William Gregg to James H. Hammond, May 30, 1849, in "Advent of William Gregg," 415–16.
169. William Gregg to Amos A. Lawrence, September 2, 1850, in "Advent of William Gregg," 421–23.
170. William Gregg to James Richardson, April 12, 1858, Gregg-Graniteville Archives, Gregg-Graniteville Library, University of South Carolina Aiken.
171. Downey, "William Gregg."
172. U.S. Department of the Interior, National Register of Historic Sites, Aiken County, Graniteville Historic District, South Carolina Department of Archives and History.
173. *Pictorial Timeline of Graniteville.*
174. Downey, "Graniteville Company," *South Carolina Encyclopedia*, 391.
175. Vaucluse Mill Village Historic District.

176. South Carolina State Board of Agriculture, *South Carolina Resources*.
177. Downey, "Graniteville Company," 391; *Pictorial Timeline of Graniteville*.
178. 27East, "Community Leader Samuel H. Swint Jr. of Southampton Dies at 76," September 22, 2010, http://www.27east.com/news/article.cfm/Southampton/302201/Community-Leader-Samuel-H-Swint-Jr-of-Southampton-dies-at-76.
179. Vaucluse Mill Village Historic District.
180. *Pictorial Timeline of Graniteville*; Downey, "Graniteville Company."
181. Jim Nesbitt, "Slope of Land Spurred Spread of Chlorine," *Augusta Chronicle*, January 23, 2005; Jeffrey B. Wallace, "The Morning that Changed a Town," *Aiken Standard*, January 9, 2005.
182. *The (Columbia, SC) State*, January 30, 2005.
183. Ibid., October 29, 2005.
184. Textile World, "Avondale Mills Closes Doors, Sells Some Facilities," July 23, 2006, www.textileworld.com/textile-world/textile-news/2006/07.

Chapter 7

185. Daniel J. Vivian, "Willis Irvin," *South Carolina Encyclopedia*, 484–86.
186. *Betty Howe's Manhattan Town Car 1942 Cadillac Fleetwood Sixty-Special with Derham Town Car Conversion*, blog, https://bettys1942cadillacderhamcar.wordpress.com/2015/03/02/155000-fpr-into-contact-karelorbillgmail-comcom.
187. *New York Times*, "Richard F. Howe Rites," January 31, 1943, 46; "Richard F. Howe, Sportsman, Dead," January 28, 1943, 20.
188. Dana Rogers, "Banksia," *Aiken Standard*, February 29, 2016.
189. Unnamed USC Aiken Branch newspaper, vol. 1, no. 2 (October 5, 1961), USCA Institutional Archives, University of South Carolina Aiken.
190. *Rebelaire*, October 31, 1961, USCA Institutional Archives, University of South Carolina Aiken.
191. Edward C. Cushman to Robert Alexander, February 20, 1985, with enclosures, Records of the Chancellor: Robert E. Alexander, USC Aiken Institutional Archives; Alexia Jones Helsley, "USC Aiken—in the Beginning," unpublished manuscript; *Rebelaire*, December 6, 1961.
192. *Herald-Tribune*, obituary of Christopher S. Sharp (1929–2012), November 20–2, 2012, www.legacy.com/obituaries/heraldrtibune; *Rebelaire*, May 1963.

193. *Augusta Chronicle*, obituary of William Cecil Casper (d. 2006), December 17, 2006, www.legacy.com/obituaries/augustachronicle.
194. *USC Aiken Magazine* (1986): 18.
195. *Rebelaire*, March 1963. DeHart also edited the student newspaper.
196. Interview with Carol McKay, June 14, 2018.
197. *Aiken Standard*, July 13, 1970; September 11, 1970.
198. Ibid., September 23, 1970.
199. Ibid.
200. *Augusta Chronicle*, September 22, 1971.
201. *USC Aiken Magazine* (1986): 20.

SELECTED BIBLIOGRAPHY

Brockington, W.S., Jr., and Judith T. VanSteenberg. *Historical Sketches of Aiken: A Collection of the Best of 150 Years of Our Southern City*. Aiken, SC, 1985.

Browder, Tonya Algerine, and Richard David Brooks. *Memories of Home: Reminiscences of Ellenton*. Savannah River Archaeological Research Heritage Series 2. Columbia: South Carolina Institute of Archaeology and Anthropology, University of South Carolina, 1996.

Brown, William H. *The History of the First Locomotive in America from Original Documents, and the Testimony of Living Witnesses*. New York: D. Appleton & Company, 1874.

Byrd, Wilkins, ed. *A Splendid Time: Photographs of Old Aiken*. Aiken, SC: Historic Aiken Foundation, 2000.

Caldwell, Norman W. "The Southern Frontier during King George's War." *Journal of Southern History* 7 (1941): 43–44.

Calmes, Alan. "The Lyttleton Expedition of 1759: Military Failures and Financial Successes." *South Carolina Historical Magazine* 77 (1976): 16.

Cashin, Edward. "Fanni Mingo." Guardians of the Valley. https://www.sc.edu/uscpress/books/2009/3821x.pdf.

Cashin, Edward J. *Guardians of the Valley: Chickasaws in Colonial South Carolina and Georgia*. Columbia: University of South Carolina Press, 2009.

———. *Lachlan McGillivray, Indian Trader: The Shaping of the Southern Colonial Frontier*. Athens: University of Georgia Press, 1992.

———. "Thomas Brown (1750–1825)." Georgia Encyclopedia. https://www.georgiaencyclopedia.org/articles/history-archaeology/thomas-brown-1750-1825.

Coker, Kathy Roe. *World War II Prisoners of War in Georgia: Camp Gordon's POWs*. Augusta, GA: Command Historian Office, U.S. Army Signal Center and Fort Gordon, 1994.

Copp, Roberta VH. *South Carolina African Americans in the Civil War: Two Sides to a Story.* Document Packet No. 6. Columbia: South Carolina Department of Archives and History, 1990.

Downey, Tom. "Graniteville Company." *South Carolina Encyclopedia*. Edited by Walter Edgar. Columbia: University of South Carolina Press, 2006, 391.

———. "Hamburg." *South Carolina Encyclopedia*. Edited by Walter Edgar. Columbia: University of South Carolina Press, 2006, 415.

———. "William Gregg." *South Carolina Encyclopedia*. Edited by Walter Edgar. Columbia: University of South Carolina Press, 2006.

Elliott, Bernard, and Joseph W. Barnwell. "Bernard Elliott's Recruiting Journal 1775." *South Carolina Historical Magazine* 17 (1916): 98.

Farmer, James O. "Aiken." *South Carolina Encyclopedia*. Edited by Walter B. Edgar. Columbia: University of South Carolina Press, 2006.

———. "Aiken County." *South Carolina Encyclopedia*. Edited by Walter B. Edgar. Columbia: University of South Carolina Press, 2006.

Georgia Historical Quarterly, "Oglethorpe's Treaty with the Lower Creek Indians" 4 (1920): 9.

Gervais, John Lewis, and Raymond Starr. "Letters from John Lewis Gervais to Henry Laurens, 1777–1778." *South Carolina Historical Magazine* 66 (1965): 21–22.

Gillam, J. Christopher, Charles Cobb, Chester DePratter and Tammy Herron. "Exploring the Native American Colonial Landscape of the Central Savannah River Area, Late 17th–Early 18th Centuries." *Legacy* 17 (2013): 24.

Gregg, William. *Essays on Domestic Industry*. Graniteville, SC: Graniteville Company, 1941.

Groover, Mark, and Jonathan Leader. "Exploring Fort Moore." *Legacy* 7, no. 8 (2002–3): 17. http://www.cas.sc.edu/sciaa.

Groover, Mark D. "George Galphin." *South Carolina Encyclopedia*. Edited by Walter Edgar. Columbia: University of South Carolina Press, 2006, 356.

Guide to Historical Markers. Columbia: South Carolina Department of Archives and History, 1998.

Hamer, Fritz. "Fort Moore." *South Carolina Encyclopedia*. Edited by Walter Edgar. Columbia: University of South Carolina Press, 2006, 335

Helsley, Alexia Jones. *Beaufort, South Carolina: A History*. Charleston, SC: The History Press, 1996.

———. "North Augusta." *South Carolina Encyclopedia*. Edited by Walter Edgar. Columbia: University of South Carolina Press, 2006, 674.

———. "A Roadside Guide to the Revolutionary War in Aiken County," *County Focus* (Winter 2017).

———. *Unsung Heroines of the Carolina Frontier*. Columbia: South Carolina Department of Archives and History, 19.

Henderson, P.F. *A Short History of Aiken and Aiken County*. Columbia, SC: R.L. Bryan Company, 1951.

———. "Some Aiken County Names." *Names in South Carolina* 7 (Winter 1960): 16.

History of North Augusta, South Carolina. North Augusta, SC: North Augusta Historical Society, 1980.

Journal of the Aiken County Historical Society. "American Railroad Journal, and Advocate of Internal Improvements, 24 August 1833" (May 2018): 3–4.

Kantrowitz, Stephen. "Benjamin Ryan Tillman." *South Carolina Encyclopedia*. Edited by Walter Edgar. Columbia: University of South Carolina Press, 2006, 961–62.

Mack, Tom. *Hidden History of Aiken County*. Charleston, SC: The History Press, 2012.

McDonald, Janice, and Paul Miles. *Aiken*. Images of America Series. Charleston, SC: Arcadia Publishing, 2011.

Meriwether, Robert L. *The Expansion of South Carolina, 1729–1765*. Kingsport, TN, 1940.

Mitchell, Broadus. "William Gregg." *Dictionary of American Biography*. Vol. 4. New York, 1931.

Morris, Michael P. *George Galphin and the Transformation of the South Carolina Backcountry*. Lanham, MD: Lexington Books, 2015.

———. "Henry Woodward." *South Carolina Encyclopedia*. Edited by Walter Edgar. Columbia: University of South Carolina Press, 2006.

———. "Indian Trade." *South Carolina Encyclopedia*. Edited by Walter Edgar. Columbia: University of South Carolina Press, 2006, 476–77.

———. "Westos." *South Carolina Encyclopedia*. Edited by Walter Edgar. Columbia: University of South Carolina Press, 2006.

———. "Yamasse War." *South Carolina Encyclopedia*. Edited by Water Edgar. Columbia: University of South Carolina Press, 2006, 1,055.

Official Gazette of the United States Patent Office 15. Washington, D.C.: Government Printing Office, 1879.

Olson, Gary D. "Loyalists and the American Revolution: Thomas Brown and the South Carolina Backcountry, 1775–1776 (continued)." *South Carolina Historical Magazine* 69 (1968): 55.

"Papers of the First Council of Safety of the Revolutionary Party in South Carolina, June–November, 1775 (continued)." *South Carolina Historical Magazine* 2 (1901): 99–100.

Peters, Kenneth. "Earthquakes." *South Carolina Encyclopedia.* Edited by Walter Edgar. Columbia: University of South Carolina Press, 2006, 280–81.

A Pictorial Timeline of Graniteville, South Carolina, 1845–1996. N.p.: Horse Creek Historical Society, 2013.

Poole, W. Scott. "Best Friend of Charleston." *South Carolina Encyclopedia.* Edited by Walter Edgar. Columbia: University of South Carolina Press, 2006, 69.

———. "Prince Rivers." *South Carolina Encyclopedia.* Edited by Walter Edgar. Columbia: University of South Carolina Press, 2008, 808.

Rey, Terry. *The Priest and the Prophetess: Abbe Ouviere, Romaine Rivere and the Revolutionary Atlantic World.* Oxford: Oxford University Press, 2017.

Riddick, Allen. *Memories of Growing Up and Living in Aiken, South Carolina.* Aiken, SC, 2011.

Rindfleisch, Brian. "George Galphin and the War in the South, 1775–1780." *Journal of the America Revolution* (September 1, 2015). https://allthingsliberty.com/2015/09/George-galphin-and-the-war-in-the-south-1775-1780.

Robbins, Walter L., and John Tobler. "John Tobler's Description of South Carolina (1753)." *South Carolina Historical Magazine* 71 (1970): 141, 149–51.

Salley, A.S., Jr. "The Calhoun Family of South Carolina." *South Carolina Historical Magazine* 7 (1906): 6.

Scott, Edwin J. *Random Recollections of a Long Life, 1806 to 1876.* Columbia, SC, 1884.

Simkins, Francis Butler, and Robert Hilliard Woody. *South Carolina during Reconstruction.* Gloucester, MA: Peter Smith, 1966; reprint of the 1932 UNC Press edition.

Smith, Mark M. "'All Is Not Quiet in Our Hellish County': Facts, Fiction, Politics, and Race: The Ellenton Riot of 1876." *South Carolina Historical Magazine* 95 (1994): 142–55.

South Carolina State Board of Agriculture, South Carolina Resources and Population, Institutions and Industries. Charleston, SC: Walker, Evans & Cogswell, 1883; reprinted Spartanburg: Reprint Company, 1972.

Spar, Ira. *New Haven's Civil War Hospital: A History of Knight U.S. General Hospital.* Jefferson, NC: McFarland & Company Inc., 2014.

Swan, Philip G. "'The Present Defenceless State of the Country': Gunpowder Plots in Revolutionary South Carolina." *South Carolina Historical Magazine* 108 (2007): 303.

Toole, Gasper Loren, II. *Ninety Years in Aiken County: Memories of Aiken County and Its People*. Aiken, SC, n.d.

Towles, Louis P. "William Aiken, Sr." *South Carolina Encyclopedia*. Edited by Walter Edgar. Columbia: University of South Carolina Press, 2006, 12.

Vandervelde, Isabel. *Aiken County: The Only South Carolina County Founded During Reconstruction*. Spartanburg, SC: Reprint Company, 1999.

Van Ruymbeke, Bertrand. "Purrysburg." *South Carolina Encyclopedia*. Columbia: University of South Carolina Press, 2006, 764.

Voigt, Gilbert P. "Swiss Notes on South Carolina." *South Carolina Historical Magazine* 21 (1920): 93–94.

Young, Willie Pauline. *Abstracts of Old Ninety-Six and Abbeville District Wills and Bonds*. Vidalia: Georgia Genealogical Reprints, 1969.

Zucek, Richard. "Ellenton Riot." *South Carolina Encyclopedia*. Edited by Walter Edgar. Columbia: University of South Carolina Press, 2006, 295.

———. "Hamburg Massacre." *South Carolina Encyclopedia*. Edited by Walter Edgar. Columbia: University of South Carolina Press, 2008, 415–16.

INDEX

A

B

C

D

E

H

M

N

O

P

Q

R

S

W

Y

Z

ABOUT THE AUTHOR

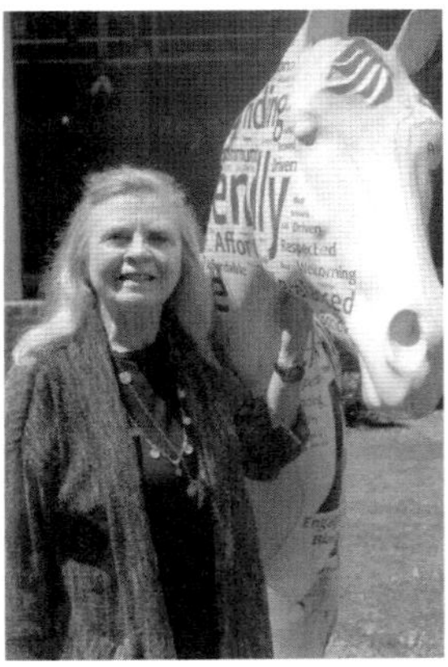

Alexia Jones Helsley, 2018.
Photographer Terry L. Helsley. Courtesy the author.

Alexia Jones Helsley, author, historian and archivist, loves to study and write about South Carolina's long and turbulent history. She grew up in Beaufort and developed a lifelong love affair with the Lowcountry. She especially enjoys beach walking, gently swinging in a hammock and listening to the surf.

Currently, she teaches history at the University of South Carolina Aiken and serves as University Archivist. Among her publications are *South Carolinians in the War for American Independence*, *Beaufort, SC: A History*, *Wicked Edisto: The Dark Side of Eden* and *Wicked Columbia*. Recently, she published "Dr. Daniel Lesesne Smith and the Spartanburg Baby Hospital: A Chapter in South Carolina Progressivism" in *Recovering the Piedmont Past II* and "A Girl, a Boy, and a Train" in *Our Prince of Scribes: Authors Remember Pat Conroy*.

A graduate of Furman University and the University of South Carolina, Helsley chairs the Old Exchange Commission and is the recipient of the Governor's Archives Award.